MOOC (Massive Open Online Courses)

Edited by Dragan Cvetković

Published in London, United Kingdom

IntechOpen

Supporting open minds since 2005

MOOC (Massive Open Online Courses)
http://dx.doi.org/10.5772/intechopen.95166
Edited by Dragan Cvetković

Contributors
Sung-Wan Kim, David Cobham, Kwamena Appiah-Kubi, Ridwan Daud Mahande, Fitrah Asma Darmawan, Jasruddin Daud Malago, Melikhaya Skhephe, Anna Siri, Rita Bencivenga, Cinzia Leone, Ramashego Shila Mphahlele, Irene C. Culaste-Quimbo, Ebba Ossiannilsson, Nor Hafiza Haron, Yusof Hafidzan, Vollan Okoth Ochieng, Maurice Mutisya, Caroline Thiong'O, Keyonda Smith, Abdullahi Abubakar Yunusa, Irfan Naufal Umar, Brandford Bervell

First published in London, United Kingdom, 2022 by IntechOpen
IntechOpen is the global imprint of INTECHOPEN LIMITED, registered in England and Wales, registration number: 11086078, 5 Princes Gate Court, London, SW7 2QJ, United Kingdom
Printed in Croatia

British Library Cataloguing-in-Publication Data
A catalogue record for this book is available from the British Library

Additional hard and PDF copies can be obtained from orders@intechopen.com

MOOC (Massive Open Online Courses)
Edited by Dragan Cvetković
p. cm.
Print ISBN 978-1-83969-737-1
Online ISBN 978-1-83969-738-8
eBook (PDF) ISBN 978-1-83969-739-5

For EU product safety concerns:
IN TECH d.o.o., Prolaz Marije Krucifikse Kozulić 3, 51000 Rijeka, Croatia, info@intechopen.com or visit our website at intechopen.com.

Meet the editor

Dragan Cvetković graduated with a degree in Aeronautics from the Faculty of Mechanical Engineering, University of Belgrade, in 1988. He obtained his Ph.D. in 1997. To date, he has published sixty-five books, scripts, and practicums about computers and computer programs, aviation weapons, and flight mechanics. He has published many scientific papers both locally and abroad. He became an assistant professor at Singidunum University, Belgrade, in 2007, and a full professor of Informatics and Computing in 2014. In 2019, he became vice-rector for teaching at the same university.

Contents

Preface

Massive Open Online Courses (MOOCs) are free online courses available to anyone who can sign up. MOOCs provide an affordable and flexible way to learn new skills, advance in careers, and provide quality educational experiences to a certain extent. Millions of people around the world use MOOCs for learning and their reasons are various, including career development, career change, college preparation, supplementary learning, lifelong learning, corporate e-Learning, training, and so on.

As MOOCs have been evolving over time, different platforms have been emerging simultaneously. There are mainly two different types of platforms. The first group, cMOOCs, allows the application of theoretical knowledge for understanding learning in the digital age (emphasizing how Internet technologies have contributed to new ways of learning). The second group, xMOOCs, resemble more traditional courses.

cMOOC platforms are based on connectivism principles that indicate that materials should be combined (rather than preselected), that different materials can be mixed and reused, and that their application reflects future potential developments (materials that are evolving should be focused on future teachings). cMOOC teaching design approaches (instruction) try to connect students with each other to answer questions or collaborate on joint projects.

xMOOC platforms have a structure that is made in a much more traditional way. Such courses have a specific goal in terms of completing the course and obtaining a specific certificate at the end of the course. They are usually presented with a clearly marked program of recorded lectures and self-test assignments. However, some providers require subscriptions as well as payment for storing materials and obtaining certificates. They use elements of the original MOOC, but, in a way, represent branded IT platforms that offer content distribution partnerships to institutions. The instructor or lecturer is a professional provider of knowledge and services, and the interaction with and among the participants is limited to seeking help and mutual counseling on difficult points.

This book is divided into two sections.

The first section, "MOOC and Education", consists of seven chapters. The themes of the first chapter are service science in education and MOOCs, education service innovation in MOOCs, education service system design for educational innovation in MOOCs, and quality management of MOOCs in the perspective of education service. The second chapter builds upon previous research that has used content analysis to assess the messages exchanged between participants enrolled in a MOOC. It focuses on uncovering the nature of the peer support that has been provided by participants and the social environment that they have established through their interactions. The third chapter is dedicated to the development of a Contextualized English Reading Proficiency Toolkit (CERPT) to help students improve their reading ability level. Chapter 4 investigates the acceptance of MOOCs and factors that might influence their use at public universities. Chapter 5 employs humanistic learning theory (HLT) to present a variety of digital teaching and learning tools that enable assessment suitable for many students in the Open Distance e-Learning (ODeL) MOOCs. Humanistic learning theory emphasizes a shift towards considering students, their characteristics, and their influence on learning. In addressing the gap created by assessments that were not focused on specific human capabilities, including creativity, personal growth, and choice, this chapter presents principles of HLT linking them with the form of assessments in MOOCs. Chapter 6 explores and presents a conceptual module to improve web developers' capabilities and knowledge of accessible digital design. Chapter 7 focuses on teachers' readiness for e-learning during the Covid-19 pandemic.

The second section, "MOOC for Lifelong Learning, Equity and Inclusion", contains five chapters. Good-quality, accessible education is a human right based on social justice and liberation and a force for sustainable development and peace. The goal of accessible education is to ensure inclusive and equitable quality education and promote lifelong learning opportunities for all as described in chapter 8. Chapter 9 is based on a systematic literature review. In this chapter, the focus is on global initiatives in education as a global common. The findings support that knowledge is a universal entity constructed by individuals that belong to anyone anywhere and at any time. Supported by a learner-centered instructional strategy, Chapter 10 explores the choices related to EDI-sensitive methods and strategies adopted to develop and implement an online education path. Theoretical and practical implications are also discussed. In Chapter 10, the authors examine articles focused on MOOCs implemented in sub-Saharan African (SSA) higher education that describe the different models of MOOCs enacted as an initiative to provide access and opportunity to acquire quality higher education across different disciplines within the sub-region. MOOCs are slowly gaining traction in education provisioning in SSA. Much of this is attributed to the governmental and institutional aim of providing quality and affordable universal education to all learners. Chapter 11 explores how MOOCs are affecting access to learning in SSA, with a particular bias to the urban education context. Chapter 12 is dedicated to a metacognitive model of learning assessment based on students' projects through the practice of blended learning. The integration of elements of metacognitive skills such as planning, monitoring, and evaluation with self–peer–teacher assessment can be a method to measure students' metacognitive thinking skills in Project-based Learning (PjBL), especially metacognitive assessment through blended learning practice MOOCs that are in accordance with the characteristics of vocational education and can be adopted by general education.

I would like to express my sincere gratitude to all the authors and co-authors for their contributions. The successful completion of this book has been the result of the cooperation of many people. I would especially like to thank Publishing Process Manager Ms. Karmen Đaleta at IntechOpen for her support during the publishing process.

Dragan Cvetković
Singidunum University,
Beograd, Serbia

Section 1

MOOC and Education

Chapter 1

What Brings about the Success of MOOCs in the Perspective of Education Service?

Sung-Wan Kim

Abstract

MOOCs passed through 'inflated expectation stage of Garner's hype cycle in 2012 and has gone 'through of disillusionment' stage. For jumping to the slope of enlightenment, MOOCs should be considered as education service focusing on service dominant logic and co-creation of value. This chapter aims to suggest a new perspective, education service science, to cope with the crisis of MOOCs. It focuses mainly on this suggestion: the principles of education service science could be applied in order for learners with MOOCs to take optimal learning experience. Themes of this paper are service science in education and MOOCs, education service innovation in MOOCs, education service system design for educational innovation in MOOCs, and quality management of MOOCs in the perspective of education service.

Keywords: MOOCs, education service science, innovation, education service design

1. Introduction

MOOCs (Massive Open Online Courses) have been popular with cost effectiveness and flexible option of online education and training opportunity. A low retention rate has been acknowledged as a tradeoff between the scalability and the effectiveness of MOOCs [1]. MOOCs passed through 'inflated expectation stage

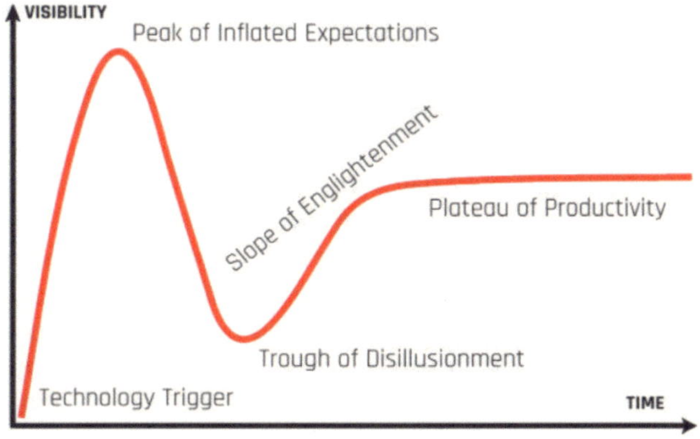

Figure 1.
Gartner hype cycle diagram for keyword "Massive open online course".

of Garner's hype cycle in 2012 when 100,000+ person enrollment [2] and has gone 'through of disillusionment' stage (**Figure 1**).

For jumping to the slope of enlightenment, new approach for the innovation of MOOCs is needed. MOOCs have been provided in the education provider's perspective rather than education demander's one. In the education process of MOOCs, instructor and learners form a relationship. But the dependency aspect in which they influence each other has not been sufficiently taken into account. In other words, co-creation of value between instructor and learners should be lit anew. In this aspect, the principles of education service science can help achieve educational innovation by solving the problems faced by MOOC through a systematic approach.

This paper presents a new perspective that MOOCs should be considered as education service focusing on service dominant logic and co-creation of value. This chapter aims to suggest a new perspective, education service science, to cope with the crisis of MOOCs. It focuses mainly on this: the principles of education service science could be applied in order for learners with MOOCs to take optimal learning experience.

2. Service science in education and MOOCs

2.1 Why MOOC should be education service rather than education?

MOOCs' the biggest weakness is that learners are not interested in completing the course [3]. This is because they do not have the inclination to do so. Only 15% or so of the enrolled students completed the course. If then, why does this happen? Absence of serious pedagogy, homogenization and depersonalization of education, and corporate influences on the academy can be mentioned and especially the issue of instructional design quality including learner motivation and support are considered very serious, which is the main reason of low rate of completion in courses [4]. Although learners in most of MOOCs do not pay money to course providers, it is believed that they are not satisfied with the MOOCs. Most of MOOC providers take a position of providing a kind of educational products. Instructors in MOOCs also focus on providing well-designed contents to learners.

Service focuses on users as well as providers and how deep and meaningful their experiences can be deployed. Accordingly, education service can focus on learners and their deep and meaningful experience. If we focus on 'education service' rather than the vague and abstract term of education, we will envision all kinds of methodologies to design learners' experiences in a meaningful way [5]. When MOOC is considered as education service rather than education, innovation of MOOC to the slope of enlightenment seems to be possible.

2.2 Why service science and education service science in MOOCs?

Service science attempts a scientific approach to services. This has been developed while responding to the economic environment in which service innovation (service economy) creates more added value than product innovation (manufacturing economy). Service science has four primary principles: Service Dominant Logic (SDL), Co-creation of value, Service System, and Service Innovation [5].

Education service science intends to incorporate the core principles of existing service science into the field of education service. Service dominant logic is different from goods dominant logic. This focuses on the value in use realized through the learner's experience rather than the value in exchange. When service dominant logic is applied, students proactively build knowledge in the teaching and learning process and take value-creating experiences. Value can be created and realized when educational service providers do not realize value, but when a number of contextual relationships are supported. The value of learning is not achieved by simple explanation and communication by the instructor. It is important how learning is realized in the context of life by the learner.

Education service science is a new interdisciplinary field aimed at maximizing the learning experience of education service users or learners through the co-creation of value between education service providers and users. It is not an ideological point of view in approaching educational phenomena, but a methodology for innovating the education service system with a focus on future-oriented improvement.

Education service science places great importance on the innovation of education services to improve the existing education service system by devising measures for the active participation and learning commitment of learners. It focuses on how to reorganize the education service system to achieve the learner's optimal learning experience. In other words, it places importance on how to innovatively recreate the learning experience, considering education service system level (learning environment service, teaching & learning service, learner experience service) and service process (input/participation experience, process/learning experience, output/value experience). Education service science approaches education service with service dominant logic and rebuilds the current education service system, thereby deriving education service innovation and ultimately creating the value of learning experience.

Many service operations providers focus on service related resources, course management, outcome goal and financial goal at the inside-out. So, the education service operation manager sees education service users as the' input' factor to be managed, and focuses on ensuring that all processing 'processes' are performed well and 'output'.

If an education service user (education service consumer or education community) approaches education service from the perspective of outside-in, the user is first interested in the optimal learning experience and outcomes for the education service. Education service users want their own optimized learning experience rather than management of input resources, processes, and outputs, and are interested in good educational outcomes (e.g. positive sense of belonging, excellent job skills, positive willingness to participate in class). During the learning experience at this time, the education service customer invests time and effort to perform high-quality learning tasks with enthusiasm, learns with peers, and under the guidance of instructors. They actively participate in the organization's education system, such as using resources and support. Finally they experience intangible values that encompass both cognition and reaction such as memories, emotions, attitudes, and behaviors.

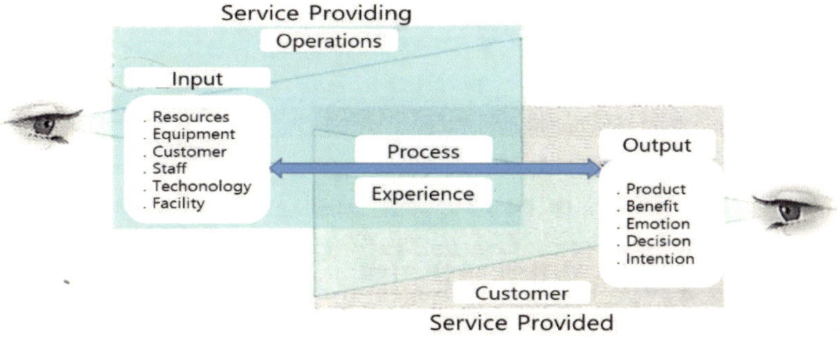

Figure 2.
Customer perspective vs. Provider's perspective. From Johnston et al., [6]. Revised by author.

Figure 2 shows how the perspectives of the provider and the user are different. It shows the contrast between the management-oriented supplier's perspective, which focuses on process efficiency, and the consumer-centered perspective, which aims to enhance experience. The effectiveness of the customer experience is focused rather than the viewpoint of resource efficiency.

Education service science aims to actively utilize 'technology' for change and innovation in educational services. For example, in order to realize customized and individualized education, the help of 'technology' is indispensable. Therefore, it can be said that MOOC has a close relationship with the direction of education service science.

2.3 Why service and education service in MOOCs?

The service breaks the boundaries between the supplier and the consumer and places importance on the relationship between their interactions. Service means creating value through an action or work. Since many educational activities so far have been centered on the acquisition of the curriculum designed with the intention of the supplier, the consumer (learner) has been merely an object of education. This forced the learners to adapt and obey instructions rather than grow and develop. This is because there is no concept of service in educational activities in the educational practice of these past days. If service is an activity that creates intangible value for customers, educational service means all efforts to create intangible value for learners. Therefore, the concept of value for learners is very important in educational services. Values that can damage the learner's existence should be excluded in MOOCs [5].

3. Education service innovation in MOOCs

A service is formless (intangible), may feel differently depending on the person providing it (heterogeneity), occurs through contact with customers (inseparability), and disappears at the same time as service delivery (perishability). In order to overcome the challenges of these characteristics, service innovation is required. For service innovation, visualization, systemic approach, contact management with users, and creation of experiences left in memory are required to respond to each challenge [7].

Educational service also has the same four characteristics (**Figure 3**). Since educational services are the result of some educational action, there is no physical entity (intangibility). It is intangible 'work done for others.' And the production of

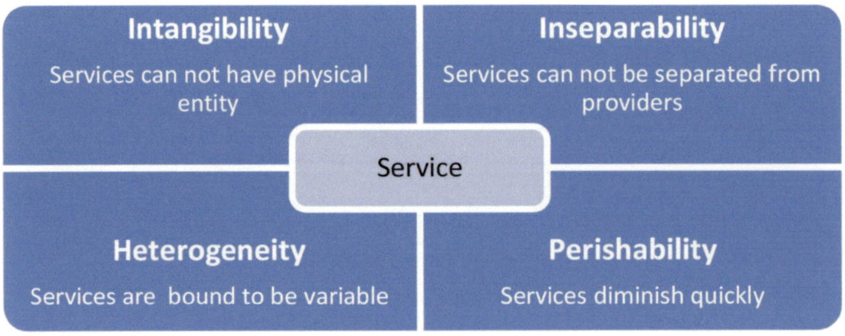

Figure 3.
Four characteristics of service.

an educational service cannot be separated from its consumption (inseparability). Educational service is felt different according to each learner (heterogeneity). Since the mechanism for delivering services is human, educational services are bound to be variable. So not everyone perceives the same value from the same service. Educational service diminishes quickly (perishability). It is needed that education service provider must work harder to ensure the value experience because of their ethereal nature.

In this section, I would like to present a concrete plan to innovate the educational service called MOOC based on those four essential characteristics of the service (intangibility, inseparability, heterogeneity, perishability) as mentioned above. For overcoming those four weaknesses, it is intended to present a one-on-one counter-measure corresponding to them.

3.1 How to cope with intangibility? Providing memorable experiences or value experiences

As mentioned in **Figure 2**, throughout the input-process-output stage of educational services from the perspective of providers, a touchpoint for participation experience, learning experience, and value experience[1] should be formed in the perspective of users. For MOOCs to overcome intangible service, they must be designed to enable learners to have memorable experiences. Learners must be able to experience value. For example, learners should be able to recognize that MOOCs are helping to improve their competency, or that classes are actually helpful. To this end, the 'experience of participation and learning' in MOOC educational activities should ultimately lead to 'value experience'. In addition, the class should provide an experience that exceeds the learner's expectations. And it is necessary to guide the learning to lead to problem- solving in life by having a sense of realism and having the experience of continuously connecting the knowledge with the actual situation.

3.2 How to cope with inseparability? Providing mutual exchange experience or user's touchpoint management

Of course, there should be no discrimination from other learners, and it is necessary to increase student's participation experiences by actively reflecting learners' opinions in the design of educational activities in MOOCs. In addition, the learner should be notified in advance when a problem occurs in the MOOC system. Responses to student's questions must be provided promptly and in good faith. A lack of learner-instructor interaction in MOOCs may lead to dropouts [8]. Rich opportunities for learner interaction with course content and peers might offset the lack of learner-instructor interaction. The decrease in learner-instructor interaction in MOOCs can be substituted by prolific learner-learner and learner-content interactions without any decrease in the quality of learning experience in MOOCs, as Anderson reported [9].

3.3 How to cope with heterogeneity? Providing systematic approach

In order to innovate the educational service of MOOC, the educational service system must be improved. According to the characteristics of education services, the quality of even the same service is not constant depending on who provides

[1] Participation experience refers to the quantity and quality of experience that is relatively more focused or more active in a task. Learning experience refers to the experience of certainty about current performance. And value experience refers to the experience of satisfying a need or value.

and uses the service when, where, and how. In order that everyone may perceive the same value from the same service, MOOC operators and designers should take a systematic and ecological approach. In order to ensure that the quality of educational services is consistently maintained, it is necessary to systematically understand how educational services create and deliver value and to intervene appropriately to solve problems. When designing MOOC services, it is necessary to consider integratively each system level (organizational environment, program, learner or instructor). For educational service design, a system design approach is required, in addition to the service design approach.

3.4 How to cope with perishability? Providing co-creation of value

Education services disappear if not used and cannot be stored. Before it disappear, value should be created. The education service system is a value creation network that creates a network of relationships. In this respect, interactions with learners, interactions between learners and learners, and interactions between learners and learning materials should be carefully designed for co-creating value.

In education systems that encourage student agency[2], which is thus defined as the capacity to set a goal, reflect and act responsibly to effect change [10], learning involves not only instruction and evaluation but also co-construction or co-agency between instructor and learner. Co-agency happens when teachers and students become co-creators in the teaching-and learning process. The expanding concept of co-agency recognizes that students, teachers, parents and communities work together to help students progress toward their shared goals.

4. Education service system Design for Educational Innovation in MOOCs[3]

The education service system design reflects the system perspective within the education service design. In other words, the methodology of service design is used to solve problems occurring at various system levels such as national, regional, college, class, and individual learning. Education service design is an area in which service systems are designed to jointly create educational values with learners, who are consumers of education.

The education service system is an aggregate composed of various people, relationships, organizations, and technologies that organically exist in the network of value creation of learning experiences. It is intended to present education service design plans for each system level of learning environment service, teaching and learning service, and learner experience service for educational innovation.

[2] "In the context of the OECD Learning Compass 2030, student agency implies a sense of responsibility as students participate in society and aim to influence people, events and circumstances for the better. Agency requires the ability to frame a guiding purpose and identify actions to achieve a goal. It is about acting rather than being acted upon; shaping rather than being shaped; and making responsible decisions and choices rather than accepting those determined by others. Student agency is not a personality trait; it is something malleable and learnable. The term 'student agency' is often mistakenly used as a synonym for 'student autonomy', 'student voice' and 'student choice'; but it is much more than these concepts. Acting autonomously does not mean functioning in social isolation, nor does it mean acting solely in self-interest. Similarly, student agency does not mean that students can voice whatever they want or can choose whatever subjects they wish to learn." [10]

[3] This section is a translated and revised some of contents which are included in a book written by author [11].

4.1 Learning environment service system: Designing environment

The learning environment service system in MOOCs, can be classified into four types, depending on the degree of technological innovation and participation in use; push-based, technology-affluent, human network-centered, and pull-based (**Figure 4**).

'Push-based service system' has a Fordism approach for mass production following mass consumption. It is a traditional pipeline system that has a fully centralized characteristic to realize economies of scale by providing curriculum to the mass market. It is a linear value chain in which value creation and movement are transferred from producer to consumer [12]. Producer designs education services and operates systems to provide the services. And the user just purchases the service. This system has a limitation that it goes toward delivery-type MOOC that is intensively produced for mass delivery. The curriculum in the provider-centered service system can be said to be mainly instructional design products based on behaviorism [13].

In order to overcome the limitations of the provider-oriented service system due to the rapid development of information and communication technology and the diverse demands of educational service users, **'technology-affluent service system'** appears. This system focuses on using technology to overcome the limitations of time and space for teaching and learning. Various information and communication devices are actively used so that individuals can choose the content and pace of learning. MOOCs on LMS (Learning Management System) belongs to technology-oriented services.

In the **'human-centered service system'**, the source of value creation focuses on the human's interaction, that is, the formation of a human network. In this type of system, instructional methods such as cooperative learning, discussion, field practice, and internships are utilized, focusing on the interaction and experiential learning between instructors and learners and between learners and learners.

'Pull-based service system' centered on co-creation of value focuses on providing an environment that creates value in the process of value in use of educational services by users. To this end, this system should be a platform to create value by creating a space (e.g. Living Lab), where educational service producers and consumers can gather and interact by using information and communication technology. Such a MOOC platform can increase user participation and provide great value to all who participate. This service has post-Fordism characteristics in that it is oriented toward a user-centered pull system that emphasizes the voluntary participation of educational service users. The curriculum, which is provided in the value co-creation-oriented service system, can be said to be a product of instructional design based on constructivism in contrast to the provider-oriented service system [13]. It also provides educational services using the latest IT technologies, such as AR (Augmented Reality), VR (Virtual Reality), AI (Artificial Intelligence), and Big Data.

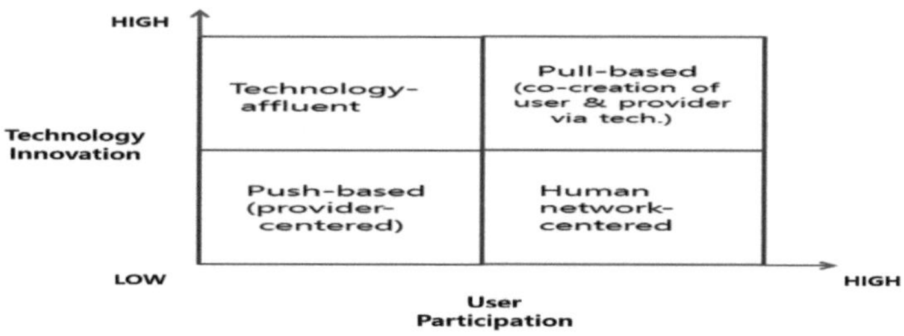

Figure 4.
Types of learning environment service system.

4.2 Teaching-learning service system: Designing education

According to the degree of two way communication orientation and program structure, the teaching-learning service system can be divided into four types: programmed, video/audio conferencing, computer-assisted, and adaptive (**Figure 5**).

'Programmed service system' focuses on the supplier-oriented and content delivery-oriented program operation. One-sided lectures using video contents are typical. There is little interaction between instructor-learners and learners-learners, comparing other systems. In addition, it has a program structure that makes it impossible for individual learners to select content, control learning speed, etc.

'Video/audio conferencing service system' has a structure that is difficult to control the needs of individual learners, and has the characteristic of providing an opportunity to interact between the instructor and the learner.

'Computer-assisted service system' supports some degree of autonomy for learners to select learning content and adjust learning speed, but it is difficult to provide opportunities for interaction between instructor and learners. Depending on the learner's response, it moves to a different text (a linear program) or a differently programmed text (a branched program) [13].

'Adaptive service system' has a high level of interaction between instructor and learners, and has the characteristics of providing educational services that meet the needs of individual learners. It is essential to support a system that provides the learning content that learners want immediately, and for this, the latest information and communication technologies such as artificial intelligence and big data must be utilized. For example, there may be an adaptive learning support program using an artificial intelligence-based chatbot. The learner also uses a very loose structure to present the structure, outcomes, and sequencing of learning activities. For example, a student taking the course 'Instructional Methods and Educational Technology' should organize and sequence each module and activity, and identify personal goals and activities to be achieved during the curriculum.

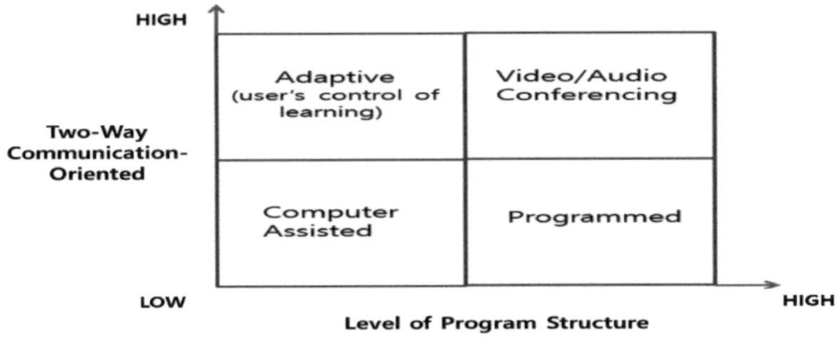

Figure 5.
Types of teaching-learning service system.

4.3 Learner's experience service system: designing experience

The learner's experience service system can be classified into four types, such as passive, active, problem solving, and value discovering, according to the level of reality and autonomy of learning (**Figure 6**).

Since **'Passive active service system'** focuses on the unilateral content delivery method of the instructor, the learner cannot actively participate in the teaching and learning process. Because the instructor systematically organizes the contents and

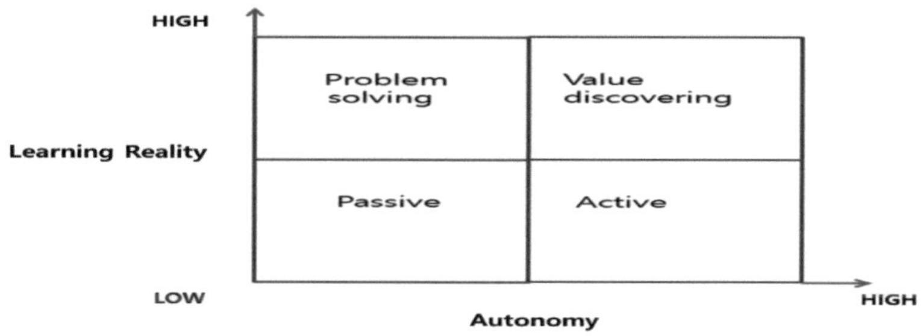

Figure 6.
Types of learner experience service system.

conveys the relationship between the contents, the cognitive process of the students is inevitably weak.

'Active service system' has high learning autonomy to participate in learning, so learner actively participates in the learning process. But there is a limitation that learning is far from the actual reality.

In **'problem-solving service system'**, the instructor presents real life problems to the learner, and the learner focuses on solving only the presented problems.

'Value discovery service system' focuses on finding practical problems by learners and then trying to solve them. MOOC class using creative problem-solving methodologies such as Design Thinking can be a representative example of value discovery. It is more important that learners create problems or activities proactively rather than pre-designed problems or activities.

5. Quality management of MOOCs in the perspective of education service

For learner to have successful experiences with MOOCs, it is important to manage and keep the quality of MOOCs. The criteria which are included in evaluation of the quality of e-learning, can be also used for the quality management of MOOCs. However, there is the absence of specific educational assessment criteria adapted to the features of a MOOC. Yepes-Baldó [14] proposed quality dimension of MOOCs which is structured into two categories (course, platform). The course category includes 14 dimensions; methodology, content organization, teaching guide, content quality, teaching resources, motivation, technical quality, chronological aspects, language, interaction, user individualization, uniqueness, values, dissemination, promotion, price. The platform category includes visual and structural design, base language, compatibility, and communication resources. The details of course category's indicators are below.

Cha [15] suggested checklists for quality assurance of K-MOOC or Korean MOOC. The quality indicator consists of four dimensions (content, activity, evaluation, supports) and twenty evaluation items. Details of Items are as follows.

Zeithaml et al., [16, 17] suggested the e-SERVQUAL model consisting of E-S-QUAL (e.g. efficiency, system availability, fulfillment and privacy) and E-ReeS-QUAL (e.g. responsiveness, compensation, and contact), for measuring e-service quality. The revised conceptual framework of e-services quality which Zemblyte [18] suggested, is composed of website quality (e.g. access, easy of use, website design, structure & layout, linkage, information accuracy), core e-service quality (e.g. privacy & security, reliability, fulfillment, efficiency, individualized attention), and e-service quality recovery (e.g. responsiveness, compensation, contact).

Dimension	Indicator	Item
Value experience	Reality	It cultivates essential competencies (e.g. communication, collaboration, creativity, critical thinking, self-direction, etc.) required in real life rather than knowledge content.
		It allows people to experience the problem-solving process rather than mere knowledge transfer.
		Dealing with the real big questions of life
	Reliability	Understand and respect students as a person
		Giving students the opportunity to grow while learning online
	Value	Explain class content professionally enough to give students confidence
		Online classes are worth noting the tuition
Mutual interaction experience	Assurance	Provides an evaluation score suitable for online student activities
		Appropriate points are given according to the evaluation criteria described in the lesson plan.
		Online classes continue to give you the same level of experience and confidence
	Empathy	Provide appropriate feedback on student questions, presentations, discussions, and outcomes of activities
		Show interest in individual students
System approach	Organizational environment	Provide a classroom environment suitable for online classes.
		Maintain the appropriateness of online content quality and sound quality
		Maintain the rigor of online test management
	Program	Clearly guide the goal, content, method, and evaluation method of the online class
		Properly present the content and volume of the online lecture
		Have students present and think about theories from different perspectives
		Strive for class based on student activity-oriented experience
		Adjust the difficulty of tests and assignments appropriately
	Learner Support	Present online activities, assignments, and materials that students may be interested in
		Encourage and praise students to build confidence
		Provide students with effective use of learning materials
		Provide opportunities for students to develop self-directed learning competencies

Dimension	Indicator	Item
Value co-creation	Reactivity	In the event of problems such as system access, notify students in advance and try to resolve them quickly.
		Actively reflect the opinions of students
		Show an active will to help students
	Collaborative co-agency	Leading classes to be with a variety of people, including local communities and industries
		Instead of blaming class problems only on students, they regard it as the professor's own problem.
		Providing opportunities for positive mutual cooperation between faculty and students
		Provide opportunities for positive student–student cooperation.
		Provides an opportunity for students to select class topics to suit student interests

Table 1.
Quality indicator for MOOCs in the perspective of education service.

Margryan and colleagues [19] proposed 10 dimensional design criteria to evaluate MOOCs quality, focusing highly on pedagogical aspect of a MOOC: Problem-centered, activation, demonstration, application, integration, collective knowledge, collaboration, differentiations, authentic resources, feedback.

To innovate the educational service called MOOC, let us consider MOOCs quality based on the essential characteristics of the service (intangibility, inseparability, heterogeneity, perishability) as mentioned above. Corresponding to each service characteristics, I suggest four MOOC quality dimension (value experience, mutual interaction experience, system approach, value co-creation) as mentioned below (**Table 1**). First, 'value experience' is required to provide tangible experience to learners. This dimension is composed of reality, reliability, and value. 'Mutual interaction experience' dimension has two indicators (assurance, empathy) about user's touchpoint management for coping with service characteristic 'inseparability'. 'System approach' dimension consists of three indicators (organizational environment, program, learner support), which are related with service characteristic 'heterogeneity'. 'Value co-creation' dimension has two indicators (reactivity, collaborative co-agency). It treats with the limitation of education service's perishability.

Author details

Sung-Wan Kim
Korea Nazarene University, South Korea

*Address all correspondence to: kimstar52@kornu.ac.kr

References

[1] Tang, H., Xing, W., & Pei, B. Exploring the temporal dimension of forum participation in MOOCs, Distance Education. 2018; 39(3): 353-372.

[2] Haber, J. *MOOCs.* Cambridge, Massachusetts; London, England: The MIT Press. [Internet]. 2014. Available from from http://www.jstor.org/stable/j.ctt9qfb6r. [Accessed: May 7, 2021]

[3] Mehta, N. What Is MOOC-Based Learning? [Internet]. 2020. Available from https://elearningindustry.com/mooc-based-learning-advantages-and-disadvantages/ [Accessed: May 9, 2021]

[4] Kim. S.W. MOOCs in Higher Education, In Dragan Cvetkovic (ed.). *Virtual Learning*, IntechOpen, DOI: 10.5772/66137. [Internet]. 2016. Available from: https://www.intechopen.com/books/virtual-learning/moocs-in-higher-education

[5] Jang. H., Baek. P., Kim. S., & Hong. J. A theoretical exploration for establishing the discipline of 'Education Service Science'. Journal of Corporate Education and Talent Research. 2018; 20(4): 125-147.

[6] Johnston, R., Clark, G., & Shulver, M. Service operations management (4th ed.). Harlow: Pearson. 2012.

[7] Kim. J. *Service experience design: I meet Steve Jobs*. Gyeonggi Paju: Ahn graphics. 2017.

[8] Hone, K., & El Said, G. Exploring the factors affecting MOOC retention: A survey study. Computers & Education. 2016; 98: 157~168.

[9] Anderson, T. Getting the mix right again: An updated and theoretical rationale for interaction. The International Review of Research in Open and Distributed Learning. 2003; 4(2): 1-14.

[10] OECD (2019). *Student agency 2030*. Available from from http://oecd.org/education/2030-project. [Accessed: March 9, 2021]

[11] Kim, S.W. *Design Thinking*. Seoul: Dongmoon-sa. 2021.

[12] Parker, G.G., Van Alstyne, M.W., & Choudary, S.P. Platform revolution: How networked markets are transforming the economy and how to make them work for you. New York, NY: W.W.Norton & Company. 2016.

[13] Kim, S.W. *Distance Education*. Seoul: Sigmapress. 2008.

[14] Yepes-Baldó, M., Romeo, M., Martín, C., García, M.A., Monzó, G., & Besolí, A. Quality indicators: developing "MOOCs" in the European Higher Education Area, Educational Media International. 2016; 53(3); 184-197,

[15] Cha, H.J. A development study of checklists for quality assurance of K-MOOC. Journal of Lifelong Learning Society. 2018; 14(4): 137-166.

[16] Zeithaml, V. Parasuraman, A. & Malhotra, A. A conceptual framework for understanding e-service quality: Implications for future research and managerial practice. Marketing Science Institute Working Paper Report No. 2000.

[17] Zeithaml, V. Parasuraman, A. & Malhotra, A. Service Quality Delivery Through Web Sites: A Critical Review of Extant Knowledge. Journal of the Academy of Marketing Science. 2002; 30: 362-375. 10.1177/009207002236911.

[18] Zemblyte, J. The instrument for evaluating e-service quality.

Procedia-Social and Behavioral Sciences, *2015; 213*, 801-806.

[19] Margryan, A., Biabco, M., Littlejohn, A. Instructional quality of massive open online courses (MOOCs). Computers & Education. 2015; 80; 77-83.

Chapter 2

A Typology of Peer Support Behaviours in a MOOC

Kwamena Appiah-Kubi and David Cobham

Abstract

This chapter builds upon a body of previous research that has used content analysis to assess the messages exchanged between participants enrolled on a Massive Open Online Course (MOOC). In particular, it focuses on uncovering the nature of the peer support that the participants provide for each other, and the social environment that they establish through their interactions. The findings of this research have led to the construction of a Typology of Peer Support Behaviours which is presented here. It is proposed that this typology can be applied across a range of contexts to assess the nature of peer support behaviours enacted by participants in those MOOCs. It is proposed that the typology could help identify any unique differences in expression of behaviours among groups of students and it could be used to assess if there is a preference towards a particular approach to, or type of, peer support.

Keywords: MOOC, peer support, typology, teaching presence, social presence

1. Introduction

MOOCs are another incarnation of the online learning paradigm. They differ from the traditional formal online learning approach which is generally closed off and only accessible to a few registered participants, and often requiring some prerequisites to be met prior to participation. Although a small proportion of MOOCs charge an enrolment fee [1], MOOCs are predominantly open and usually free to participate in; as a result they tend to attract a large number of participants. The MOOC format was conceived in 2008 by George Siemens and Stephen Downes when they developed and deployed their inaugural course Connectivism and Connective Knowledge (CCK08) which attracted over 2000 participants [2, 3]. MOOCs have gained a stronghold and drawn much attention to learning analytics research and the open education resource movement. In their current and popular manifestation, conceived by Stanford professors Sebastian Thrun and Peter Norvig, MOOCs do not deviate far from the traditional online learning model, but through technological innovation have opened up access to educational content with a low barrier of entry [3, 4]. George Siemens categorises MOOCs into three distinct groups based on their approach in facilitating learning for their participants: *Connectivist*, *Instructivist* and *Open Learning Resources* [3].

- Connectivist MOOC (cMOOC): the initial conceptualisation of MOOCs as developed and deployed by George Siemens and Stephen Downes allows participants to network and collaborate among themselves to identify their individual learning needs, then create and follow their own learning path. Learning in this MOOC format is self-directed, the instructor does not define learning paths or outcomes but is available and involved in the process to facilitate the participants' learning. Using the interaction equivalency theorem, Miyazoe & Anderson benchmark cMOOCs as having low student-teacher interactions, medium student-content interaction but high student–student interactions highlighting the nature of the cMOOC variant as student–student interaction driven [5].

- Instructivist MOOC (xMOOC): these follow the traditional online learning model closely. Learning paths and goals are predefined by the facilitator featuring reading materials and instructional videos often interspersed with quizzes and end-of-module assessment. The course is often scheduled to run for a set duration, usually over the course of three to twelve weeks. Some courses though are self-paced without a hard deadline or end date, allowing participants to follow along on their own schedule. Miyazoe & Anderson benchmark xMOOCs high for student-content interaction, low for student-teacher interaction and low-to-medium for student–student interaction [5]. They highlight that for xMOOCs participants are drawn to the content which is usually video recording of lectures by academics renowned in their fields.

- The third MOOC variety, according to Siemens, is open learning resources made openly available such as MIT's Open Courseware [5]. These are generally dumps of video recorded lectures and assessments in the form of documents that can be downloaded to use. These resources are made freely available to anyone to use. Usually there is not a structured community of participants as found in the other two variations of MOOCs, and assessments are not graded as is found in xMOOCs. They may also not be updated as frequently as xMOOCs will be. Reference to MOOCs from this point onwards (unless otherwise stated) will be in Ref. to xMOOCs only.

MOOCs attract a myriad of participants from various age groups and with varying levels of experience, interests and motivations [6, 7]. Though some prerequisites may be set, they are not used to bar any participant from entry if they are not met. As such it is not surprising that the major issue faced by providers of MOOCs is a high attrition rate, aptly conceptualised as "the funnel of participation" [8] where a MOOC course attracts several thousands of participants, but only a few follow through to completion, with conservative estimates pegging this figure at about 10%. Time constraints feature as a major driver of attrition especially when participants were faced with other priorities in their daily lives [9].

2. Interactions in MOOCs

In an online learning environment, participants need an avenue to interact with fellow learners, to share ideas and seek assistance with challenges in the course. Discussion forums have been the dominant platform where these interactions take place [10]. They are usually built into the online learning platform, are usually text-based and asynchronous in nature. This allows participants the flexibility to freely share and attend to each other's inquiry at a time that is convenient.

Unlike in traditional online learning platforms with comparatively fewer students, the large number of participants taking part in a MOOC can generate voluminous amounts of communication which can lead to data overload for the participants [11, 12]. There has been increasing interest in research focusing on this phenomenon and how it may impact the learning process and learning outcomes of participants in a MOOC.

MOOC students interact with the discussion forum in various degrees and levels. The interaction pattern that occurs in the discussion forums can be used to categorise participants as: *active participants*, *lurkers* and *passive participants* [13, 14]. Studies have highlighted that the majority (about eighty per cent) of participants are lurkers who do not participate in “visible” forum activities such as publishing posts or commenting [13, 15, 16]. They usually do not follow the course actively but engage with the content at a slower pace, and search through or peruse content on the forum created by the other participants. Lurking may result from personal commitments that may hamper frequent participation in the course. However, some lurkers do so by choosing to consume and reflect rather than actively participate and benefit from ongoing discussions that ensue in the forum [13, 17]. Compared to lurkers, who will only follow a discussion and do not usually initiate one, passive participants follow and contribute to ongoing discussions or start their own, albeit their participation is less frequent and irregular. Active participants, so-called “superposters” [18] or “wholly engaged” learners [16] exhibit above-average engagement patterns by starting, facilitating or contributing quality content to discussions. Though they comprise a small subset of the population, they contribute the majority of relevant discussions on the forum and provide helpful assistance to their fellow participants.

The interactions of the participants are also relevant for their socialisation process, which can facilitate the establishment of a community and thus create a conducive social climate that fosters free and open expression of thoughts and ideas. However studies that examine participant interactions indicate overall participation in forum discussion decreased over time, and noted participants came together and dispersed in a crowd-like pattern rather than as a cohesive community, and that a majority of the discussions were carried out by students who were high-performing [19]. This peer-led discussions in the forum have been observed to promote discussions and engagement as well as active learning [20].

Only a few of the total registered participants interacted in the discussion forum, leading the researchers to wonder how or why more participants were not drawn to interact in the forum and possible remediation strategies. Some have noted that by virtue of the minimal information participants have about each other, save for what is shared in the forum, “experts” who could be approached to act as mentors to foster deeper learning and collaboration are not identified [21].

3. The Community of Inquiry framework

In late 1999 Randy Garrison, Terry Anderson and Walter Archer, three researchers focused on distance education, were confronted with a challenging issue: to make sense of interactions in a new online graduate program offered by their faculty. This had the effect of aligning their research to issues around the use of online text-based platforms to facilitate teaching, interaction and learning. Thus came to be the research team whose seminal work was the Community of Inquiry framework [22]. According to Garrison [23], the framework is predominantly based on the collaborative and constructivist ideas of John Dewey [24] in that meaning or knowledge is constructed and shared through interactions. The framework has been developed over the years and is much favoured by online learning researchers for its holistic approach to online learning research [22, 25]. It comprises three overlapping components that Garrison et al. postulate as needful in an online learning environment, with the intersection of the components posited as producing a meaningful learning experience. These three components - Teaching presence, Social presence and Cognitive presence - encapsulate the modalities of interactions in an online learning environment.

Social Presence captures the development of social interactions to create a productive social environment. In a mediated environment where participants are unable to infer nonverbal cues of other participants in an interaction, participants convey their sense of self through the thoughts and ideas they share. By projecting their personal identities through their interactions, participants are able to identify with each other and the community thus establishing a trusting environment that allows participants to interact freely. This can allow inter-personal relationships to develop which fosters group cohesion. The development of group cohesion is ideal if participants are to interact productively and meaningfully to facilitate their learning [26].

Teaching presence captures the facilitation and organisation of the course and actions of the instructor for the advancement of the learning process. Teaching presence serves a mediating role of balancing (and fostering) the social presence of participants (needed for free and open discourse) and guiding their cognitive presence towards achieving their learning goals. Teaching presence is predominantly enacted by the instructor and occurs not only in the online learning environment but offline as well, such as during the instruction design and preparation of the course syllabus and specification of learning outcomes [25]. The teaching presence role however is not limited to the instructor but can be carried out by participants through their interactions hence the reference to this component as "teaching" rather than "teacher" presence [27, 28]. Through their interactions, learners may assist each other to navigate the course content, providing helpful guidance and direction [27]. This may be institutionalised through the appointment of student moderators or teaching assistants from the cohort. This peer support is needful in an online learning environment where instructors may not be able to attend to each student individually and where learners can take the course in their own time. This

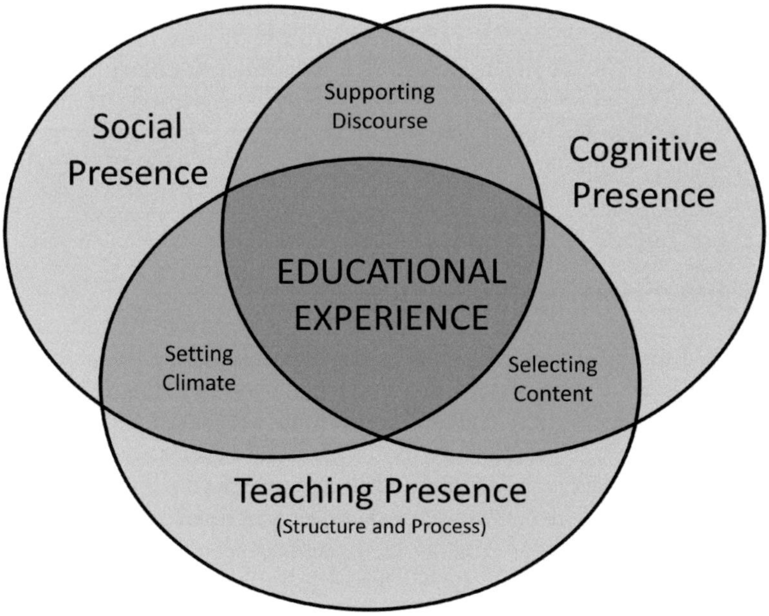

Figure 1.
Elements of the Community of Inquiry framework [29].

essentially necessitates an open environment where participants have the freedom to speak freely and express their opinions, to be able to provide assistance to other participants when required.

Cognitive presence captures the meaning-making process which the participants engage in to facilitate their learning. Cognitive presence highlights the development of critical thinking when students are able to engage successfully in inquiry-based learning [29]. Though the three presences all influence one another in various ways and degrees, cognitive presence has been observed to be heavily influenced by social presence and teaching presence.

The Community of Inquiry framework has evolved and has been adapted over the years from its beginnings as a tool to evaluate the effectiveness of online learning environments to a framework shedding light on learning patterns in online learning environments [30, 31] and recommending strategies to enhance the effectiveness of participants engaged in the learning process [32, 33]. The framework is described as a process model because it "embraces a constructivist orientation in which the emphasis is on how we construct knowledge" [34] and reflects the dynamism of the learning process that is to be encountered in an online learning environment as reflected by the interplay between the three components of the Community of Inquiry framework. A conducive learning environment that fosters free and open communication with other participants is the main function of the social presence element. Discourse is then able to ensue, allowing the participants to express cognitive presence. Via interaction with the course content and communication with fellow participants, teaching presence facilitates the other two elements in the framework to support the learning experience (**Figure 1**).

4. Findings from previous research

Below we present the findings of a study carried out to gain an insight into interaction behaviours of MOOC participants towards enacting peer support and social presence. With limited course staff consisting of one facilitator and four teaching assistants, all of whom were based in the United States of America, providing adequate support for a large proportion of participants would be a difficult undertaking for the team hence participants relied on other learners in their cohort for support. Interaction logs of discussion forum usage were processed using statistical models to categorise participants interaction pattern. The Community of Inquiry framework was then utilised in a content analysis to assess the messages exchanged by participants in the discussion forum. Themes extracted are from this process are presented below.

4.1 Social presence served as a utility to facilitate learning rather than to foster interpersonal bonds for community development

Open Communication was identified as the most frequent of social presence indicators exhibited, comprising 70% of the interactions coded in the dataset. This was followed by the *Group Cohesion* indicators (15%) that reflect self-identification with the group, which is an essential requirement for collaborative learning in MOOCs. In the Community of Inquiry framework, group cohesion is demonstrated by the use of vocatives, referring to the group using inclusive pronouns, phatic, salutations and greetings, course reflections and social sharing. Social sharing interactions where participants share portions of their personal lives (such as birthdays, vacations etc.) unrelated to the course content were absent in the dataset studied. This absence may be the result of a possible weak interpersonal bond among the participants; nonetheless, the high presence of open communication does indicate participants freely expressed themselves.

Affective indicators were exhibited by the participants in this study. Indicators under the Affective category capture the use of unconventional expressions to reflect emotion and humour. Affective indicators also highlight the disclosure of personal information, such as personal experiences related to the course content and challenges they may be facing. In a text-based discussion forum that is devoid of visual and auditory cues such as body language and tone in voice, affective indicators serve to transmit a participant's moods, feelings and emotions. Indicators found within this component allow the learners to express their opinions, emotions and perceptions freely, thus promoting open communication and collaboration among them. Phatic expressions, greetings and salutations comprised over fifty per cent of group cohesion indicators identified. Coupled with low densities of course reflection and referencing the group using inclusive pronouns, it may indicate weak (or the absence of) interpersonal bonds as such interactions predominantly become polite or formal social exchanges, a situation highlighted in [35].

4.2 Distributed teaching: facilitating learning with clarifications and relevant external resources

The teaching presence was enacted primarily through the facilitation and organisation of the course content and serves to promote knowledge sharing among the participants. Teaching presence is not limited to facilitators alone but "all participants assume teaching and learning roles and responsibilities to varying degrees" [23]. Indeed, with industry experts and some participants taking the course as a refresher, there were opportunities for knowledge sharing in the forum. *Direct Instruction* appeared to be the most expressed teaching presence indicator comprising 65% of all messages coded for teaching presence. This involves knowledge sharing on the subject matter by the participants. This involved interactions such as making explicit reference to outside material that the sharer found to be useful and relevant. This indicator was followed by giving information that clarifies issues with the course materials and offering useful illustrations that facilitate in the clarification exercise.

Facilitating Discourse expressions can be employed to steer interactions towards learning objectives by the instructor. In this study it was enacted by participants primarily as a way of encouraging, acknowledging and reinforcing contributions from other participants, and drawing in participants, promoting discussions. Participants expressing this indicator may only be focused on the current context of the message being replied to and may not have an overarching learning goal that a facilitator or instructor will hope to achieve.

Assessment indicators were lacking in this study. This was anticipated as students did not have provision to assess or evaluate other learners' test submissions or results. This is a critical concern in MOOC learning, where peer-grading could play a significant role in re-enforcing learning. Some MOOC platforms (such as Coursera) utilise peer assessment to this end, though their primary design was to surmount the technical challenge of grading value-based subjective coursework [19, 36].

4.3 Peer support: openness and willingness to explain and provide examples

The demographic profile of participants in the study were predominantly young and well educated, some to Master's and PhD level. The presence of these participants, especially those with an economics background, could have been an avenue for support to other participants.

One of the primary limitations of the dataset, and hence this study, was the lack of an identifying link between demographic information and messages in the forum. This could have been used to assess the contributions of participants by their academic level. This can highlight, for example, whether participants with higher degrees (or experience in the area) carry out more peer support. In this study, only a few participants actively contributed in the discussion forum. A majority of participants' interactions in the forum was focused on searching and reading with very few posting or replying to messages of other participants. With such a large number of participants, it may be that participants are able to find a query to have already been asked and answered hence lowering the need to post a message. This behaviour requires further investigation to assess the correlation (if any) between the number of participants in a course and volume of messages in the forum. This pattern of use may highlight the discussion forum as a utility to obtain support rather than to collaborate for community building.

Some of the participants, with or without intention, demonstrated teaching presence to the notice of other participants. This was captured in the below message of a student requesting assistance from another student via another student's thread:

> *Hey [student's username], can you answer a question I posted in this thread: [web link to question in the forum].*
>
> *Thanks.*

Anderson et al., part of the initial collaborators on the Community of Inquiry framework, highlighted this duality of students to act as teachers when developing the framework [27]. However, this dynamic role that a participant may play was not given much focus, granted at the inception of the framework online classes were not as large as MOOCs have become.

The teaching presence category consists of the following elements: *Instructional Design and Organisation*, *Facilitating Discourse*, *Direct Instruction*, and *Assessment*. The course facilitators are chiefly responsible for designing the course and organising the curriculum, resources and assessments hence it was anticipated (and was observed) that the teaching presence indicators that will be exhibited by participants would be concentrated within the Facilitating Discourse and Direct Instruction categories. A closer look revealed these expressions were concentrated within a few indicators.

More than 65% of messages coded for teaching presence were in the direct instruction category. This category comprises indicators such as providing valuable analogies, offering useful illustrations, supplying clarifying information and making explicit reference to outside material. These indicators classify messages that are intended to make the course material comprehensible or accessible to other participants. MOOC participants come from diverse backgrounds and experiences. In this study, a number of experienced professionals from various industries were observed to disclose their background and experience in an effort to clarify a point or share an experience in line with the course material; an example extract is produced below. This was in response to another student's submission to a discussion prompt:

> *At 5:30 during the lecture 'Are the competitive markets efficient?', Professor Taylor refers to MRIs as 'magnetic research imaging scanners', but MRI actually stands for magnetic resonance imaging. I know this is rather pedantic, but my many years in radiology requires that I call your attention to this point. It is certainly true that there are far more MRI scanners in the US compared with either the UK*

or Canada, but this is primarily a function of our for-profit healthcare delivery system as well as insatiable patient demand in this country for the latest medical technologic advancement regardless of the cost (usually borne by a third party or received as an untaxed benefit from their employer).

Participants sharing their experiences can help make the course content accessible to other participants by reformulating the course material or by providing relevant and relatable examples from their personal lives and work experience. Participants utilised social elements frequently in their enactment of peer support, highlighting social presence as a core component of teaching presence with a wider overlap in its role in facilitating discourse within the discussion forum [37].

Another interesting observation was the sharing of external resources mainly in the form of web links to articles, documents and videos which show a willingness of some participants to assist other students in the course with relevant material they had found useful. This was the most frequent activity carried out by participants in their peer-support efforts. Though the facilitator may be expected to provide extra resource materials, this may not satisfy the needs of all participants. Participants may most likely share external resources that may be localised to the specific need of the student requesting assistance. The following two extracts from the forum demonstrate participants sharing helpful resources to other participants:

True. I think we will learn more about this later but here is the Gini coefficient for the US against time [link to an image of a graph]. The Gini coefficient is a measure of inequality. You can see how the U.S. has changed towards more income inequality in the past 40–50 years.! Income Gini Ratio, U.S., Investormill.com: https://investormill.com/data/income-gini-ratio-households-by-race-of-householder/

I did some further online searching and found a good article at http://www.popcouncil.org/uploads/pdfs/frontiers/Capacity Bldg/WTP Manual.pdf on how Willingness to pay is actually collected. It does not deal with the case here of increasing numbers of bananas - but it [does] convince me that the data here is misleadingly displayed and that the Marginal Benefit = Willingness to Pay for additional item is the question that was actually asked and the data that was used to build the misleadingly labelled 'Willingness to Pay column'. If this is not the case then the argument given here for deriving the Demand curve is simply wrong.

As has been observed so far, participants provided rich comments and responses to their peer's submissions, some of which can be seen in the use of illustrations and analogies to reformulate and explain concepts to fellow participants. With a large number of participants with varied experiences, there is the likelihood of a participant having the background and experience that can better explain a point, concept or idea from the course material. This characteristic is also manifested through demonstrations by example, the clarification of information, and the use of illustrations and analogies to simplify course material to assist other participants in the course. The dataset that was used in this research did not tag each participant to the messages they shared; this limits the ability of this study to identify and characterise at an individual level participant's peer-support behaviour however the overall impact can be observed. The following message extract shows a participant stepping in to help another student whose query had received no response for an extended period of time. The responder may have chanced upon the participant's query while searching for answers to their own query, and it may also be the responder may have sought out forum posts that had received no responses, by using the filter and sort functionality available. Note that the course spanned an eight-week period, hence this intervention may have arrived at the tail end or after the course:

> *I'm surprised that no one has responded to your request after 2 months. Marginal cost is what it costs to produce one more unit of a good or service. So if, say, one unit of a good costs a firm $3 to produce and two units together costs $7 to produce, then the marginal cost of producing the second good is the $7 cost for producing two units minus $3 for producing just one unit or $7 - $3 = $4 for producing the second unit of the good.*

The majority of the teaching presence indicators were enacted in the direct instruction category. We observe that some participants actively reformulated the course content for those who needed assistance and frequently provided additional resources to supplement their feedback. The student's expectation of the teacher is to provide "content knowledge that is enhanced by the teacher's personal interest, excitement and in-depth understanding of the content" [27], qualities that may be exhibited by knowledgeable peers that participate in a MOOC out of interest or as a refresher as discussed in the literature review.

Anderson et al. defined facilitating discourse as the component "that stimulates social process with a direct goal of stimulating individual and group learning" and is a shared activity between teacher and students [27]. This definition aptly describes the overlap of the social presence and the teaching presence, which is described as providing intellectual and scholarly leadership towards the growth of knowledge of the students. The Community of Inquiry framework posits that the teacher ought to be not only a content deliverer but also an active member of the community engaging with the participants by commenting with supportive responses to facilitate their learning, a role that experienced and knowledgeable participants can be encouraged to fulfil.

Of the eight indicators that form the facilitating discourse component, only four were exhibited by the participants in the forum. The absence of these indicators was not surprising. These indicators: *Present follow up topics for discussion*, *Refocusing discussion on specific issues*, *Seeking to reach consensus* and *Setting climate for learning*, may require deliberate effort by a facilitator, enacted to steer participants towards attaining a learning outcome. A student providing peer support may not deliberately embark on enacting these indicators. Furthermore, the student providing peer support may lack requisite toolset and professional skills to carry out these indicators. Out of the four indicators that were expressed in facilitating discourse category, *Drawing in participants* and *Encouraging, acknowledging or reinforcing student contributions* were the most frequently expressed indicators. The discussion prompts which were employed as part of the pedagogy of the course provided an opportunity for students to share their thoughts, and while perusing the contributions of others could chime in an acknowledgement or contribution their own submission. The following is an extract from a contribution by a student who was adding to the responses by two others that had responded to a contribution submitted by another student:

> *Thanks [Student 1] and [Student 2] for your insightful comments. If I recall correctly, Specialisation, Division of Labor and Comparative Advantage apply for 'better trade'. Does it apply also to the 'economy?' In the example that [Student 1] articulates here yes, the economy gains when income is freed up for other expenditures, ...*

The results of the study highlight that very few participants were actively engaged in the discussion forum, a scenario that has been observed in previous studies [15, 16]. However, these few active participants account for only a few of the responses that participants received. The majority of messages and responses are submitted by the larger pool of participants that would have made a submission about once or twice for the duration of the course. Social presence expressed was superficial and primarily served to facilitate interaction and not utilised for community building. Further studies are required to develop a more complete picture of social presence enactment in MOOCs, especially studies that investigate the social presence of active and passive participants separately. Teaching presence also was distributed in that it was expressed by several participants with most participants enacting it once or twice. Though this is beneficial for the facilitators (by reducing load) and for the participants (by benefiting from other experienced participants) further research is required to investigate in more depth how this can be fully actualised and its impact in a MOOC.

5. A typology of peer support behaviours in a MOOC

This section presents a typology that builds upon the findings highlighted earlier. Once developed, the typology then can be reused in other MOOC contexts and settings to assess the enactment and nature of peer support activities. The typology is influenced by the Community of Inquiry framework. Though the Community of Inquiry highlights that participants can carry out teaching presence the Community of Inquiry framework is focused on teaching presence carried out by the teacher or instructor. An opportunity, therefore, exists to address this gap in the framework to provide a means of assessing student–student interactions that are geared towards facilitating the learning of other participants. A typology capturing the behaviours of participants engaged in this type of activity is a step towards addressing this gap.

MOOCs exemplify the reduced capability of teachers and instructors to provide adequate support to learners via direct interaction with each student and the increasing role of learners to support each other through the learning process. This typology aims to focus on the peer support carried out by participants as opposed to the entire learning process which is the focus of the Community of Inquiry framework. The typology hence acts as an add-on or extension to the Community of Inquiry framework to capture peer support interactions. A reusable tool provides consistency in use across different environments and contexts useful for benchmarking and comparisons when utilised across different contexts.

Research into the nature of peer support in MOOCs is ongoing and evolving; as such there are a number of reasons that a typology will be useful for the ongoing research in peer support behaviours that are enacted by MOOC participants. First, a typology provides a simple way to organise and make sense of peer support behaviours to provide a coherent description of the behaviours enacted by participants. A typology can also facilitate communication between both researchers and practitioners who are exploring pedagogical strategies. A typology can also help identify interplays between the observed behaviours and by extension predict possible behaviours that could occur. The typology provides a framework for accessing peer support behaviours carried out by participants in a MOOC discussion forum. The typology has applications for future researchers in building upon the body of knowledge of participants interaction behaviours in a MOOC context. The typology is presented as a descriptive framework with no stipulated hierarchy nor does inclusion of a characteristic suggests importance. The typology is envisioned as a tool to compare peer support behaviours carried out by participants in different MOOC contexts that can inform pedagogical strategies employed to facilitate achieving learning outcomes and objectives especially from the participants perspective.

5.1 Extracting peer support behaviours

The constituents of the typology are derived from the coding of discussion forum interactions carried out by participants in the MOOC used in the study. This coding was carried out using the Community of Inquiry framework. To extract the typology the indicators are further summarised and organised into behaviours with respect to the learner providing peer support. These are behaviours exhibited by the participant while carrying out the task of facilitating the learning process for another learner. With a sample size of one MOOC (of one variety) this typology may not be exhaustive and will require review and refinement in future studies. The typology comprises three elements that interact with each other *Openness*, *Re-Contextualisation of Course Content* and *Transactional Exchanges*. The purpose of each element and relevance is discussed below.

Teaching presence is not enacted in isolation, but in concert with social presence hence social discourse forms an integral component in the enactment of teaching presence [37]. Participants utilised a range of social presence indicators to convey their thoughts and ideas. For example, when providing assistance participants sometimes drew from their personal experience of their work in industry or personal knowledge to provide the help required (self-disclosure, personal advice). The diversity of participants enriches the learning process for those requiring support as the responses can be localised to the asker with information that meets or suits their needs. The willingness of responders to share from their personal experience and knowledge demonstrates that participants felt comfortable sharing in the discussion forum. This behaviour, the co-occurrence of social presence with teaching presence, is collectively referred to as *Openness*.

Openness by responders providing peer support was also enacted through the encouragement they provided to other participants for example when they posted their response to discussion prompts. Discussion prompts serve to reinforce the learning of the course content while creating opportunities to further learn through discussion. The acknowledgement and encouragement offered by responders can provide a morale boost and recognition of the efforts of participants who may be undertaking the course in isolation.

Through *Openness*, the interactions of participants are less formal when they inject humour or express emotion in their response. These behaviours demonstrate an openness by participants to freely express themselves. This behaviour can be high in a MOOC where participants are able to comfortably express themselves, or low where participants show restraint or are formal with their interaction providing an opportunity for MOOC facilitators to further investigate if such behaviour was not an expected outcome. The richness of participants background was brought to bear in this MOOC through the support they provided. Diverse participants utilised knowledge from their personal experience to explain course content or answer questions asked by other participants. Participants stepped in to clarify course content which posters had flagged as challenging. They sometimes conducted demonstrations (for example through a worked example), and provided useful illustrations and analogies through which the course material was made accessible to learners requesting assistance.

Responders also frequently shared materials and links to external resources they found useful and relevant to address the query they were responding to. In carrying out these teaching presence indicators, participants were using the tools at their disposal (personal knowledge, industry experience, external content they had found useful) to address a message posted (such as a question or response to discussion prompt) in a form that makes the course content accessible to their fellow learners. The indicators under direct instruction are collectively referred to as *Re-Contextualisation of Course Content* capturing the various approaches responders utilised to deliver responses to queries. Currently in the typology emphasis is not placed on the method used, rather choosing to identify any approach that can be utilised to make the course content accessible to other learners. This behaviour can be high: where participants are actively engaging with and supporting the learning process of fellow learners, or low: where few participants engage in providing assistance to other participants needing support.

Messages exchanged on the discussion forum appear to be of a transactional nature. The majority of participants provided responses only once or twice, with very few participants posting frequently (more than twice) indicating that participants were not engaged in back-and-forth discussions. They reply one time, or a second time, and may not reply again. The asynchronous nature of interactions on the forum means queries can be addressed at any time by anyone who is available and/or has the expertise to address the query. It may be that when a query receives a response there is little motivation to add on, that a discussion does not ensue, hence discussion threads consist primarily of queries and answers.

The frequent use of vocatives and expressions of appreciation could also indicate the orientation of interactions towards query and response. With the majority of participants submitting just about one query each, submission is thus being received from "new" participants each time. Though responses tend to be short, long-form exploratory answers were observed as well. Participants were not habitual posters on the discussion forum but only stepped in to provide support when seeking answers to their own questions through searching the discussion forum. Thus, this interaction behaviour of participants appears to be transactional in nature: providing support to others while seeking out answers to their own queries. From this the *Transactional Exchanges* behaviour of participants is derived. This highlights the engagement pattern that may be exhibited by participants providing peer support. This behaviour could be high: where exchanges are of one-time assistance, or low: where participants actively deliberate with each other. Where MOOC providers anticipate a level of engagement and interaction by participants, this behaviour in the typology can highlight if this outcome was achieved.

5.2 Typology of peer support behaviours

Table 1 below summarises the extracted behaviours earlier discussed. As an add-on to the Community of Inquiry framework, this table serves to guide researchers on how to map their coding carried out using the Community of Inquiry framework into the peer support behaviours for this typology. In **Table 1** below each *Behaviour* (typology element) maps to a *Coding Categorisation*. The coding categorisation directs how the indicators from the Community of Inquiry framework are to be categorised to derive the behaviour. *Example of Enactment* in **Table 1** below provides an example at the indicator level of the social and teaching presence within the Community of Inquiry framework. The three behaviours are not enacted in isolation but can be acted with one or all of the other behaviours.

In the provision of peer support, each of the behaviours occurs at different levels, for example, where transactional exchange is high, *Openness* by participants may be low. **Figure 2** on the following page captures the interplay between each of the behaviours. At the centre of behaviours is the peer support carried out. The diagram can be read as.

behaviour x influences level of behaviour y due to factors a, b, c etc.

Behaviour	Example of Enactment	Coding Categorisation
Openness	1. Self-disclosure when encouraging other participants 2. Use of humour when offering useful illustrations 3. Sharing personal advice when making explicit reference to outside materials	Overlap of teaching presence and social presence categories enacted by participants
Re-contextualising Course Content	1. Providing valuable analogies 2. Offering useful illustrations 3. Conducting supportive 4. demonstrations 5. Supplying clarifying information 6. Making explicit reference 7. to outside material	Any of indicators within direct instruction category of teaching presence
Transactional Exchanges	1. Brief/short responses 2. Short discussion thread 3. One-time feedback	Through assessment of messages per participant and average length of thread

Table 1.
Typology of peer support behaviours in a MOOC.

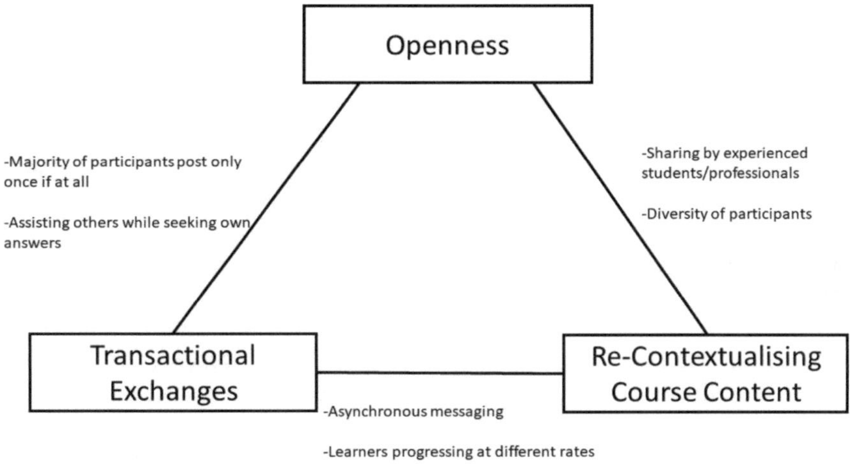

Figure 2.
How peer support was enacted by participants in this study.

For example, *Transactional Exchanges* influence *Re-Contextualisation of Course Content* due to the asynchronous messaging nature of discussion forum. **Figure 2** is not static but depends on the MOOC context where the typology is applied. It summarises the factors at play in the MOOC being studied. Researchers are encouraged to model the typology per their interaction with each other.

5.2.1 Openness

Participants engaged in the discussion forum primarily respond to discussion prompts, and raise questions about challenges they encountered. In their provision of assistance, respondents utilised details from their personal life and experience. These respondents would most likely be professionals taking the course out of interest. The platform provided a comfortable environment to share their personal experiences. *Openness* in their interaction also allowed respondents to express themselves freely, such as with humour to reformulate course content to "soften" what may have been a hard topic. The messages were informal but polite, usually initiated and concluded with a salutation and focused on the course content. This interplay between *Openness* and Re-contextualising Course Content is captured in **Figure 2** above.

Though participants were open in their interactions, not all types of messages were shared. The primary focus of the exchanges was on the course. Personal details and experiences shared to explain or make the course content accessible were limited to the context of the course. Messages about personal events, such as holiday trips or birthday announcements, were absent. Very few participants were frequent posters with the majority of participants sharing on average only once if at all hence interpersonal bonds that may develop are weak. This highlights the interplay between *Openness* and *Transactional Exchanges* by participants in the Principles of Economics MOOC as depicted in **Figure 2**. When *Transactional Exchanges* are high, social interactions may be limited to superficial and formal expressions, this may be an artefact of participants taking a moment to respond to a fellow learner while seeking out answers to their own questions rather than seeking to engage with other learners. *Openness* by participants is needful in MOOC discussion forums where individually participants share infrequently. Comfortably sharing their thoughts, encouraging other participants or drawing from their experience to support other learners is valuable even if this happens as a one-time activity for the learner.

5.2.2 Re-contextualisation of course content

Participants showed a capacity to explain course materials to fellow learners sometimes utilising information from their personal life and informal social language to reformulate the course content in their responses. On limited occasions, participants provided detailed explanations consisting of several paragraphs drawing on examples from their life or experience in an effort to make a concept accessible to the question-asker reflecting the openness by responders captured by the interaction between *Openness* and Re-Contextualising Course Content represented in **Figure 2**. Responders can localise responses to the requester using references that make the explanation accessible to the recipient, for example, using alternative definitions of content highlighted in the course and worked examples of math-based problems.

The diversity of backgrounds and experiences of participants makes available a pool of knowledge to address a variety of needs that may arise in the discussion forum, they can bring the course to life with their industry experience. Participants voluntarily helping each other can alleviate the load on the course facilitators in providing assistance. Respondents providing assistance also made reference to materials (for example, books) and shared web links to external resources (such as web articles and videos) in their responses. These resources are specific to the query being addressed by providing extra content that precisely addresses the needs of the requester. The respondent may have personally utilised these resources or has assessed them to be relevant to the query.

External resources provided are hence specific and relevant to the needs of the requester. The interplay between *Transactional Exchanges* and *Re-Contextualisation of Course Content* may be influenced by the asynchronous nature of the discussion forum which allows responders to provide feedback when they are in the position to do so, hence responses are not instantaneous, and neither is the feedback if any from the learner receiving the assistance. Participants could have progressed further with their learning by the time they receive a response at which point the desired period when the information may have been useful (for example undertaking a quiz) may have elapsed.

5.2.3 Transactional exchanges

Exchanges in the discussion forum were not directed towards community building. An exchange was usually initiated by a submission for a discussion prompt or query then immediately concluded in the immediate reply when an answer to the query was provided. Messages in response to discussion prompts were usually followed by expressions of agreement that did not build on the initial post. Hence discussion threads were usually short comprising usually of a question and an answer or a comment. With participants progressing through the course at different rates, follow-ups if at all desired may be a challenge as new questions come through from the large number of participants. It may be that peer support happens sporadically while participants browse through the forum searching for answers to their own challenges.

The high attrition in MOOCs may not couple well with asynchronous messaging as participants drop out over time resulting in one or both participants involved in a discussion not being available to follow up. As discussed under *Openness* above, the enactment of *Transactional Exchanges* can influence the level of *Openness* participants exhibit with *Openness* being low if participants only interact if required rather than actively engaging with each other. The influence of *Transactional Exchanges* on *Re-contextualisation of Course Content* will be the subject of further investigation; it is anticipated that the level of *Transactional Exchanges* may influence the mode of re-contextualisation utilised by participants. For example, will use of analogies and illustrations be high when the level of *Transactional Exchanges* is low? Will participants in a high *Transactional Exchanges* environment utilise reference to outside materials more?

5.3 Utilising the typology

The following procedure is recommended for the application of the typology in future studies. The typology is derived from the Community of Inquiry framework hence utilises the Community of Inquiry coding scheme. Users are encouraged to utilise a whole message of a post for a more robust and consistent coding process. Multiple coding of the same message with different indicators is also encouraged given the expected overlap between social and teaching presences. The typology can be used to compare peer support behaviour across multiple MOOCs. An example of the outcome from the application of the typology is discussed at the end of this section.

To utilise the typology in a research study:

1. Obtain the messages exchanged by participants within the MOOC discussion forum for the period of interest.

2. Messages should be grouped into threads comprising of the head (the initial post being a submission or a question) and ensuing responses to maintain context of messages exchanged.

3. Utilise the social and teaching presences of the Community of Inquiry framework to code each message.

4. Using **Table 1** map the coding from Step 3 to the behaviours in the typology.

5. Tabulate results and summarise the behaviours of the typology as:

$$Behaviour\left(eg.Opennes\right)=\frac{count\ of\ messages\ coded\ for\ behaviour}{number\ of\ messages\ coded} \tag{1}$$

6. Item 5 above will yield percentage scores. These can be mapped to behaviour levels using the following bands. The score ranges are indicative only, researchers can adapt as required to suit their context (**Table 2**).

7. Repeat for each course under investigation then compare output of summary of codes across the courses.

5.4 A typology use example

An example use of the typology is applied to the theoretical interactions of students (and hence peer support) that may be carried by participants in a cMOOC and xMOOC. Referencing Miyazoe & Anderson's Interaction Equivalency [5] as a benchmarking guide for student–student interaction this example compares the enactment of each behaviour for peer support. Miyazoe & Anderson indicate cMOOCs experience high student–student interaction as learners connect with each other.

Students in cMOOCs are encouraged to contribute resources that are added to the collection shared with other learners. A cMOOC usually has medium student-content interactions because learning is focused on interaction with other students in the network. In the context of the peer support typology, this can be translated as high *Openness* by students in the cMOOCs environment as participants are

Score range (%)	Behaviour level
0–30	Low
30–60	Medium
60–100	High

Table 2.
Mapping scores to behaviour level.

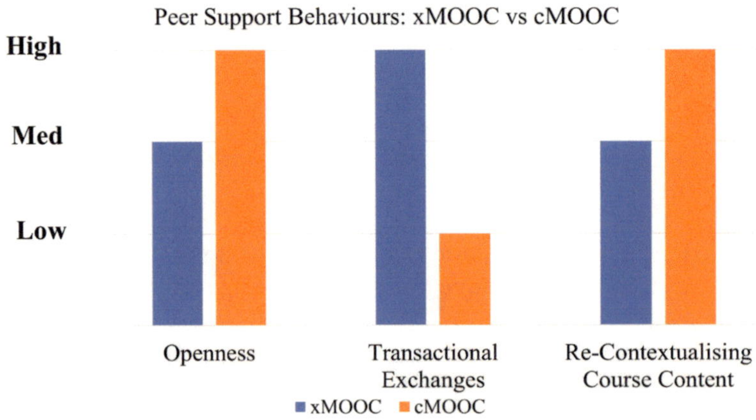

Figure 3.
Example result: Comparing peers support behaviours in xMOOC and cMOOC.

encouraged to actively network and interact with each other to facilitate their learning. As such, *Transactional Exchanges* will be low as students frequently interact with each other. *Re-Contextualisation of Course Content* is high in a cMOOC as learners are encouraged to contribute resources that everyone in the learning network can benefit from.

In contrast, xMOOCs have low-to-medium student–student interaction, as effective tools to support the large number of participants remains a challenge. Student-content interaction is high usually driven by the prestige and experience of the instructor whose lessons have been pre-recorded. From this we can expect that *Openness* by participants providing peer support in an xMOOC will be low-to-medium and *Transactional Exchanges* will be high. Nonetheless, this research study has shown participants providing peer support put in the effort to share extra resources they have found useful or provide answers to their peers asking questions, however, given that a large number of queries go unanswered, *Re-Contextualisation of Course Content* is pegged at medium for xMOOCs. **Figure 3** presents this information in graphical format.

Acknowledgements

The content of this Chapter is based on research carried out by Kwamena Appiah-Kubi for the award of PhD. The original thesis can be found at reference [38] below. Both authors have contributed to the writing of the paper and have approved the final version.

Author details

Kwamena Appiah-Kubi and David Cobham*
University of Lincoln, Lincoln, UK

*Address all correspondence to: dcobham@lincoln.ac.uk

References

[1] Rhoads RA. MOOCs, High Technology, and Higher Learning. In Johns Hopkins University Press; 2015. p. 185.

[2] McAuley S, Stewart B, Siemens G, Cormier D. The MOOC model for digital practice. Massive Open Online Courses Digit ways knowing Learn. 2010;1-64.

[3] Siemens G. Massive open online courses : innovation in education? Massive open online courses Innov Educ. 2013;1833:5-16.

[4] Glance DG, Forsey M, Riley M. The pedagogical foundations of massive open online courses. First Monday. 2013 May 6;18(5).

[5] Miyazoe T, Anderson T. Interaction Equivalency in an OER, MOOCS and Informal Learning Era. J Interact Media Educ. 2013;2013(2):15.

[6] Pursel BK, Zhang L, Jablokow KW, Choi GW, Velegol D. Understanding MOOC students: motivations and behaviours indicative of MOOC completion. J Comput Assist Learn. 2016 Jun;32(3):202-217.

[7] Shapiro HB, Lee CH, Wyman Roth NE, Li K, Çetinkaya-Rundel M, Canelas DA. Understanding the massive open online course (MOOC) student experience: An examination of attitudes, motivations, and barriers. Comput Educ. 2017;110:35-50.

[8] Clow D. MOOCs and the funnel of participation. In: Proceedings of the Third International Conference on Learning Analytics and Knowledge - LAK '13 [Internet]. New York, New York, USA: ACM Press; 2013 [cited 2014 Dec 1]. p. 185-9. Available from: http://dl.acm.org/citation.cfm?id=2460296.2460332

[9] Eriksson T, Adawi T, Stöhr C. "Time is the bottleneck": a qualitative study exploring why learners drop out of MOOCs. J Comput High Educ. 2017;29(1):133-146.

[10] Salmon G. E-Moderating: The Key to Online Teaching and Learning. 3rd ed. E-Moderating. Routledge; 2012. 288 p.

[11] Gillani N, Yasseri T, Eynon R, Hjorth I. Structural limitations of learning in a crowd: Communication vulnerability and information diffusion in MOOCs. Sci Rep. 2014;4:1-7.

[12] Wise AF, Cui Y, Vytasek J. Bringing order to chaos in MOOC discussion forums with content-related thread identification. In: Proceedings of the Sixth International Conference on Learning Analytics & Knowledge - LAK '16. New York, New York, USA: ACM Press; 2016. p. 188-197.

[13] Koutropoulos A, Hogue RJ. How to Succeed in a MOOC - Massive Online Open Course (Oct 12). 2012.

[14] Milligan C, Littlejohn A, Margaryan A. Patterns of Engagement in Connectivist MOOCs. MERLOT J Online Learn Teach. 2013;9(2):149-159.

[15] Breslow L, Pritchard DE, DeBoer J, Stump GS, Ho AD, Seaton DT. Studying learning in the worldwide classroom: Research into edX's first MOOC. Res Pract Assess. 2013;8(March 2012):13-25.

[16] Deng R, Benckendorff P, Gannaway D. Linking learner factors, teaching context, and engagement patterns with MOOC learning outcomes. J Comput Assist Learn. 2020 Oct 29;36(5):688-708.

[17] Kop R. The Challenges to Connectivist Learning on Open Online Networks : Learning Experiences during a Massive Open Online Course. Int Rev Res Open Distance Learn. 2011;12(3):19-38.

[18] Huang J, Dasgupta A, Ghosh A, Manning J, Sanders M. Superposter behavior in MOOC forums. Proc first ACM Conf Learn @ scale Conf - L@S '14. 2014;117-126.

[19] Gillani N, Eynon R. Communication patterns in massively open online courses. Internet High Educ. 2014 Oct;23:18-26.

[20] Onah DFO, Sinclair JE, Boyatt R. Exploring the Use of MOOC Discussion Forums. Proc London Int Conf Educ. 2014;1-4.

[21] Kellogg S, Booth S, Oliver K. A social network perspective on peer supported learning in MOOCs for educators. Vol. 15, The International Review of Research in Open and Distributed Learning. 2014.

[22] Garrison DR, Anderson T, Archer W. The first decade of the community of inquiry framework: A retrospective. Internet High Educ. 2010 Jan;13(1-2):5-9.

[23] Garrison DR. E-Learning in the 21st Century. 2nd ed. Routledge; 2016.

[24] Dewey J. My Pedagogic Creed. J Educ [Internet]. 1925 Apr 10;101(18):490-490. Available from: http://journals.sagepub.com/doi/10.1177/002205742510101803

[25] Arbaugh JB, Hwang A. Does "teaching presence" exist in online MBA courses? Internet High Educ. 2006 Jan;9(1):9-21.

[26] Garrison DR. Online Community of Inquiry Review : Social , Cognitive , and Teaching Presence Issues. J Asynchronous Learn Networks. 2007;11(1):61-72.

[27] Anderson T, Rourke L, Garrison DR, Archer W. Assessing teaching presence in a computer conferencing context. J Asynchronous Learn Netw. 2001;5(2):1-17.

[28] Shea P, Pickett A, Pelz W. A Follow Up Investigation of "Teacher Presence" in the SUNY Learning Network. J Asynchronous Learn Networks. 2003;7(2):61-80.

[29] Garrison DR, Anderson T, Archer W. Critical thinking, cognitive presence, and computer conferencing in distance education. Am J Distance Educ. 2001;15(1):7-23.

[30] Akyol Z, Garrison DR. The Development of a Community of Inquiry over Time in an Online Course: Understanding the Progression and Integration of Social, Cognitive and Teaching Presence. J Asynchronous Learn Networks. 2008;12(3-4):3-22.

[31] Armellini A, Rodriguez BCP. Are Massive Open Online Courses (MOOCs) pedagogically innovative? J Interact online Learn. 2016;14(1):17-28.

[32] Arbaugh JB, Cleveland-Innes M, Diaz SR, Garrison DR, Ice P, Richardson JC, et al. Developing a community of inquiry instrument: Testing a measure of the Community of Inquiry framework using a multi-institutional sample. Internet High Educ. 2008 Jan;11(3-4):133-136.

[33] Lambert JL, Fisher JL. Community of inquiry framework: Establishing community in an online course. J Interact Online Learn. 2013;12(1):1-16.

[34] Akyol Z, Arbaugh JB, Cleveland-Innes M, Garrison DR, Richardson JC, Swan K. A Response to the Review of the Community of Inquiry Framework Learning Processes vs . Learning Outcomes. J Distance Educ. 2009;23(2):123-136.

[35] Rourke L, Anderson T, Garrison DR, Archer W. Assessing Social Presence In Asynchronous Text-based Computer

Conferencing. Int J E-Learning Distance Educ. 1999;14(2):50-71.

[36] Khalil H, Ebner M. MOOCs Completion Rates and Possible Methods to Improve Retention - A Literature Review. In: World Conference on Educational Multimedia, Hypermedia and Telecommunications. 2014. p. 1305-1313.

[37] Armellini A, De Stefani M. Social presence in the 21st century: An adjustment to the Community of Inquiry framework. Br J Educ Technol. 2016;47(6):1202-1216.

[38] Appiah-Kubi K, Thesis for the award of PhD, Available on request from University of Lincoln library.

Chapter 3

Contextualized English Reading Proficiency Toolkit (CERPT): Enhance Learners' English Reading Proficiency

Dr. Irene C. Culaste-Quimbo

Abstract

The Department of Education has introduced numerous intervention and remediation programs to address the reading needs of learners. Despite these, data showed that majority of the learners still have reading problems when they reach higher grade levels. Henceforth, the study experimented on the innovation – Contextualized English Reading Proficiency Toolkit (CERPT) to help the learners of Kibacania Elementary School improved their reading ability level. All the pupils were exposed to CERPT. A pre-experimental research design was employed in this study. Findings revealed that the learners' reading ability level enhanced from frustration to instructional. There was a significant difference in the learners' reading ability levels before and after exposure to CERPT. Thus, the study commends the use of CERPT to help in the improvement of the learners' reading ability level.

Keywords: contextualized, reading ability level, reading toolkit, frustration, instructional

1. Introduction

Success in reading is critical to the success in school and reading problems will influence every facet of a child's academic achievement. Therefore, early reading is so important. Children who learn to read early go on to develop exceptional reading skills and achieve greater academic success in school. When kids fall behind in reading, they also lag in other subject areas, and will struggle with schoolwork. They become discouraged, lose motivation, fall further behind, and it becomes a vicious cycle downwards.

DepEd has presented programs to affect the reading needs of learners. It issued DepEd Order No. 45 s. 2002 or Every Child A Reader Program (ECARP) as a national program with a goal that every child will be a reader by the time, they finish grade three. Numerous intervention and remediation programs had been conducted by teachers to address the call of DepEd. However, data showed that most of the learners reaching grades four and above still have difficulties in their reading proficiency level.

In fact, the Philippine – Informal Reading Inventory (Phil-IRI) English Post-Test result in Kibacania Elementary School for the academic year 2018–2019 revealed that 24% of the grades four to six learners were frustrated readers, 31% were instructional readers, and 36% were independent readers. When examined closely by the class advisers through the individual oral reading of graded passages, it was found out that the frustrated readers were having word recognition problems on words with consonant blends and consonant digraphs. It was also found out that both frustrated and instructional readers had problems with fluency, vocabulary and reading comprehension. This result emerges and replicates a depressing level of reading proficiency by the learners.

Krause et al. (2016) [1] conversed that the use of content contextualization is supported by three principles: prior knowledge, promoting conceptual change, and promoting metacognition. Firstly, contextualized content instruction activates the learners' prior knowledge and promote more effective problem solving. Student can retain information better if things can be related to their daily life. Secondly, an improvement in learning is evident when content contextualization activities are interactive and engaging that motivates students with a concept relevance. Thirdly, contextualization of content helps students reflect on their learning to link ideas from a recognizable tangible context of an abstract idea so they can distinguish their own personal association to these ideas.

Bonganciso, 2016 [2] conducted a study on the effects of Contextualized Teaching and Learning on the reading comprehension performance of the thirty-three Bachelor of Science in Information Technology students. Results revealed that there was a significant increase on the reading comprehension performance of the students from pretest to posttest. Hence, positive effects on the learners' reading comprehension performance are visible when reading tasks given were contextualized.

Subsequently, this gave light to the researcher to design a Contextualized English Reading Proficiency Toolkit (CERPT) to address the English reading needs of the learners. Reading resources shall be within the concern and within the context of the learners to foster higher performance in reading proficiency.

Particularly, the purpose of this study was to see if the use of CERPT greatly enhances the English reading proficiency level of grades one to six learners in Kibacania Elementary School for the academic year 2019–2020. Thereby making them independent readers.

2. Action research questions

The study aims to help the grades one to six learners of Kibacania Elementary School in the academic year 2019–2020 enhance their English reading proficiency level through the Contextualized English Reading Proficiency Toolkit. Thereby making them independent readers.

The research questions providing focus for this study are:

1. What is the English reading proficiency level of grades one to six learners in Kibacania Elementary School in terms of word reading and comprehension before and after using the Contextualized English Reading Proficiency Toolkit?

2. Is there a significant increase in the English reading proficiency level of grades one to six learners in terms of word reading and comprehension after using the Contextualized English Reading Proficiency Toolkit?

3. Hypothesis of the study

The hypothesis of this study was tested at 0.05 level of significance.

There is no significant increase in the English reading proficiency level of grades one to six learners in terms of word reading and comprehension after using the Contextualized English Reading Proficiency Toolkit.

4. Description of Contextualized English Reading Proficiency Toolkit (CERPT)

The Contextualized English Reading Proficiency Toolkit (CERPT) is an English reading resource made by the researcher. This is an initiative to address the gap in English reading proficiency levels of the Kibacania Elementary School learners from grade one to grade six. It focuses on the development of phonemic awareness, beginning reading, word recognition, fluency, vocabulary and reading comprehension skills.

The CERPT consists of four workbooks: the phonemic awareness for workbook 1, beginning reading for workbook 2, word recognition and comprehension for workbook 3, and developing reading comprehension for workbook 4.

The first workbook which is the Phonemic Awareness was designed to help the struggling readers memorize all the consonant letter names and sounds. This workbook offers brilliant exercise with phonemic awareness skills for beginning and ending sounds. One of the most important Kindergarten skills is complete memorization of all consonant letter sounds since this is the backbone to reading success in first grade. It is also recommended that this toolkit be reviewed for the first month of first grade before any word reading takes place.

Phonemic Awareness denotes to being able to recognize where a certain sound occurs in the word: beginning, middle, or end. It is a critical skill for spelling unknown words and is helpful in deciphering new reading words. Children who do not have satisfactory phonemic awareness skills will not only suffer slower reading progress but will become severely frustrated when trying to spell words while writing sentences, paragraphs, or stories.

The second workbook is on the development of Beginning Reading. It was designed to help the grade one and struggling readers how to blend the sound of every letter to read the word or what we call decoding. It utilized the "stop at the vowel" strategy and consists of five parts. The pupils would learn how to read CVC words.

The third workbook is the Word Recognition and Comprehension Development. It includes short vowel words in CVC pattern, consonant blends, consonant digraphs, long vowel words ending in silent e, words with vowel digraphs, and words with vowel diphthongs. This workbook is designed for the grades two and three pupils as well as the struggling readers in grades four, five and six.

Finally, the fourth workbook is the Developing Reading Comprehension. It includes graded reading comprehension passages that addresses the literal, inferential and critical skills. This toolkit was designed to augment the English reading proficiency level of grades four, five and six learners as well as of the struggling readers.

5. Methodology

A pre-experimental research design was employed in this study. All the participants in the study were exposed to the innovation which was the use of Contextualized English Reading Proficiency Toolkit. The Phil-IRI assessment tool pre-test and post-test result were utilized for data analysis.

Purposive sampling was employed in determining the participants of this study who were the grades one to six learners of Kibacania Elementary School for the academic year 2019–2020. **Table 1** shows the detailed breakdown of the participants of this study. The study was conducted on July 1, 2019 to December 12, 2019.

The Phil-IRI Assessment Tool pretest and posttest adopted from DepEd Phil-IRI Manual 2018 for grades four to six were utilized as well as the Phil-IRI Manual 2011–2012 for grades one to three were used to determine the reading proficiency level of the participants in this study before and after the implementation of the innovation. The Phil-IRI reading test uses predetermined set of criteria in identifying the reading level of each student for each passage. These criteria include the percentage of word recognition accuracy and the percentage of correct answers to comprehension questions.

To calculate the word reading score in percentage, formula 1 below was used.

Equation 1: Word reading score

$$Word\ Reading\ Score = \frac{(total\ number\ of\ words\ in\ the\ passage - number\ of\ words\ miscues)}{total\ number\ of\ words\ in\ the\ passage} X\ 100 \quad (1)$$

To compute the reading comprehension score in percentage, formula 2 was followed.

Equation 2: Reading comprehension score

$$Reading\ Comprehension\ Score = \frac{number\ of\ correct\ answers}{number\ of\ questions} X\ 100 \quad (2)$$

To determine the proficiency level of learners in word reading as well as in reading comprehension, the percentage scores were analyzed following the rating scale shown in **Table 2** basing from Phil-IRI Manual, 2018.

Grade level	Male	Female	Total
I	16	10	26
II	8	10	18
III	10	4	14
IV	10	6	16
V	16	11	27
VI	6	7	13
Total	66	48	114

Table 1.
Participants of the study.

Proficiency level	Word reading		Reading comprehension	
	Score (in %)	Mean score	Score (in %)	Mean score
Independent (Ind)	97–100%	97.00–100	80–100%	80.00–100
Instructional (Ins)	90–96%	90.00–96.99	59–79%	59.00–79.99
Frustration (F)	1–89%	1.00–89.99	1–58%	1.00–58.99
Non-reader (NR)	0%	0.00–0.99	0%	0.00–0.99

Table 2.
Criteria in determining the learners' proficiency level in word reading and reading comprehension.

Reading proficiency level	Word reading level	Reading comprehension level
Independent (Ind)	Independent (Ind)	Independent (Ind)
Instructional (Ins)	Independent (Ind)	Instructional (Ins)
Instructional (Ins)	Instructional (Ins)	Independent (Ind)
Frustration (F)	Instructional (Ins)	Frustration (F)
Frustration (F)	Frustration (F)	Instructional (Ins)
Frustration (F)	Frustration (F)	Frustration (F)

Table 3.
Criteria in determining the learners' reading proficiency level.

Afterwards, the learner's reading proficiency level in general was determined using the criteria presented in **Table 3** basing from Phil-IRI Manual, 2018 [3].

Further, descriptive statistics particularly mean was employed to answer question number one. While inferential statistics specifically paired t-test was utilized to treat question number two.

6. Results/findings of the study

6.1 Reading proficiency level of learners before and after using CERPT

The reading proficiency level of learners in general and in terms of word reading as well as in reading comprehension are presented in **Table 4**.

Legend:

Proficiency level	Word reading mean score	Reading comprehension mean score
Independent (Ind)	97.00–100	80.00–100
Instructional (Ins)	90.00–96.99	59.00–79.99
Frustration (F)	1.00–89.99	1.00–58.99
Non-Reader (NR)	0.00–0.99	0.00–0.99

Reading proficiency level	Word reading level	Reading comprehension level
Independent (Ind)	Independent (Ind)	Independent (Ind)
Instructional (Ins)	Independent (Ind)	Instructional (Ins)
Instructional (Ins)	Instructional (Ins)	Independent (Ind)
Frustration (F)	Instructional (Ins)	Frustration (F)
Frustration (F)	Frustration (F)	Instructional (Ins)
Frustration (F)	Frustration (F)	Frustration (F)

As gleaned in **Table 4**, the reading proficiency level in general for grades two to six is frustration except in grade one which is non-reader before they used the Contextualized English Reading Proficiency Toolkit.

In terms of word reading, the proficiency level of grades two to six is frustration with mean values of 46.67, 41.79, 52.81, 57.96, and 64.85 respectively. While for

Grade level	Pre-test					Post-test				
	Word reading		Reading comprehension		Reading proficiency level	Word reading		Reading comprehension		Reading proficiency level
	Mean	Level	Mean	Level		Mean	Level	Mean	Level	
I	0.00	NR	0.00	NR	**NR**	47.77	F	31.23	F	**F**
II	46.67	F	27.72	F	**F**	81.89	F	61.56	Ins	**F**
III	41.79	F	29.14	F	**F**	90.00	Ins	60.29	Ins	**Ins**
IV	52.81	F	36.25	F	**F**	91.69	Ins	61.88	Ins	**Ins**
V	57.96	F	39.81	F	**F**	81.30	F	55.04	F	**F**
VI	64.85	F	42.38	F	**F**	91.08	Ins	65.54	Ins	**Ins**

Table 4.
Reading proficiency level of learners before and after using CERPT.

grade one level, their word reading proficiency level is non-reader with the mean value of 0.00.

In terms of reading comprehension, the proficiency level of grades two to six is also frustration as supported with its mean values of 27.72, 29.14, 36.25, 39.81, and 42.38 respectively. As to grade one, they were still non-reader as supported with its mean value of 0.00.

After the learners were exposed to the use of Contextualized English Reading Proficiency Toolkit, some developments were observed in general particularly in grades one, three, four, and six. The reading proficiency level in grade one improved to frustration from being non-reader, and the grades three, four, and six improved to instructional level from frustration level. For grades two and five, the reading proficiency level remains in the frustration level though an increase in the mean scores of both word reading and reading comprehension are visible.

In terms of word reading post-test result, the grade three (mean = 90.00), grade four (mean = 91.69), and grade six (mean = 91.08) learners' word reading proficiency level is instructional as strengthened with its corresponding mean values. There was also an alleviation in grade one (mean = 47.77) from non-reader to frustration as supported by its mean value. As to grades two (mean = 81.89) and five (mean = 81.30) levels, the word reading proficiency level remains frustration nonetheless the mean values increased compared to the pre-test mean values.

In terms of the learners' reading comprehension proficiency level in post-test, it progresses to instructional level particularly in grade two (mean = 61.56), grade three (mean = 60.29, grade four (mean = 61.88), and grade six (mean = 65.54). For grade one (mean = 31.23), the mean value has increased as well as its proficiency level to frustration from non-reader. As to grade five (mean = 55.04), the mean value also increased but the proficiency level remains frustration.

Results implies that the contextualization of reading materials helps the learners in the development of their word reading skills as well as their reading comprehension skills. The learners were able to make connections to what they were reading. The lesson or the reading text were related to the learners' interest and were familiar to them since they were able to somehow comprehend on it. As what Perin (2011) [4] suggests that lower-skilled schoolchildren benefit from contextualization, not because it helps them become flexible students but because it upsurges their mastery of basic skills as well as rises the probability of transmission of basic skills to content courses that is not happening in old-style, decontextualized learning situations.

6.2 Significant increase on learners' reading proficiency level after using CERPT

The significant increase on learners' reading proficiency level after using the CERPT was determined using paired t-test. **Table 5** shows that there is indeed a significant increase in the reading proficiency level of grades one to six learners of Kibacania Elementary School in terms of word reading and reading comprehension. The word reading t-value is −8.588 with a significant value of 0.000, which means that it is highly significant at 0.05 level. The same is true in reading comprehension with t-value of −9.507 and significant value of 0.000. Hence, the null hypothesis which states that there is no significant increase in the English reading proficiency level of grades one to six learners in terms of word reading and comprehension after using the Contextualized English Reading Proficiency Toolkit is rejected.

This result is in consonance to the study of Bonganciso (2016) [2]. Results of his study revealed that there was a significant increase of the reading performance of the students from pretest to posttest after using contextualized reading materials.

Test	N	Word reading				Reading comprehension			
		$\overline{X}$	SD	t-value	Sig	$\overline{X}$	SD	t-value	Sig
Pre-test	114	44.01	23.04	−8.588	.000	29.22	15.43	−9.507	.000
Post-test	114	80.57	16.71			55.92	12.56		

Table 5.
Significant increase on learners' reading proficiency level in terms of word reading and reading comprehension after using CERPT.

Henceforth, contextualizing the reading tasks of the learners had positive effects on their reading performance. Contextualized teaching and learning are recommended in helping learners improve their performance in reading.

7. Reflection

I learned that teaching reading comprehension is difficult especially when the learner has difficulty in word recognition because the teacher needs to go back to the basics of teaching reading. As a result, the teacher and learner need to double time in order to cope up with the competencies that were not yet developed by the learner. If the teacher and the learner will not double time, the learner will be left behind of the competencies and skills that he/she is expected to learn in his/her present grade level.

I realized then that teachers in every grade level must do all means in order to materialize the competencies needed by the learner so he/she will be ready in the next grade level. By that, the learner will have more time mastering the competencies he/she needed.

The facilitative aspect of the action research that contributed much to its success was the cooperation of my colleagues and learners. The teachers were very much cooperative in every activity and instructions given to them were followed without any complain. The learners were looking forward for the reading time every Tuesday and Thursday, they keep reminding me to have our reading time every time I missed it.

It would have been better if the intervention was done for the whole school year so there will be an ample time to make up with those missed reading competencies by the learners in the previous grade level.

8. Conclusions

Based on the findings delineated in the study, the following conclusions are drawn:

In terms of word reading, the learners' reading proficiency level before using the Contextualized English reading Proficiency Toolkit was non-reader for grade one, and frustration for grades two to six. After using the CERPT, the proficiency level improved to instructional for grade three, grade four, as well as in grade six. An improvement to frustration level was also observed for grade one. While it remained in the frustration level for grades two and five.

In terms of reading comprehension, the learners' reading proficiency level before using the CERPT was non-reader for grade one and frustration for grades two to six. After using the CERPT, the learners' proficiency level developed to instructional level for grades two, three, four, and six. A development was also evident for grade one from non-reader to frustration level. However, for grade five, the proficiency level remains frustration.

There was a significant increase on the learners' reading proficiency level in terms of word reading as well as in reading comprehension after using the CERPT.

Acknowledgements

This study is funded by Basic Education Research Fund.

Author details

Dr. Irene C. Culaste-Quimbo
Division of Bukidnon, Department of Education – Region 10, Philippines

*Address all correspondence to: irene.quimbo@deped.gov.ph

References

[1] Krause, S. J., et al. (2016). Effect of Contextualization of Content and Concepts on Students' Course Relevance and Value in Introductory Materials Classes. American Society for Engineering Education 123rd Annual Conference & Exposition. New Orleans, LA. Paper ID # 14943. Available from Effect of Contextualization of Content and Concepts on Students' Course Relevance and Value in Introductory Materials Classes American Society for Engineering Education (asee.org)

[2] Bongancisco, R. (2016). Effects of contextualization on the reading comprehension performance of Filipino learners. ASIA Pacific Higher Education Research Journal. Volume 3, Issue No. 1. Available from https://www.researchgate.net/publication/310671685

[3] Phil-IRI Manual (2018). Available from www.deped.gov.ph/

[4] Perin, D. (2011). Facilitating Student Learning Through Contextualization. Community College Research Center. Teachers College, Columbia University. Working Paper No. 29. Available from http://ccrc.tc.columbia.edu.

Chapter 4

The Acceptance of MOOC in Teaching and Learning Process: A Case Study at Malaysian Public University

Nor Hafiza Haron and Yusof Hafidzan

Abstract

The aim of these studies is to investigate the acceptance of MOOC and factors that might influence the use of MOOC at Public Universities. A quantitative technique which is a survey method was conducted at the selected public university where data were collected from 400 respondents. The analysis was then conducted by using Smart PLS software. Meanwhile, the Technology Acceptance Model was implemented as to obtain the findings of this study. The results showed that performance expectancy, effort expectancy, social influence and facilitating condition are factors influencing MOOC usage among students at the particular university. The findings also show that the acceptance level of MOOC learning at this particular university was substantial due to some factors might influence the usage and encouragement of these technologies. The result also shows that there is an area of improvement in term of MOOC learning at these universities in order to make the technologies useful and can be beneficial for long term sight and lifelong learning especially in the context of distance education.

Keywords: MOOC, technology acceptance, smart PLS, lifelong learning, distance education

1. Introduction

Over the past decade, open educational resources or Open Educational Resources (OER) have brought innovation and technology in online-focused education. According to [1], OER is an open source of education by using material for teaching or learning is in the public domain or under a license that allows it to be used, modified or shared with others freely. As a result of this open source education initiative, MOOCs (Massive Open Online Courses) began to grow. Among the OER projects are such as portal sites, databases, MOOCs, Open Courseware (OCW), open textbooks (e-books) and tutorials. In the next chapter the word MOOCs will always be used in this thesis. MOOCs in Malay means courses Open in Massive. Massive or large-scale online Open Courses are an educational innovation in technology and didactic strategy [2].

Along with the development of global technology, education can be expanded by applying elements of lifelong learning that provide access to every individual widely.

According to [3] in open, distance, flexible and online education, including e-Learning providers are also influential in initiating the movement of OERs and MOOCs for both its categories or models. MOOCs are opportunities and playgrounds that perceive such learning as interactions between different people and groups in new ways [4].

The term 'MOOCs' means access or access that is open, global, free and contains video-based instructional materials, has problem sets as well as online forums to a large number of participants who aim to pursue a course or education [5]. Most MOOCs can be accessed by anyone for free online. In addition, this global level of online learning also wants to be applied in education in our country to take advantage of the use of internet access to something more scientific. This approach also offers diverse learning according to the inclinations of each individual [6]. With the changes and evolution in various technologies and methods in online teaching and learning, public universities in Malaysia have kept pace with developments that have taken place specifically in e-Learning programs [7]. To date, almost all public and private universities have applied e-Learning in teaching and learning using various methods and platforms. Furthermore, blended learning method is one of the relatively popular methods in teaching and learning, especially in institutions of higher learning [7].

With blended learning methods, teaching can be done online such as using LMS systems, MOOCs and other appropriate methods. Malaysia was also among the first countries in the world to undertake a global strategy to integrate MOOCs with classes in public institutions later known as blended MOOCs or 'blended MOOCs' [8]. To coordinate the use of MOOCs between public universities, Australia-based OpenLearning has partnered with the IPTA e-Learning Coordinating Council (MEIPTA) to develop a portal of MOOCs in public universities [8]. Therefore, MOOCs are said to be a self -learning platform that is a trend because it is applied in various disciplines, especially at the tertiary level [9]. It is also one of the most ideal learning methods today. This is because of the easy way by simply accessing the learning materials online or online. Furthermore, MOOCs have been used by all groups of students of all ages across the country because of their benefits and having different learning experiences compared to traditional learning [10].

In general, MOOCs can be categorized into two types or models namely cMOOCs and xMOOCs. cMOOCs are a first generation model i.e. it started in 2008. Basically, cMOOCs are an earlier or older type or model, as developed by Siemens [11]. Its main purpose is to create and generate knowledge through interaction among participants or users. In cMOOCs, students take a greater role in shaping their learning experience than in traditional online courses, while facilitators focus on fostering space for learning connection to take place [12]. This is so because cMOOCs are the first models to be developed by previous researchers. According to [13], the term Massive Open Online Courses (MOOCs) describes an evolving ecosystem of open online learning environments, spanning the spectrum of course design ranging from distributed online resource networks (cMOOCs) to platform -centered structured learning pathways digital (xMOOCs). cMOOCs are platforms that focus on the generation of distributed knowledge while xMOOCs are centralized knowledge. Both these types and models of MOOCs have their respective advantages and disadvantages. According to [14], cMOOCs are based on network theory (connectivism) while xMOOCs are based on behaviorist theory. This statement is supported by [15], that the concept of MOOCs is based on two pedagogical foundations in education namely connectivism and behaviorism. In this model of cMOOCs, participants or users are encouraged to use a variety of technologies that can reflect their learning, following the principle of connectivism which considers intense interaction between participants as the basis for knowledge construction [16].

MOOCs are a learning system that adapts the structure of learning content to the desires of individual students because this system is said to model students [17].

In addition, this approach is widely used as an information system and database system to manage, deliver content, interact or facilitate as well as conduct teaching and learning activities [18]. Thus, the purpose of this study is to investigate the factor that might influence the use of MOOC at Public Universities. A quantitative technique which is a survey method was conducted at the selected public university. The response from 400 respondents were analyzed. The analysis was then conducted by using Smart PLS 3.0 version of the software. For now, the Technology Acceptance Model was implemented as to obtain the findings of this study. The result indicated that factor in the UTAUT model act as an important tool to determine the uses of MOOC. The result also shows that there is an area of improvement in term of MOOC learning at these universities in order to make the technologies useful. Furthermore, it can be beneficial for long term sight and encourage lifelong learning especially in the context of distance education and online learning.

2. Technology acceptance

Now days, theory of technology acceptance has been widely used to evaluate the acceptance of technology. It has been widely used to understand and make predictions about consumer acceptance of a new technology [19]. Acceptance of technology is closely related to how a person receives and uses the technology. User acceptance or better known as User Acceptance is an important factor that affects the success of the implementation of a technology [20].

This can show the effectiveness of a technology developed. It is also a general acceptance model for several types of technology such as describing the use of information technology, the use of microcomputers and the use of the internet [21]. Furthermore, technology acceptance theory is also often used in studies related to the application of technology in society [22]. Several theories and models have been designed and are popularly used by most researchers to understand the factors that affect the acceptance and use of technology [23]. Here are some popular technology acceptance theories:

- Theory of Reasoned Action (TRA);
- Motivational Model (MM);
- Theory of Planned Behavior (TPB);
- Decomposed Theory of Planned Behavior (DTPB);
- Technology Acceptance Model (TAM);
- Technology Acceptance Model 2 (TAM2);
- Combined TAM and TPB (C-TAM-TPB);
- Model of PC Utilization (MPCU);
- Social Cognitive Theory (SCT);
- Innovation Diffusion Theory (IDT) and;
- Unified Theory of Acceptance and Use of Technology (UTAUT).

The UTAUT model intentions to study technology acceptance is based on eight theories [24]. Historically, the theory and model such as the Theory of Reasoned Action (TRA), the Technology Acceptance Model (TAM), the Motivational Model, the Theory of Planned Behavior (TPB), the model of Personal Computer Utilization, the Innovation Diffusion Theory and the Social Cognitive Theory were derived from the UTAUT [25]. Past studies show that many studies have applied the UTAUT model in various fields. Unfortunately, very limited research applying the UTAUT model especially in the sector of Education in Malaysia [26]. It is since the use of Information Communication and Technology (ICT) in the Malaysian education system is quite ambiguous [26].

Therefore, the study on the adoption and acceptance use of information technology (IT) is one of the most established streams of information systems (IS) research [27]. In particular, the UTAUT draws on the combination of one or more popular theories such as the Technology Acceptance Model (TAM), the Motivational Model, the model of Personal Computer Utilization, the Innovation Diffusion Theory and the Social Cognitive Theory [28]. The acronym of UTAUT is a Unified Theory of Acceptance and Use of Technology. The UTAUT model as illustrated in **Figure 1** was developed by Venkatesh, Morris, Davis and Davis in 2003 to address the limitations of the Technology Acceptance Model (TAM) and other popular models used in the study of information systems adoption [28]. According to Venkatesh et al. [29] the discrepancy in intention to use described by the contributing models ranged from 17 to 53%. The UTAUT model was found to perform better in terms of variance in intention to use which is related to the technology compared to any of the other eight models. **Figure 1** illustrate the UTAUT Model.

Meanwhile, **Table 1** below refer to the main construct or variables used in this model.

The outcome of the previous studies shown that by using the UTAUT model the effects on behavioral intention were significant to almost for the four construct. The significance of the studies was related to the use of e-learning systems. So in this context, it would also have applied at MOOC. Thus, the study's assumption could be as follows:

a. Performance has an important influence on students' Behavioral Intention concerning MOOC usage.

b. Effort has an important influence on students' Behavioral Intention concerning MOOC usage.

c. Social influence has an important influence on students' Behavioral Intention concerning MOOC usage.

d. Facilitating condition has an important influence on the MOOC usage.

e. Behavioral Intentions has an important influence on the MOOC usage.

In this study, Behavioral Intention refers to the pre-determined decision (*antecedent*). It means that the individual action to use the MOOC is determined by their intention. Behavioral intention is theorized to result in Use Behavior, which is MOOC. Furthermore, a few concepts and models have promoted a direct influence of behavioral Intention on Use Behavior; such as Technology Acceptance Model (TAM), Theory Plan Behavior (TPB), UTAUT and UTAUT2.

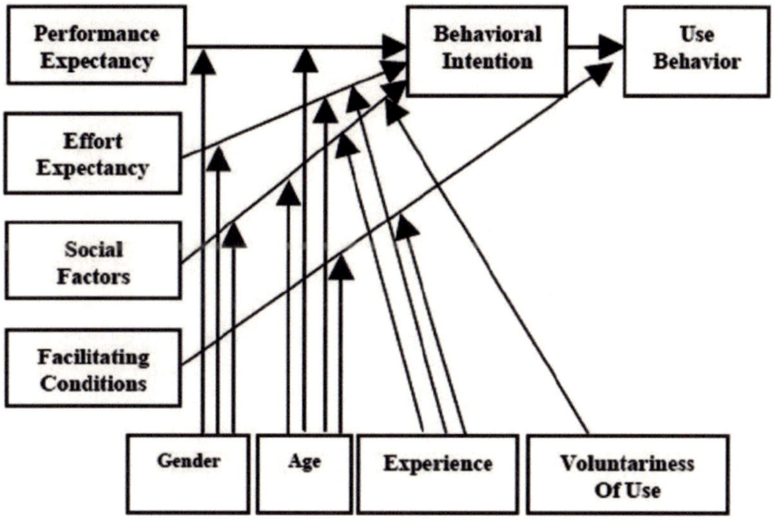

Figure 1.
The unified theory of acceptance and use of technology (UTAUT).

Construct used	Explanation related to the construct
Performance	Performance mean the level of an individual's belief in the extent to which technology can help to improve her or his job performance.
Effort	Effort is related to the convenience used of certain technology
Social Influence	Social influence is related to the encouragement and support from others to use the particular technology.
Facilitating Condition	Facilitating condition is related to the infrastructural support to use the particular technology.

Table 1.
UTAUT construct.

3. Methodology

This study investigates the technology acceptance of MOOC among students. It implemented at Public Universities. The purpose is to recognize the factors that might affect the use of MOOC among student. Meanwhile, the framework of this research illustrated as in **Figure 2**.

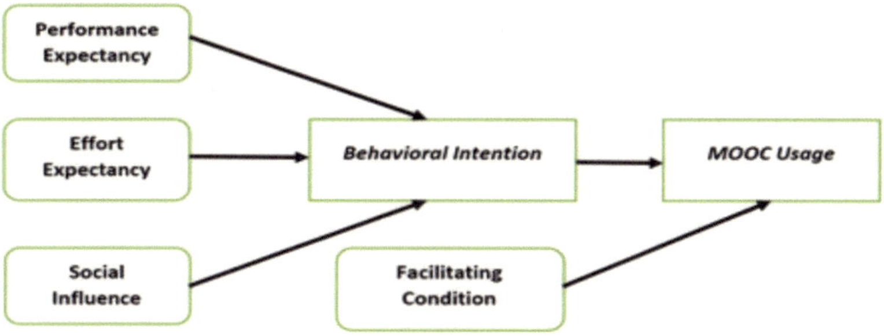

Figure 2.
Research framework.

The quantitative method was used as a methodology in this study. The total sample consists of 400 respondents of the survey. It took students as a sample and the survey being administered at Universiti Kebangsaan Malaysia (UKM). A questionnaire was used in this survey, which consists a part of the item regarding technology acceptance as mentioned before. The Likert-Scale was used in the measurement of the item in the variables and construct used in the questionnaire.

4. Result

In this part, the analysis of the result will be discussed. At the first, the software used for analyze data is Smart PLS version 3. This software has been selected because it's used second-generation statistical technique that enables researchers to examine causal relationships between latent variables [30]. As far as the concern, the results are reflected according to the UTAUT factors that has been discussed earlier. As general, two major methods were used in order to analyze the data which is a measurement and structural model of the statistical technique. **Figure 3** demonstrated the diagram of the construct in the model in the research framework which has been implemented. The implementation of the framework into the path model was done by using the above mentioned software.

The second step was to evaluate the reliability and validity of the construct in the model. These would also include the discriminant validity and convergent validity of the construct. For the meantime, the consistency of the constructs was assessed using Alpha Cronbach.

Table 2 shown that the value of Alpha Cronbach is in the range of 0.7 to 0.9. Thus, the initial step which is the measurement model shows that the value of the construct was good and reflect the study being done.

The next picture displays the factor loading of the item used in the construct is shown in **Figure 4** below. It shows that the factor loading for all construct meet the requirement setting.

Henseler et al. [30] specify that the average variance extracted (AVE) value should be greater than 0.5. It should be reflected for each latent construct in the measurement of convergent validity. So that, **Table 3** shows the AVE values for all constructs were encountered. Then, the technique of Fornell-Larker was applied. This was to assess a discriminant validity of the construct. Again, the value of AVE

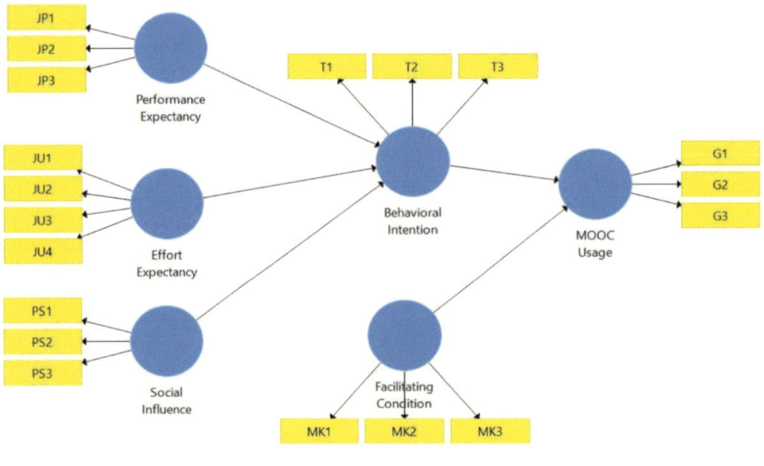

Figure 3.
Measurement model.

Construct	Item	Composite reliability	Cronbach's Alpha
Behavioral Intention	3	0.944	0.910
Effort	4	0.905	0.860
Facilitating Condition	3	0.892	0.818
MOOC Usage	3	0.939	0.902
Performance	3	0.942	0.907
Social Influence	3	0.936	0.897

Table 2.
Construct reliability and consistency.

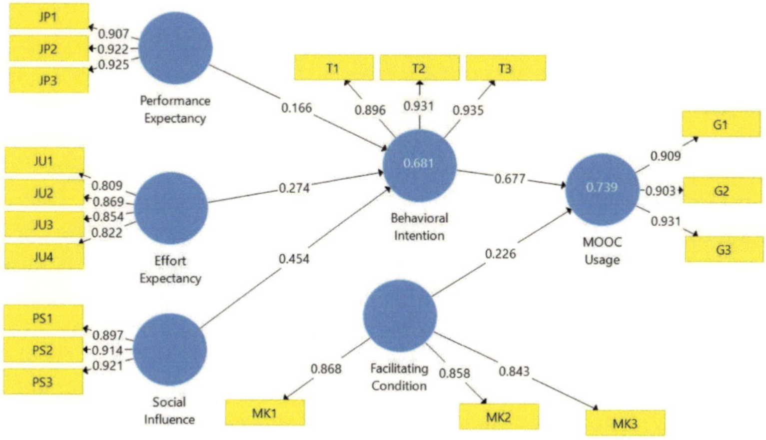

Figure 4.
Factor loading for item in construct.

Construct	AVE	BI	EE	FC	MU	PE	SI
Behavioral Intention_	0.848	0.921					
Effort	0.703	0.748	0.839				
Facilitating Condition	0.733	0.751	0.720	0.856			
MOOC Usage	0.837	0.847	0.743	0.734	0.915		
Performance	0.843	0.719	0.786	0.668	0.706	0.918	
Social Influence	0.830	0.785	0.757	0.696	0.784	0.743	0.911

Table 3.
Discriminant validity using Fornell-larker technique.

should be greater than the highest formed correlations between any other construct [30]. It can also be seen from the table as well. From the result also, the measurement model implemented and assessed shows a good validity of the construct used in the study.

The second step which are structural model then was implemented. In this part, the purpose of structural model was to confirm the significance of path coefficients. The technique of bootstrapping was conducted. These was to determine the significance of each estimated path. The R squared or (R^2) then was considered to estimate the model created. It is to administrate the detailed explanation of the research model. Thus, **Table 4** indicate the detailed results of hypothesis.

Hypothesis path	Path coefficient (B)	T statistics	P values	Results
Behavioral intention → usage behavior	0.677	14.363	0.000	Supported
Effort → behavioral intention	0.274	4.760	0.000	Supported
Facilitating condition → behavioral intention	0.226	4.528	0.000	Supported
Performance → behavioral intention	0.166	2.399	0.008	Supported
Social influence → behavioral intention	0.454	8.202	0.000	Supported
R square (behavioral intention) = 0.681				
R square (mooc usage) = 0.739				

Table 4.
Hypothesis testing.

5. Discussion

The results of the study show that anticipates using the technology of MOOC depends and influenced by certain factors or variables involved in it. It also indicated that factor in the UTAUT model was important to determine the uses of MOOC especially in teaching learning process. For instance, the behavioral intention was essential in order for students use MOOC. The behavioral intention act as antecedent for MOOC usage in term of factors in the UTAUT model such as performance, effort, social influence and facilitating condition.

The social was determined to be an important factor in this study. This is due to student support and encourage each other in order they use MOOC. This would also the concept of online learning which required social interaction in the learning process. Furthermore, a relationship between facilitating conditions and behavioral intention means that the students were also supported by the infrastructure which is exists within their campus. Another important element is that a good internet resource and access to MOOC convenience has made a good reinforcement to a user's apply MOOC. The effort factor is also determined as good influence in the acceptance of MOOC technology as well as performance factor. The finding indicates that students managed to handle and operate the MOOC as well as they believe that the technology can help them perform better in learning.

6. Conclusion

Technology acceptance is a concept of understanding the adoption of technology. As a technology used in this context where MOOC act as a system for e-learning purposes. Many factors that can be contributed in order to influence the user to use MOOC. In this study, the technology acceptance factors remain as per discussed. These factors are very important as they were significant to the MOOC usage. As for the conclusion, the instructor of MOOC especially lecturer who conduct a course online should be exposed more on how to manage the courses online.

To improve the research conducted it will suggest that the further study could be applied at another university in Malaysia. These could clearly understand the MOOC acceptance of online learning as far as the concern of continuance of the technology. Thus, it would have recommended that this method could be used for lifelong learning. Furthermore, this type of technology is very imperative in teaching and learning process due to many countries getting through the Covid-19 pandemic. The concept of teaching and learning online is very crucial especially in the Industrial Revolution 4.0 era and in the context of distance education. The last but not least, an institution or higher learning is the biggest influence in any e-learning project and indirectly gives an impact or effect on the implementation of e-learning. In the context of MOOCs, the institution actually has a role to ensure that elements of infrastructure requirements such as hardware, software, internet facilities on campus are available to encourage the use of MOOCs and cultivate the learning of MOOCs.

Author details

Nor Hafiza Haron* and Yusof Hafidzan
Kolej Universiti Poly-Tech MARA, Kuala Lumpur, Malaysia

*Address all correspondence to: afieza@kuptm.edu.my

References

[1] Butcher, N. & Moore, A. 2015. Understanding Open Educational Resources. Commonwealth of Learning.

[2] Lubis, A. H., Zulkarnain, S., Idrus, S. & Rashid, S. A. 2020. The Exposure Of MOOC Usage In Indonesia 9(02): 2716-2720.

[3] Ossiannilsson, E., Williams, K., Camilleri, A. & Brown, M. 2015. Quality Models in Online and Open Education around the Globe: State of the Art and Recommendations. Online Submission.

[4] Griesbaum, J. & Görtz, M. 2015. MOOCs as a tool to connect higher education and professional experience? Experiences from a student made MOOC on E-Learning (2006): 111-120. doi:10.4995/head15.2015.324

[5] Baturay, M. H. 2015. An Overview of the World of MOOCs. Procedia - Social and Behavioral Sciences 174: 427-433. doi:10.1016/j.sbspro.2015.01.685

[6] Shah Rulbani, Mohd Isa & Khadijah. 2017. Penggunaan ICT dalam Pengajaran dan Pembelajaran Pensyarah Pendidikan Islam di Politeknik Zon Selatan. Tinta Artikulasi Membina Ummah 3(1): 29-41.

[7] Zulkifli, N. Z., Mohamed Maidin, F. B., Abd Halim, A. H., Ali, U. H. & Ahmad Kuthi, H. A. 2019. Students' readiness in using MOOC for teaching and learning. Journal of Counseling and Educational Technology 2(2): 42. doi:10.32698/0281

[8] Habibah Ab Jalil, Alyani Ismail, Norasiken Bakar & N. A. Kasma Azizan K. A. Nasir. 2016. Evaluation of Malaysia Pilot MOOC (Final Report). CADe UPM Serdang.

[9] Fatin Nabilah, A. W., Rohani, A. A., Ruslina, I., Helmi, N. & Norazah, N. 2017. Kajian Tinjauan Sistematik Mooc Bagi Kajian Terpilih Tahun 2013-2016 (September): 563-574.

[10] Al-Shami, S. A., Sedik, S., Rashid, N. & Hussin, H. 2018. An empirical analysis of MOOC adoption from the perspective of institutional theory. Journal of Advanced Research in Dynamical and Control Systems 10(6 Special Issue): 332-343.

[11] Kay, J., Reimann, P., Diebold, E. & Kummerfeld, B. 2013. MOOCs: So many learners, so much potential. IEEE Intelligent Systems 28(3): 70-77. doi:10.1109/MIS.2013.66.

[12] Aharony, N. & Bar-Ilan, J. 2016. Students' Perceptions on MOOCs: An Exploratory Study. Interdisciplinary Journal of e-Skills and Lifelong Learning 12: 145-162. doi:10.28945/3540.

[13] Veletsianos, G. & Shepherdson, P. 2015. Who studies MOOCs_ Interdisciplinarity in MOOC research and its changes over time _ Veletsianos _ The International Review of Research in Open and Distributed Learning. doi: 1492-3831.

[14] Nordin, N., Norman, H. & Embi, M. A. 2016. Technology Acceptance of Massive Open Online Courses in Malaysia. Malaysian Journal of Distance Education 17(2): 1-16. doi:10.21315/mjde2015.17.2.1.

[15] Abu-Shanab, E. A. & Musleh, S. 2018. The Adoption of Massive Open Online Courses. International Journal of Web-Based Learning and Teaching Technologies 13(4): 62-76. doi:10.4018/ijwltt.2018100104

[16] Bozkurt, A. & Keefer, J. 2017. Participatory learning culture and community formation in connectivist MOOCs. Interactive Learning Environments 0(0): 1-13. doi:10.1080/10494820.2017.1412988.

[17] Alzaghoul, A. & Tovar, E. 2016. A proposed framework for an adaptive learning of Massive Open Online Courses (MOOCs). Proceedings of 2016 13th International Conference on Remote Engineering and Virtual Instrumentation, REV 2016 (February): 127-132. doi:10.1109/REV.2016.7444452.

[18] Umbit, A. F. & Taat, M. S. 2016. Faktor-faktor Yang Mempengaruhi Penerimaan E-Pembelajaran Dalam Kalangan Pelajar Di Institut. Jurnal penyelidikan IPGK BL 1-14.

[19] Dulle, F. W. & Minishi-Majanja, M. K. 2011. The suitability of the unified theory of acceptance and use of technology (utaut) model in open access adoption studies. Information Development 27(1): 32-45. doi:10.1177/0266666910385375.

[20] Sedana, I. G. N. & Wijaya, S. W. 2012. Penerapan Model Utaut Untuk Memahami Penerimaan Dan Penggunaan Learning Management System Studi Kasus: Experential E-Learning of Sanata Dharma University. Jurnal Sistem Informasi 5(2): 114. doi:10.21609/jsi.v5i2.271.

[21] Raida, R. E. & Néji, B. 2013. The Adoption of the E-Banking: Validation of the Technology Acceptance Model. Technology and Investment 04(03): 197-203. doi:10.4236/ti.2013.43023.

[22] Ishak, M. S. 2014, December. Pemodelan Penerimagunaan Maklumat Berkaitan Islam Di Internet: Pengaplikasian Model Penerimaan Teknologi (TAM). Journal of Techno Social, V O L . 6 (N O . 2).

[23] Aslina Saad, E. D. 2016. Kepelbagaian Model Penerimaan Teknologi dan Sistem Maklumat. International Conference on ICT in Education.

[24] Khalid R, Raman A, Hussin F, Ghani M, Don Y and Omar M S 2014. Technology Acceptance on Smart Board among Teachers in Terengganu Using UTAUT Model. Asian Social Science 10(11): 71-85.

[25] Hamdan, A., Din, R., Manaf, S. Z. A., Salleh, N. S. M., & Kamsin, I. F. (2015). Pendidikan: Satu Ulasan Sistematik (UTAUT Applications in the field of Education: A Systematic Review). Journal of Advanced Review on Scientific Research, 5(1), 10-29.

[26] Mohamad M, Hamdan N A, Shaharuddin S and Khalid F 2015 Hypermedia reading strategies of TESL undergraduate students in Malaysia. Turkish Online Journal of Educational Technology 2015: 301-310.

[27] Venkatesh V, Thong J Y L and Xu X 2016 Journal of the IS association for information systems Unified Theory of Acceptance and Use of Technology: A Synthesis and the Road Ahead. Journal of the Association for Information Systems 17(5): 328-376.

[28] Venkatesh V, Morris M G, Davis G B and Davis F D 2003 User acceptance of information technology: Toward a unified view. MIS Quarterly: Management Information Systems 27(3): 425-478.

[29] Mohamad, M., & Rahim, M. K. I. A. (2018). Factors Affecting MOOCs Continuance Intention in Malaysia: A Proposed Conceptual Framework. Journal of Humanities, Language, Culture and Business, 2(7), 1268147.

[30] Henseler J, M R Cristian and Sarstedt M 2009 Partial Least Squares Equation Model.

Chapter 5

Innovative Tools to Assess a Large Number of Students in the Open Distance and e-Learning MOOCs

Ramashego Shila Mphahlele

Abstract

The literature on students registered in the Open Distance and e-Learning (ODeL) institutions suggests many obstacles related to their summative-driven assessments, which give insufficient time for study, difficulties in access and use of innovative assessment tools, ineffective feedback, and lack of feedback of study materials. These challenges lead students to learn just enough to get grades without understanding the topics or acquiring knowledge and skills. On the other hand, massive Open Online Courses (MOOCs) give students, who have to fulfil multiple roles and are affected by the barriers of distance, cost and time, an opportunity to pursue their studies online. This chapter employed humanistic learning theory (HLT) to present a variety of digital teaching and learning tools that enable assessment suitable for a large number of students in the ODeL MOOCs. Humanistic learning theory emphasises a shift towards considering students, their characteristics, and their influence on learning. In addressing the gap created by assessments that were not focused on the specific human capabilities, including creativity, personal growth, and choice, this chapter first presents principles of HLT linking them with the form of assessments in MOOCs. Secondly, the ways to assess a large number of students in ODeL MOOCs are outlined. Lastly, various digital tools that can assess a large number of students are discussed, considering students as sources of authority.

Keywords: Assessment tools, humanistic learning theory Massive Open Online Courses and Open Distance and e-Learning

1. Introduction

Millions of higher education students are taking distance education courses from different institutions around the world. Qayyum and Zawacki-Richter (2019) [1] confirmed that 23 million students enrolled in distance education courses from institutions in the twelve countries. This increase in enrolment calls for a paradigm shift to meet the needs of assessments. It should be noted that assessment is no longer used for only grading and certification; instead, it has linked with the learning and skill development of the students (Chaudhary & Dey, 2013) [2]. This chapter employs the Humanistic Learning Theory (HLT) to explore the students' capabilities to set their learning standards and evaluate their work. HLT, often called Humanism, necessitates that the teaching and learning experience help students develop positive relations with their peers (Hare, 2019) [3]. Humanism is a philosophical and ethical stance that emphasises the value and agency of human beings, individually and collectively (Slakmon & Schwarz, 2018) [4]. Furthermore, HLT describes learning in terms of personal growth and the full development of each human's potential not on just an intellectual level but also on an emotional, psychological, creative, social, physical, and even spiritual level (Gould and Roffey-Barentsen) [5].

The humanistic learning theory was developed by Abraham Maslow, Carl Rogers, and James F. T. Bugental in the early 1900s in response to the typical educational theories at the time, which were behaviourism and psychoanalysis. Maslow [6] emphasised that HLT encourages innovation and creativity while purporting that every student is responsible for their learning and the learning of those around them. Against this background, this chapter highlights the link between HLT and Open Distance and e-Learning (ODeL) assessment, where students need to engage in self and peer assessment activities. However, the following need to be considered:

- Due to the physical distance between the students and teachers in the ODeL, feedback is vital to generate a spirit of consciousness and motivation

- Teachers' examination of students' performance at every stage of their study and progress successfully to attain the course objectives

- monitoring the effectiveness of academic programmes and adopting appropriate strategies to accomplish institutional objectives.

- Development of a positive attitude towards the institutional system

2. The humanistic assessments in ODeL MOOCs

The meaning of assessment has been consistent throughout the years. Nevertheless, the implementation of assessments varies depending on the teaching and learning environments. This chapter focuses on assessment as legitimate activities within the HLT, which emphasises growth, subjectivity, agency and student centredness (Friedman & MacDonald) [7]. Having humanistic assessments implies incorporating humanistic strategies and interactive activities in ODeL MOOC assessments, as highlighted by Davis, Chang, and McGlothlin [8], who further attest that humanistic assessments help demonstrate the utility of practical humanistic knowledge and skills. It should be noted that is HLT, as confirmed by Johnson [9], is concerned with personal growth and includes attention to students' affective dimensions such as self-concept, values, and emotions. Against this background, it is safe to conclude that humanistic assessments should include self-assessments for personal growth and self-concept. They should also include peer assessments because [9] maintain that students do not take away from the other; instead, they both serve to enhance the other. While implementing the self and peer assessments in the ODeL MOOCs, one should consider many student enrolments. The following section put forward the principles of HTL linked with the forms of assessments in ODeL MOOCs.

3. Principles of HLT linked with forms of assessments in MOOCs

Several essential principles are involved in the HLT that the author found to connect with assessment forms in ODeL MOOCs. First, assessment in MOOCs does not necessarily have to be about course completion. Instead, students can be assessed on time-on-task, student-course component interaction, and a certification of the specific skills and knowledge gained from a MOOC (Chauhan, 2014) **Table 1** [10]. presents the summary of the link between the principles of HLT and forms of assessments in ODeL MOOCs.

Table 1 shows how the principles of HLT connects with the form of assessment described by [6]. The link is described in detail below.

3.1 Student choice

According to Maslow [6], student choice is central to the HLT. Given the fact that humanistic learning is student-centred, students are encouraged to take control over their learning. Students can control their learning by using various online teaching, learning and assessment tools to develop their learning networks. The online tools will help students to make choices that can range from daily activities to future goals also to find motivation and engagement in their learning,

3.2 Fostering engagement

The HLT relies on teachers to fosters engagement, encouraging them to find things they are passionate about so they are excited about learning to inspire students to become self-motivated to learn. When students are self-motivated to learn, it will be easier for them to use mobile technologies to access course content and assessment activities and knowledge creation and sharing within the network of their peers. Learning in a MOOC offers students various online media and interactive tools for student participation and engagement.

3.3 The importance of self-evaluation

Maslow [6] For most humanistic teachers, grades do not matter. Self-evaluation is the most meaningful way to evaluate how learning is going. Grading students encourages students to work for the grade instead of doing things based on their satisfaction and excitement of learning. Routine testing and rote memorisation do not lead to meaningful learning in HLT and thus are not encouraged by humanistic teachers. Instead, humanistic teachers help students perform self-evaluations so they can see how students feel about their progress.

3.4 A safe learning environment

Because humanistic learning focuses on the entire student, humanistic teachers understand that they need to create a safe environment to have as many students need to be met as possible. The adaptive assessments cater for diverse learners

Principle of HLT	Form of assessment in MOOCs
Student choice	Personal learning networks
Fostering engagement	mobile learning on MobiMOOC
The importance of self-evaluation	Automated assessments
A safe learning environment	Adaptive assessments

Table 1.
The link between the principles of HLT and forms of assessments in MOOCs.

because they address different difficulty levels. Based on each assessment item's response, most adaptive assessments decrease or increase the difficulty level to match learner ability and potential.

There are some critics on the quality of assessment in MOOCs; for example, MOOCs automated grading tools for straightforward testing, such as multiple-choice, true/false, and short problem sets. Linking the principles of HLT with forms of assessment in this chapter aims to address some of these criticisms. The following section presents the current ways to assess a large number of MOOCs before focusing on the innovative tools to assess a large number of students in ODeL MOOCs.

4. Ways to assess a large number of students in ODeL MOOCs

Given the large numbers of students in MOOCs, the following assessments, according to Admiraal, Huisman and Pilli [11], are implemented:

- Self-assessment
- Peer assessment
- Summative assessment

4.1 Self-assessment

Some studies declare that the use of self-assessment in MOOCs is underestimated to some extent; Ventista [12] argue that it is the most suitable assessment method to correspond to the needs of these self-regulated students and a potential solution to the high attrition rates and the patriotic grading bias during peer-assessment. Nevertheless, Admiraal, Huisman and van den Ven [13] corroborate the declaration of undervalued self-assessment in MOOCs because their study suggested a bias of self-assessments that led them to conclude that self-assessments might not be an excellent way to assess students' performance in MOOCs. As highlighted in the section of HLT principles, humanistic teachers believe that grades are irrelevant and that only self-assessment is meaningful.

4.2 Peer-assessment

Perr assessment is a form of assessment where students receive marks from their peers (Habib & Sanzgiri) [14].

Furthermore, they mark their peers in returnVentista [12] notes that peer assessment does not appear to be implemented in the ideal conditions in the case of MOOCs. According to Comer and White, [15] peer assessment can be beneficial for the students when they reflect on and evaluate the work of their peers but could not be used as a summative indicator of students' achievement. Much of the current literature on MOOCs pays particular attention to limitations in giving students feedback in MOOCs due to the large enrolment. Piech, Huang, Chen, Do, Ng and Koller [16] recommend using peer assessment, which they refer to as a form of assessment historically used for logistical, pedagogical, metacognitive, and affective benefits. In MOOCs, peer assessment is viewed as a promising solution that can scale the grading of complex assignments for many students (Sadler & Goo [17]. Some students view peer assessment as a motivating element due to helpful feedback and fair grades (Luo & Robinson) [18].

In terms of HLT principles presented in the previous section, peer assessment fosters students' engagement. Taken together, the note by [12] and recommendation by [15], it seems possible that peer assessment can develop more expert-like evaluative judgement (critique, analyse, provide feedback). This chapter also notes that with peer assessment, students can demonstrate expertise through the creation of non-automatically gradable materials (e.g., video presentations, essays, reports, reflections, designs).

4.3 Summative assessment

The term summative assessment has come to be used to refer to assessments of learning, which record students' cumulative progress. Xiong and Sueng [19] differentiate between formative and summative assessments in MOOCs by emphasising that the stakes involved in the summative assessment are usually higher than those in a formative assessment because the former leads to course grade assignment. In general, summative assessment is defined as evaluating what students have achieved after a period of study relative to the learning aims and in accordance with a national qualification framework. Within MOOCs, summative assessments can employ either one or multiple assessment types. Combining multiple assessment types can help reduce the time and cost of marking per student and provide more chances for students to obtain helpful and meaningful feedback.

In MOOCs, summative assessment is viewed as cost-effective because it reduces the cost of marking per student and offers opportunities for instant feedback depending on the tasks. MCQ tests allow automatic evaluation of group and individual performance. The online media and interactive tools enable the humanistic approach in the assessment activities. In addition, some Learning Management Systems (LMS) used to host the MOOCs offer various assessment tools that enable integration of teaching, learning and assessments. The assessment tools are discussed in the section below.

5. What are innovative tools to assess a large number of students in ODeL MOOCs?

Most MOOCs offer automated grading tools for straightforward testing, such as multiple-choice, true/false, and short problem sets. However, when assessments wade into more complex territory--such as student essays--the grading solutions take on the controversy. In this section, some tools that can be used to conduct the assessments presented in the previous section. **Table 2** summarises the link between the assessment tool, types of assessment and HLT principles.

Table 2 illustrates how and when the innovative tool to assess a large number of students in ODeL MOOCs can be used. This chapter assessments for a large number of students in ODeL institutions should not be a nightmare but should encourage innovation, creativity and responsibility. As shown in **Table 2** that Blogs and discussion forums are not yet used as a summative assessment because summative assessments are almost always formally graded and often heavily weighted. The innovative assessment tools discussed below can be used either for formative or summative assessments. With the formative assessments, teachers can assign them either self or peer assessment, particularly for many students.

5.1 Quizzes

Quizzes in Moodle are used to evaluate student understanding of the material. Chauhan and Goel [20] regard quizzes as some of the primary elements of MOOCs

Assessment tool	Type of assessment	HLT principle	Grading
Quiz	Formative and summative	Student choice The importance of self-evaluation Fostering engagement mobile learning on MobiMOOC	Teacher and computer
Discussion Forum	Formative	Fostering engagement A safe learning environment	Teacher and peer
Blog	Formative	Fostering engagement A safe learning environment Personal learning networks	Teacher and peer
e-Portfolio	Formative and summative	Fostering engagement	Teacher and peer

Table 2.
Summary of innovative tools to assess a large number of students in ODeL MOOCs.

for evaluating the students' knowledge. In addition, Gamage, Ayres, Behrend and Smith [21] attest that quizzes can be used to improve student engagement addition, Gamage et al. [21] attest that quizzes can be used to assess students' competencies during the various stages of a study period through automated marking and easily extractable statistics as well as improve student engagement. Chauhan and Goel [20] established that quizzes are used for two reasons; first is for evaluating students' performance, second for practice purpose to provide instant feedback to the students for self-evaluation, without worrying about the effect of their score on final score outcome. With a large ODeL MOOC class, the teacher can set up a computer-graded quiz with feedback for each question or only correct and incorrect question feedback. The students will receive feedback either immediately after each question or after submitting it for grading. That will depend on the teacher's settings. The same quiz can be used as a self-assessment activity where the students can use the feedback provided to perform personal, unguided reflection on performance to generate an individually derived summary of one's level of knowledge, skill, and understanding in a particular area (Andrade) [22].

5.2 Discussion forums

MOOCs have focused on social interactions between students due to the physical distance and large enrolments and, most importantly, improving learning outcomes [21]. However, some researchers do not associate discussion forum with assessment. Lan, Spencer, Chen, Brinton and Chiang [23] posit that discussion forums are tools to facilitate social learning in MOOCs. Similarly, Onah, Sinclair, and Boyatt [24] view discussion forums as a primary means of interaction among students and teachers in MOOCs. The study conducted by [24] using data from a specific MOOC run by the University of Warwick revealed low discussion forums and inadequate peer support. Another concern about discussion forums in MOOCs raised by Lan et al. [23] is being structured instead ofo being generic. According to Brinton, Chiang, Jain, Lam, Liu, and Wong [25], discussion forums are mostly centred around course content, assignments, and course logistics. This chapter argues that discussion forums can also be used as an innovative assessment tool and peer or teacher graded. For a teacher to enter a grade and feedback for each student in a discussion forum assessment for a large number of students in ODeL MOOC can be a monumental task. In keeping with their significance to MOOCs, where students are scattered across the globe, such as in ODeL institutions, teachers should create peer-graded discussion forums to empower the students to test out new concepts, galvanise ideas and reinforce new thinking (Sharif & Magril) [26].

5.3 Blog

Much literature has been published on Blogs deeming them as communication and learning tools in MOOCs. Mak, Williams and Mackness [27] reflect on several definitions of a Blog from various sources and maintain that blogs are associated with creating personal space for personal learning, quiet reflection and developing personal relationships with bloggers and others. Depending on the LSM used for the MOOC, blogging for assessment can be effective to a certain extend. For example, in the ODeL environment, it might be ideal to use a blog for peer and self formative assessments. The blogging activity does not only encourage students to engage but also enhances their digital literacy skills.

It should be noted that the blogs that can be used for assessments are those embedded in the LSM; however, they should still allow self-motivated bloggers to freely and easily post ideas, individual experiences, and opinions. The teacher can ask the students to create a blog or respond to a blog that they created to be graded through peer or teacher grading. Some of the LMSs hosting the MOOCs incorporated a peer review system in their learning platform that guides students using grading rubrics to evaluate and provide feedback for each other's work. The teacher can set up a blog activity and ask each student to grade at least three other students or more blog posts. In this activity, students can be allowed to evaluate their blog post and allocate self-grading scores.

5.4 E-portfolio

There is some evidence to suggest that e-portfolios in ODeL MOOCs are used mainly for summative assessments. Nevertheless, Cheng [28] validates that e-Portfolio-based formative assessment can record students' progress to offer teachers and students information about how students' proficiency improves and enhance students' autonomy in learning. In line with the first statement, Downes (2013) [29] explains e-portfolio in a MOOC can serve as a resource that a student has to present as proof of his or her learning. A portfolio can be graded with a peer or teacher grading. In the LMS like Moodle, a teacher can use a workshop tool for students to submit their portfolios to distribute among peers for assessment based on a specific grading scale or rubric.

5.5 Game-based assessment

There are millions of learning games in the online learning environment. Although game-based assessment, according to Smith [30], is mainly Game-Based assessments, or GBAs, use gaming technology to help assist employer decisions during their recruitment processes. They form part of the puzzle as to how suitable a candidate is for the role and company.

The most commonly used game-based assessment tool in ODeL MOOCs is Kahoot. It is a game-based approach for learning and assessment. Students can even create their own "kahoots" to share with classmates, creating an interactive experience. In addition, the game-based assessments can be integrated with the quizzes.

6. Conclusions

This chapter put forward the principles of HLT in related forms of assessments in ODeL MOOCs. The section touched on the criticism made by some researcher about the quality of assessments in MOOCs. In concluding this chapter, it addresses those criticisms by associating them with the reliability and validity of assessments. Luo, Robinson and Park [31] affirm that the joint efforts of multiple student graders can produce fairly consistent grading results using MOOCs' peer review systems. Their study of investigating the reliability and validity of peer grading found high levels of agreement between student-assigned scores and teacher-assigned scores measured by the correlation coefficients, which support the validity of peer grading in the MOOC context.

The ways of assessing a large number of students in ODeL MOOCs presented in this chapter are not new to the general teaching and learning environment. However, in this chapter, self, peer and summative assessments were linked with HLT principles and how they can be used in ODeL MOOCs. Lastly, the chapter depicted innovative tools to assess a large number of students in ODeL MOOCs. Some examples are given on how a large number of students can use the tools.

Since humanistic teachers are passionate about helping students meet as many of their needs as possible, using the innovative tools mentioned in this chapter may assist the students to adapt to learning and measure their performance.

Conflict of interest

I declare no conflict of interest.

Author details

Ramashego Shila Mphahlele
University of South Africa, South Africa

*Address all correspondence to: emphahrs@unisa.ac.za

References

[1] Qayyum A., Zawacki-Richter O. (2019) The State of Open and Distance Education. In: Zawacki-Richter O., Qayyum A. (eds) *Open and Distance Education in Asia, Africa and the Middle East. SpringerBriefs in Education*. Springer, Singapore.

[2] Chaudhary, S.V.S. & Dey, N. (2013). Assessment in Open and Distance Learning System (ODL): A Challenge. *Open Praxis*, 5(3), 207-216

[3] Hare, C. (2019). An Introduction to Humanistic Learning Theory. https://medium.com/age-of-awareness/an-introduction-to-humanistic-learning-theory-1489cdde6359

[4] Slakmon, B. & Schwarz, B.B. (2018). An Outline of Assessment in Humanistic Conversations: Definitions, Aims and Design. In R. Wegerif & L. Kerslake (Eds.), Theory on Teaching thinking: International Perspectives (pp. 134-150). Routledge.

[5] Gould, J., & Roffey-Barentsen, J. (2014). *Achieving your diploma in education and training* (1st ed.). London: Sage Publications Ltd.

[6] Maslow, A. (1971). The farther reaches of human nature. New York: Viking Press.

[7] Friedman, H. L., & MacDonald, D. A. (2006). Humanistic Testing and Assessment. *Journal of Humanistic Psychology*, *46*(4), 510-529.

[8] Davis, K., Chang, C. & McGlothlin, J.M. (2011). Teaching Assessment and Appraisal: Humanistic Strategies and Activities for Counselor Educators. *Journal of Humanistic Counseling*.

[9] Johnson, A.P. (2014). *Education Psychology: Theories of Learning and Human Development*. Mankato: Minnesota University.

[10] Chauhan, A. (2014) Massive Open Online Courses (MOOCS): Emerging Trends in Assessment and Accreditation. *Digital Education Review*, 25(1), 7-18.

[11] Admiraal W, Huisman B and Pilli O "Assessment in Massive Open Online Courses" *The Electronic Journal of e-Learning,* 13(4), 207-216.

[12] Ventista, O.M. (2018). Self-assessment in Massive Open Online Courses. *E-Learning and digital media,* 15(4), 165-175.

[13] Admiraal, W., Huisman, B. & van de Ven, M. (2014). Self- and Peer Assessment in Massive Open Online Courses. *International Journal of Higher Education,* 3(3):119-128.

[14] Habib, M. and Sanzgiri, J. (2020). *Compendium on good practices in assessing and recognising MOOCs for the EU labour market (EMC-LM deliverable 4.1). EMC-LM Project. CC-BY 4.0.* https://emc.eadtu.eu/images/publications_and_outputs/EMC-LM_Compendium_on_good_practices_final.pdf.

[15] Comer, D.K. & White E.M. (2016) Adventuring into MOOC writing assessment: Challenges, results, and possibilities. *College Composition and Communication* 67(3): 318-359.

[16] Piech, C., Huang, J., Chen, Z., Do, C., Ng, A. & Koller, D. (2013). Tuned Models of Peer Assessment in MOOCs. https://arxiv.org/pdf/1307.2579.pdf

[17] Sadler, P.M & Goo, E. (2006)The impact of self-and peer-grading on student learning. *Educational assessment*, 11(1):1-31.

[18] Luo, H., & Robinson, A. C. (2014). Is peer grading a valid assessment method for Massive Open Online Courses (MOOCs)? Paper presented at

the 7th Annual International Symposium. Emerging Technologies for Online Learning. Retrieved from http://sloanconsortium.org/conference/2014/et4online/peer-grading-validassessment-method-massive-open-online-courses-moocs.

[19] Xiong, Y. & Suen, H.K. (2018). Assessment approaches in massive open online courses: Possibilities, challenges and future directions. *International Review of Education.* 64(2), 241-263.

[20] Chauhan, J. & Goel, A. (2017). Quiz in MOOC: An Overview. *International Research Journal of Engineering and Technology,* 4(7), 1-7.

[21] Gamage, S.H.P.W., Ayres, J.R., Behrend, M.B. and Smith, E.J. (2019) Optimising Moodle quizzes for online assessments. *Internation Journal of STEM Education* **6**(27) (2019)

[22] Andrade, H. (2019). A Critical Review of Research on Student Self-Assessment. *Frontiers in Education,* 4(87), 1-13.

[23] Lan, A.S., Spencer, J., Chen, Z., Brinton, C.G., & Chiang, M. (2018). Personalised Thread Recommendation for MOOC Discussion Forums. *ECML/PKDD.*

[24] Onah, D., Sinclair, J. & Byatt, R. (2014). Dropout Rates of Massive Open Online Courses: Behavioural Patterns. In *Proceedings of the 6th International Conference on Education and New Learning Technologies (EDULEARN14,* Barcelona, Spain.

[25] Brinton,C.G., Chiang, M., Jain, S., Lam,H., Liu, Z. & Wong. F. (2014). Learning about social learning in MOOCs: From statistical analysis to generative model. IEEE *Transactions on Learning Technologies*. 7(4), 346-359.

[26] Sharif, A. & Magrill, B. (2015). Discussion forums in MOOCs. *International Journal of Learning, Teaching and Educational Research,* 12(1), 119-132.

[27] Mak, S.F.J., William, R. & Mackness, J. (2014). Blogs and Forums as Communication and Learning Tools in a MOOC. *Proceedings of the 7th International Conference on Networked Learning 2010,*

[28] Cheng, J. (2017). An e-Portfolio-based Model for the Application and Sharing of College English ESP MOOCs. *Hinger Education Studies,* 7(2), 35-42.

[29] Downes, S. (2013). Assessment in MOOCs [Web log post]. Retrieved from http://halfanhour.blogspot.com.es/2013/05/assessment-in-moocs.html.

[30] Smith, M. (2020). Game-Based Assessments: what, why and how to succeed. https://blogs.lse.ac.uk/careers/2020/10/19/game-based-assessments-what-why-and-how-to-succeed/#:~:text=What%20is%20a%20Game%2DBased,based%20games%20can%20be%20used.

[31] Luo, H., Robinson, A.C. & Park, J. (2014). Peer Grading in a MOOC: Reliability, Validity, and Perceived Effects. *Journal of Asynchronous Learning Network*, 18(2):1-14.

Chapter 6

A Conceptual Model for Conformance with Accessible Gamification

Keyonda Smith

Abstract

There currently remains limited Gamification awareness and training for developers on WCAG conformance. Studies indicate an increased interest from developers to raise their acceptance, awareness, and technical abilities for designing accessible digital products. This article explores and presents a conceptual module to improve web developers' capabilities and knowledge of accessible digital design. By leveraging the standards put forth by WCAG 2.0, developers can create accessible content for users who identify with various forms of abilities. Four primary principles comprise WCAG 2.0 and 12 standards, and 12 standards deliver fundamental objectives as best practices for developers. These guidelines were employed for gaming content design and development, permitting users to regulate reality and Gamification associations whereas immersing in the game. The goal is to apply diverse processes for each stage of the game to allow challenges and motivation for users to determine novel processes while understanding the guidelines. Assistive Technology was used to navigate each stage. To suit independence or self-reliance, the conceptual model supports players' personalization while completing the game activities. Likewise, employing complex, advanced, and reward dashboards satisfies the proficiency component, and social network communications to other players provide the opportunity for interconnectedness. The conceptual model presented in this paper underpins Gamification and the potential to incorporate evidence-based accessibility principles developed by W3C. The previous examinations focused on instruments (e.g., software, feature, components) to achieve WCAG conformance. This examination presents a distinction from prior studies as this conceptual model recognizes consciousness and self-determination as the initial starting point.

Keywords: Gamification, accessibility, eLearning, ADA, disability

1. Introduction

The expansion of accessible e-learning and its components presents challenges and barriers recognized by the World Wide Consortium (W3C) and similar compliance organizations. A recent Centers for Disease Control and Prevention (CDC) [1] study results suggested that over 60 million adults live within the United States and identify as possessing a disability. These results indicate that most adults in the United States seeking higher education may experience barriers and challenges when presented with digital learning tasks. Sallafranque-St-Louis & Normand [2] research revealed that approximately 25 percent of disabled adults lacked access to the Internet, compared to over 10 percent of non-disabled adults. This disproportion for Internet access demonstrates an essential disadvantage, particularly when considering age.

Additionally, these statistics forecast an increase as people are living longer. The lack of accessibility provisions validates a significant digital gap for adults that identify with a disability. Even though there are continuous improvements, less than 20 percent of public websites conform to the World Wide Consortium (W3C) Web Content Accessibility Guidelines (WCAG) 2.0/2.1 guidelines [3]. This statistic suggests insufficient compliance for most web developers' inability to comply with the guidelines. The Americans with Disabilities Act (ADA) necessitates specific public and private entities to ensure published web content is accessible for those who identify with various levels of blindness, deafness, dexterity abilities, cognition, or using assistive technology. However, there is a continued overall deficiency of consciousness regarding accessibility resources such as training and developers' incentive to practice accessible design.

Moreover, Dror et al. [4] argue that the most recent global pandemic exposed how assistive device and technology marketplaces remain disjointed and largely cost-prohibitive, resulting in digital products lacking compliance to accommodate all users. These issues demonstrate the critical state of accessibility and developers' capacity to implement and assimilate accessible features for digital products. Considering that accessible and compliant digital products increase the UX (UX) by over 30 percent [5], verify positive returns when integrating content that meets accessibility standards and guidelines. To improve user results, engagement, and the general experience, developers incorporate Gamification features within digital products. Nacke & Deterding [6] defines Gamification as employing 'game design elements in a non-game context.' As research increases and practice improves, there remains scant guidance on the appropriate design and implementation of accessible digital gamification elements using game design elements (e.g., leaderboards, points, progression indicators, leaderboards). Organizations and institutions generally leverage Gamification to enhance learning, provide training, increase employee enrichment and inspiration, and research projected its growth to over $19.4 billion by 2023 [7].

There currently remains limited Gamification awareness, and training [8], for developers on WCAG conformance. Studies indicate an increased interest from developers to raise their acceptance, awareness, and technical abilities for designing accessible digital products. This article explores and presents an engaging resolution to improve web developers' capabilities and knowledge of accessible digital design.

2. The literature

2.1 Accessibility background

Developers employ various conventions to mitigate accessibility issues. As an endeavor to commiserate and perceive users' requirements, this proposal suggests the deployment of avatars. Zhang et al. [9] examined the adoption of sensible methods to further this concept. Their research focused on implementing accessibility and its corresponding users to navigate a Gamified platform named '**CoMove.**' CoMove is a virtual living space atmosphere for players who identify with differing cognitive abilities. Coincidentally, researchers continue to explore mechanized online accessibility review tools [10, 11] without requiring user intervention that measures accessibility using WCAG standards and guidelines. Automated tools lack complete compatibility with current WCAG standards and with constraints to only evaluating select elements.

In contrast, current tools often present limitations, steep learning curves, and often require clarification, resulting in issues and non-compliance. Undeniably, research has demonstrated that the current standards present as vague, abstruse, and unnecessarily challenging to decipher. There is a deficient examination to refine the convoluted and arduous process to mitigate digital products when leveraging WCAG standards. The effort to improve digital accessibility centers on employing approaches and procedures that consolidate the recommended standards; yet, these tactics fail to confront encouragement and absence of consciousness by developers', which present various barriers and challenges.

2.2 Gamification and eLearning

Usability and UX act as essential characters concerning the quality of ubiquitous access to digital materials. Several models underpin how UX, internally and externally, supports motivation and inspiration when conducting specific activities. However, Wigfield's [12] examination of the Expectancy Value Theory of Motivation (EVTM) published results grounded on acknowledging that inborn inspiration is most desirable due to leveraging three central rational requirements - aptitude, self-sufficiency, and empathy. When satisfied, the user expresses increased satisfaction and inspiration. The examination of Gamification advantages meant to engage users is not novel. Further exploration has indicated that Gamification aids in self-efficacy, empathy, compassion, and engagement. Research also indicated that Gamification enhanced stimulation.

In practice, there are a few instances of this hypothesis. For example, to help individuals become familiar with another dialect, the software Duolingo utilized Gamification. Microsoft [13] integrated and introduced Gamification to nearly 1,000 employees to enhance its Windows interpretation program, where they completed over 25,000 assignments. This strategy exhibited that their employees completed assignments over 130 percent more rapidly than the benchmark group. These results concluded an over 60 percent increase in participation when engaging with Gamification. Online training also demonstrated increased participation in course activities when employing Gamification by over 60 percent.

Prior research purported that boundaries exist when comparing an assignment to reality [14, 15]. A more prominent construct among the present reality situation and a gamified task may improve UX and satisfaction. However, it may conceivably increase challenges and difficulty for accomplishing the coarse learning objectives. Games with realistic scenarios present fewer challenges when working towards accomplishing the course objective, yet the user experiences, engagement, and commitment may decline. Nakamura et al. [16] assessed Gamification and the UX's viability in learning management systems by measuring UX and usability. Their research introduced several models applied to appraise knowledge attainment and learning conditions.

In this article, the author furthers this exploration by constructing a scheme outlining realistic Gamification components to increase accessibility consciousness and improve acceptance of WCAG's accessibility standards.

3. Aligning WCAG principles and Gamified solutions

As a methodology, Gamification demands the development of a practical solution centered on the foundations of Gamification. The standards put forth by WCAG 2.0 provides a conduit for developers to create accessible content that is and increasingly available for users who identify with various forms of abilities. Four primary principles comprise WCAG 2.0 and 12 standards. The 12 standards deliver fundamental objectives as best practices for developers. In the context of this article, the standards are central to achieving accessibility.

This scheme intends to employ gaming content design and development, permitting users to regulate reality and Gamification associations whereas immersing in the game. The game entails various stages, individually plotting to each of the WCAG standards. The goal is to apply diverse processes for each stage to allow challenges and motivation for users to determine novel processes while understanding the guidelines. Assistive Technology observes and aids users as they navigate each stage. Assistive Technology is acting as the sole and primary guide. Assistive Technology provides motivation and clarity on comprehending strategy and design in numerous stages.

The projected plotting among how the game operates and WCAG 2.1 consists of the below criteria.

a. Perceivable - WCAG explains the perceivable principle as ensuring the content and interface presents intuitively. Additionally, this principle encompasses four standards, plotted against how the game operates for the users (Accessibility Principles [17]).

- *Alternative Text:* Present all non-text content to users with text alternatives. This standard maps to the '**Facebook® Live Trivia**' game, where users are positioned in a dark room viewing an unclear picture. The Assistive Robot will explain what is on the image, and the player transcribes the explanations in the image 'ALT tag' to move forward.

- *Synchronization:* Time-based media, or synchronization, contains characteristics that allow corresponding alternatives (e.g., Audio or Video content). This corresponding measurement tool is the '**Facebook® Live Trivia**' game, which contains ambiguous videos. By viewing this multimedia in a noisy and loud environment, Assistive Technology then connects the text and player to complete the 'ALT Text' and obtain information from the video that provides access to the next stage.

- *Flexible:* Create various content types (e.g., more straightforward layout) without losing information or structure. The game **'Braid'** aligns with the 'Flexibility' standard. Braid is a puzzle game where the user receives tasks to open three doors in a specific sequence, using two keys. The first key in the cadence is the most difficult. However, users have access to a rewinding feature, which allows the user to reverse any mistakes.

- *Differentiate:* Create a simple, user-friendly experience that distinguishes the foreground content from the background. The **'Sift Heads Cartels'** game measures and links to the 'Differentiate' standard. The user identifies a unique target in a mass of targets. All targets are homogenous and require filtering to allow visualization. Alternatively, other features require fine-tuning by the user, such as audio.

b. Operable – WCAG outlines the 'Operable' principle to comprise of four standards and posits that the user interface, its elements, and navigation are generally operational (Accessibility Principles [17]).

- *Focus:* Keyboard focus and usability connect to the '**Discovery! A Seek and Find Adventure**' game, whereby players accept a duty to restore a keyboard to submit the security information. To accomplish this particular task, the player must discover the misplaced keys. The assistive technology recommends applying keyboard shortcuts. The game consists of specific zones that disallow keyboards and mice, challenges expected for the player to conquer.

- *Efforts:* Users are allowed adequate time and effort to consume the content. Adequate time links to the '**Defenders 2: Tower Defense CCG**' game. In this game, players must terminate a specific number of opponents within the predetermined time allowed. To win the assistive technology is required to guide them by helping them lengthen the permitted time.

- *Flashing:* By evaluating the **'Cyberpunk 2077'** game and its potential seizure-causing elements, players may further understand this phenomenon. The game features a highlighted attribute called "braindance." Braindance initiates with sequential blinking lights, similar to those employed by professional neurologists to induce seizures during diagnostic sessions. Although computer device solutions potentially decrease the likelihood of seizures for those who identify as epileptic, there are no native or inherent in-game settings to control this.

- *Manipulation:* Afford methods to assist users with maneuvering and navigation for players when locating game materials or features and allow independent regulation of their location within the game. Navigation corresponds with the '**Discovery! A Seek and Find Adventure**,' which initiates with the player experiencing various spaces and rooms. For players to move on and accomplish each activity, they must post or access (download) a file. The assistive technology provides suggestions and recommendations to assist players in locating the home screen, identifying page headings, and accessing breadcrumb tracking links.

c. Understandable – WCAG describes three fundamental standards that define the 'Understandable' principle when considering and planning game development and its accompanying user interface or platform (Accessibility Principles [17]).

- *Comprehensive*: To understand the game material and its contents, it must sustain readability. This standard correlates with the **'7 Little Words'** game, which requires the player to locate the URL to alter the instructions' language.

- *Intuitive:* The game pages and screens must operate intuitively and expectedly. The 'Intuitive' standard connects with the **'Escape the Crate'** game. The game initiates with the player situated in a room that is locked. The exit has a dashboard located adjacently. First, there is a code which the player needs to locate. Conversely, the entry field requires unlocking to allow the play to input the secret code. Lastly, a submission control containing the appropriate tag is required to enter the secret code.

- *Form Entry Ability*: Assistive Technology seeks to aid players in preventing and adjusting errors. The game '**2 For 2: Connect The Numbers**' corresponds with this standard. For this game, players receive instructions to match to solve for the sum of those numbers. This task involves the player associating where the player needs to connect verifications, proof, and tags to specific areas to advance to the next phase.

d. Robust – WCAG summarizes one essential standard to define the 'Robust' principle. This classification characterizes the game materials as consistent for translation by assistive technology and the most ubiquitous group of individuals (Accessibility Principles [17]).

- Congruency – This standard aligns with the '**Metro Exodus**' game. In this game, players must unlock an electric door. However, the power supply is not functioning. Therefore, the player's task is to repair the component. The assistive technology software does not recognize this screen and lacks any notification to the player. If the player somehow realizes this error, they can remediate this by repairing user identification labels or tags to allow the assistive technology to recognize what is occurring on the screen and the required next steps.

3.1 Gamification tools, features, and measure

Lastly, the final phase entails the incorporation of Gamification technology. A study conducted by van Roy & Zaman [18] acknowledged several Gamification features and their correlation to EVTM.

Correspondingly, to suit independence or self-reliance, the conceptual model supports *players' personalization* while completing the game activities. Likewise, employing *complex, advanced, and reward dashboards* satisfies the proficiency component, and *social network communications to other players* provide the opportunity for interconnectedness **Figure 1**.

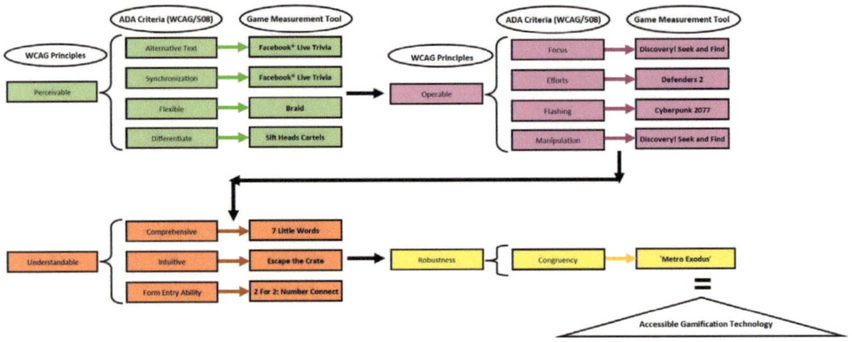

Figure 1.
The conceptual model.

4. Discussion

The conceptual model presented in this paper underpins Gamification and the potential to incorporate evidence-based accessibility principles developed by W3C. The previous examinations focused on instruments (e.g., software, feature, components) to achieve WCAG conformance. This examination presents a distinction from prior studies as this conceptual model recognizes consciousness and self-determination as the initial starting point.

Section 508 of the Rehabilitation Act of 1973, amended in 1998, mandates federal agencies to comply with providing accessible information technology to people with disabilities. This mandate comprises both employees and the public. Section

508 underwent a significant revision in 2017 and commissioned that by January 2018, all federal and contracted service providers conform to WCAG 2.0 A/AA. Therefore, this conceptual model reinforces and supports Gamification and gamified learning equity for active participation and engagement to increase WCAG 2.0/2.1 knowledge. The prediction based on this remedy is a treatment for future accessibility in a digital environment. It is recommended to researchers to examine further an exhaustive treatment for accessibility in conjunction with developers. Moreover, researchers should further review the Unified Theory of Acceptance and Use of Technology (UTAUT) and its relationship to M-learning -Usability and User Experience Encountered in Mobile Educational Context (MUUX-E).

Author details

Keyonda Smith
Trident @ American InterContinental University, Fairfax, VA, USA

*Address all correspondence to: kmsmithphd@gmail.com

References

[1] Centers for Disease Control and Prevention. Disability and Health Data System (DHDS) [Internet]. 2018 [cited 2021]. Available from: http://dhds.cdc.gov

[2] Sallafranque-St-Louis, F., & Normand, C. L. (2017). From solitude to solicitation: How people with intellectual disability or autism spectrum disorder use the Internet. *Cyberpsychology: Journal of Psychosocial Research on Cyberspace*, *11*(1).

[3] Acosta, T., Acosta-Vargas, P., Salvador-Ullauri, L., & Luján-Mora, S. (2018, January). Method for accessibility assessment of online content editors. In *International Conference on Information Technology & Systems* (pp. 538-551). Springer, Cham.

[4] Dror, A. A., Morozov, N. G., & Layous, E., (2021). United by hope, divided by access: Country mapping of COVID-19 information accessibility and its consequences on pandemic eradication. Frontiers in Medicine, 7, 1133.

[5] Chandrashekar S, McCardle L. How WCAG 2.1 Relates to Online User Experience with Switch-Based Tools. Journal on Technology and Persons with Disabilities [Internet]. 2020 [cited 2021];**8**:223-36. Available from: http://hdl.handle.net/10211.3/215990

[6] Nacke, L. E., & Deterding, C. S. (2017). The maturing of gamification research. *Computers in Human Behavior*, 450-454.

[7] Wünderlich, N. V., Gustafsson, A., Hamari, J., Parvinen, P., & Haff, A. (2020). The great game of business: Advancing knowledge on Gamification in business contexts.

[8] Larson, K. (2020). Serious Games and Gamification in the corporate training environment: A literature review. *TechTrends*, *64*(2), 319-328.

[9] Zhang, L., Fu, Q., Swanson, A., Weitlauf, A., Warren, Z., & Sarkar, N. (2018). Design and evaluation of a collaborative virtual environment (CoMove) for autism spectrum disorder intervention. *ACM Transactions on Accessible Computing (T-ACCESS)*, *11*(2), 1-22.

[10] Parajuli, P., & Eika, E. (2020, July). A comparative study of accessibility and usability of Norwegian university websites for screen reader users based on user experience and automated assessment. In *International Conference on Human-Computer Interaction* (pp. 300-310). Springer, Cham.

[11] Souza, N., Cardoso, E., & Perry, G. T. (2019). Limitations of Automated Accessibility Evaluation in a MOOC Platform: Case Study of a Brazilian Platform. Revista Brasileira de Educação Especial, 25(4), 603-616.

[12] Wigfield, A. (1994). Expectancy-value theory of achievement motivation: A developmental perspective. *Educational psychology review*, 6(1), 49-78.

[13] Microsoft (2018). Limitations of Xamarin.iOS - Xamarin | Microsoft Docs. https://docs.microsoft.com/en-us/xamarin/ios/internals/limitations [2020-2104-6].

[14] Liu, S., Saito, S., Chen, W., & Li, H. (2019). Learning to infer implicit surfaces without 3d supervision. *arXiv preprint arXiv:1911.00767*.

[15] Markowitz, D. M., Laha, R., Perone, B. P., Pea, R. D., & Bailenson, J. N. (2018). Immersive virtual reality field trips facilitate learning about climate change. *Frontiers in psychology*, *9*, 2364.

[16] Nakamura, W. T., de Oliveira, E. H. T., & Conte, T. (2017, April). Usability and User Experience Evaluation of Learning Management Systems-A Systematic Mapping Study. In *International Conference on Enterprise Information Systems* (Vol. 2, pp. 97-108). SCITEPRESS.

[17] Accessibility Principles. (2021). Accessibility Principles. https://www.w3.org/WAI/fundamentals/accessibility-principles/

[18] van Roy, R., & Zaman, B. (2017). Why Gamification fails in education and how to make it successful: Introducing nine gamification heuristics based on self-determination theory. In *Serious Games and edutainment applications* (pp. *485-509)*. Springer, Cham.

Chapter 7

Teachers' Readiness for e-Learning during the COVID-19 Pandemic, South Africa

Melikhaya Skhephe

Abstract

The event of the COVID-19 pandemic and the respective implementation of social distancing protocols resulted in a rapid transition to online teaching and learning for most education institutions around the world, independent of whether teachers were prepared. The Corona Virus Disease –19 (COVID-19) has interrupted educational processes worldwide. The impact of COVID-19 on the educational system has gained crucial relevance in research, with the intention of identifying a scientifically based solution to this problem. This study is based on the notion that, while the pandemic's effect is broad, a unit-level analysis can provide some insight. As a result, this study thus investigated the teachers' readiness for e-learning during the COVID-19 pandemic. A qualitative approach, in particular a case study research design was employed, with sampling consisting of six teachers being purposively and conveniently selected. The findings revealed that teachers do not understand what e-learning is all about and how it can be implemented within the classroom. Another finding was that classrooms do not promote e-learning. The researchers recommend that; education officials need to organize continuous e-learning workshops for teachers. Classrooms need to be redesigned in order to promote e-learning.

Keywords: covid-19 pandemic, e-learning, teachers, teachers' readiness and classroom

1. Introduction

E-readiness is the capability of e-learning users to adapt to a new learning environment, using new technologies, and be involved in self-directed learning [1]. E-learning is the feature of the 21st century and all institutions worldwide are looking for innovative and more effective ways to deliver education and to connect more broadly learners and other stakeholders [2]. Rosen [1] supports this notion that the 21st century is characterized by the pervasive influence of technology across all spheres. As a result, utilization of technology offers an uncompromising alternative form of instruction, especially in the developed world. However, Glenda [3] argues that e-learning has become an essential feature in the delivery of education, particularly in the 21st century. Glenda [3] further observe that e-learning effectiveness relies on a stable network with specific software, a repository for managing the delivery of content, and a good social environment created by the online interaction among learners. Hammond [4] over the past two decades, technology has transformed education systems. Mncube et al. [5] revealed that the usage of digital tools and resources revealed that school teachers do not use digital tools and devices for exploring curriculum content, and this has something to do with their readiness. Dagada and Chigona [6] supported this finding that most teachers do not make use of digital tools because they lack the understanding of the complex relationships between content, pedagogy, and the technology to be integrated into the curriculum delivery. Dagada and Chigona [6] further reveal that there is a need for schools to assist teachers to improve their technological pedagogical content knowledge if the institutions are to successfully domesticate e-learning platforms. Kiilu and Muema [7] opine that e-learning is a powerful enabling tool for educational change and reform and many of the productivity gains in the developed world economies over the past decade to a great extent can be attributed to the impact of technology. Cloete [8] teachers' readiness is achieved by providing the requisite infrastructure and ensuring the populace has access to technologies. Njagi [9] states that heads of state worldwide and educational organizations are supporting the view that incorporating e-learning in teaching and learning is an important aspect of keeping the curriculum relevant and preparing learners for the future. Kaur and Abas [10] teachers' readiness for e-learning helps their schools to design e-learning strategies comprehensively and to implement its technology goals effectively. Kaur and Abas [10] learners must also be ready for e-learning so that a coherent and achievable strategy, tailored to meet their needs, may be implemented. Kaur and Abas [10] went further that once teachers and learners become technology ready this helps in providing key information to the classroom to supply solutions that can cater to the specific needs of each learning group. Amir and Krish [11] argue that in the 21st century teachers' readiness for technology teaching should be considered an important feature of the 21st century and e-learning connections should be ready all the time. To understand teachers' readiness for e-learning in more detail, examining its relations to these factors is critical [12]. Moreover, these factors may not affect all teachers in the same way. Teachers in schools are not a homogeneous group, the different important relationships affecting one group may be completely different for another, given different backgrounds, experience with e-learning. To be able to provide appropriate support, understanding some of the reasons why teachers do or do not adopt new e-learning practices is necessary [13]. Scherer et al. [14] assert that e-learning teaching understanding is positively related to teachers' general self-efficacy and their attitudes toward e-learning. Carril [15] confirm that showed that more e-learning teachers' understanding also has higher self-confidence in their pedagogical competencies to teach online. Shea [16] reported that teachers with little understanding of e-learning have high levels of struggle related to communication and interaction, and unfamiliarity with effective online pedagogy and technology. A study conducted by Martin et al. [17] showed that experience and understanding from teaching online impact online subject design and facilitation, that is, aspects of teaching practice and presence. However, little or no online teaching experience and understanding are associated with lower self-efficacy. De Villiers [18] further observe that lack of critical non-technical skills are among the things that need to be addressed in the teaching of education. According to Kassim et al., [19] overemphasis on the content-driven approach in which textbooks are cases of academic dishonest have become among the prime subjects of constant debates in the academic domain. Kozma [20] asserts schooling has been recognize as one of the nationalize sectors most affected by technological developments and it's a subject that has also been influenced by this shift as well. Kozma [20] further observes that improvement of technological use in the schooling sector and improvement in schooling attainment achievement are prime to states' compound for worldwide, technology-based changes in all sections. Were et al. [21] argue that, formation of information and communication technology blueprint in schooling much as inserted in the international technology plans of the of each state, is seen to be critical as technology take part in a major role in preparing solidarity in school for the workstation. Online teaching, if cautious integrated into schooling, has a future to facilitate the acquisition of relevant life skills that buttress the development process in the prevailing economic and information order. Hare [22] observes that in many African countries there is a deficiency of a determined strategy for online use within the schooling zone despite acknowledging technology as an enabler in improving access and quality of schooling. Hare [22] further observes that one of the challenges facing online teaching is the insufficiency of perception, coupled with a shortage of qualified teachers within information communication technology knowledge, which has resulted in the deficiency of interest and seeming lethargy related to adopting ICT in the classroom. Mangesi [23] reveals that online teaching in the classroom is not controlled by any accepted framework. Mangesi

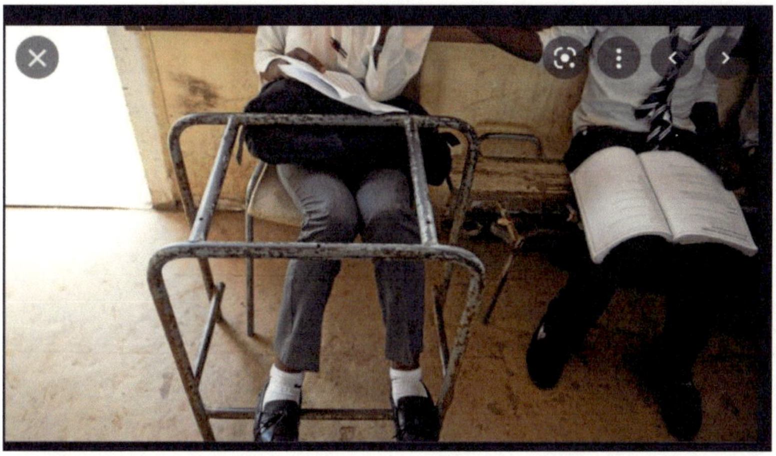

Source: Mail & Guardian 8 March 2013

Source (News 24, 8 April 2015)

Source (News 24, 8 April 2015)

Source (Daily Maverick, 03 March 2016)

[23] further stated that various schools led their own enterprise mainly funded on bilateral terms between the school and their donors'. In the western countries of Africa, there are strategies and proposals to ensure that school curriculum is on compact disc to ease access across the nation without distributing it as a hard copy [23]. Farrell [24] reveals that in many secondary schools, technology studies are offered as a different subject, focusing on expanding respective capabilities. At the end of the year, the learners are expected to be familiar with internet usage and presenting their work using technology in a different way as well as, using technologies with data and information processing [24]. Farrell [24] further observes that these learners are also expected to bear on the idea, understanding, and expertise of technology on a day-to-day basis; provide answers to challenges using technology and indicate promptness to possess up to date with recent growths and matters related to daily use of technology.

It is against this background that the researchers wanted to explore teachers' readiness for e-learning during the Covid-19 pandemic in South Africa.

2. Research framework

Based on global expectations, and changing realities related to the way in which technology influences teaching in the era of COVID-19 and in the 4IR [25] developed the technology acceptance model (TAM). Having considered the stated research question, the researchers who authored this article deemed TAM ideal for underpinning their study, which is reported here. TAM is used to predict or determine why someone might use technology, while another individual may decline to do so [25]. To have a better understanding of how teachers relate and think of technology, the TAM theory was explored. TAM is a theoretical model that is popularly employed by researchers to critique the usage and the acceptance of technological systems by its intended users [25]. TAM has been proven over time by many researchers as a good model to explain the users' attitude and behavioral intention to use a particular system of technology [26]. According to Davis et al. [27], technological systems do not serve their purpose of improving organizations if they are not utilized. Similarly, this study is holding the premises that educational technologies are only fully utilized if their potential is to be realized. This view is supported by Davis [27] who observed that the potential benefits of technological systems are often not realized because of the intended users' lack of will to utilize them. Davis et al. [27] further highlighted that users shy away from using systems because they either do not believe they will help improve their jobs or believe they are difficult to use, as a result, TAM uses the two variables as the main determinants of the attitude and the behavioral intension to use the system. Collectively this evidence presented in this section suggests that TAM is possibly relevant to explain the relationship between the teachers and the educational technologies. Moreover, Davis et al. [27] raise the concern that organizations will not realize the gains of technological systems if the intention of using those systems is not realized. TAM takes into account only users versus the system, whereas in the context of this study the users (being the teachers) also have the responsibility to be concerned about the other users (being the learners) expected to utilize some of the systems. The teachers' main responsibility is to transfer knowledge to the learners [28], with the aim of realizing learners' excellence with regard to their academic responsibilities. As a result, it is assumed by this study that from the lecturer's perspective, each intervention to improve any aspect of the learners' learning, should be in the interest of successful knowledge transfer and the achievement of good academic results by their learners. According to the view of TAM [27], the two external variables are recognized as the determinants of the users' attitude and behavioral intention to use the system. The TAM concept has been expanded by other scholars to accommodate furthermore variables. In the context of this study, another external variable being the "perceived response and benefit" of the other users' (learners) is also a key determinant of their attitude and behavioral intention to use educational technologies. This study reserves a view that it would be unbeneficial to the teachers to utilize a system that would not be beneficial to their learners, or the learners are somehow unable to respond expectantly to the system. Also, the adequate facilitation and support of the systems play a key role in determining the actual use of the system.

3. Material and method

3.1 Context and participants

South Africa is a developing country with a majority of the teachers working in rural schools where there is no infrastructure [29]. The majority of teachers and learners do not own, have access to or lack adequate computer or internet facilities at home. With the introduction of e-learning, teachers have to be the instructors in order to offer blended learning (classroom-based or computer laboratory-based with online components). Learners in either cohort can completely become computer experts once e-learning is taken place at school. This study analyzed teachers' readiness for e-learning during the COVID-19 pandemic, South Africa.

4. Methodology

Research design: A case study research design was used in this investigation. As Leavy [30], a case study is a form of qualitative analysis that focuses on providing a detailed account of a single case or numerous cases.

Sample: The sample of the study consist of 10 accounting teachers. Educators were chosen specifically because they held the data needed for the study. They were selected from 5 high schools in Eastern Cape Province, South Africa.

Instruments: Interviews were employed to gather data for this article. Bogdan and Biklen [31] define interviews as a conversation between two or more people that is moderated by one person with the goal of obtaining information from other people. They were semi-structured interviews. However, it is important to mention that since the study was conducted during the COVID-19 pandemic, interviews were conducted online in order to comply with COVID-19 protocols.

Reliability and validity: In order to validate the instrument, researchers shared the data collection instrument to check for consistencies after which it was administered to seven in-service student teachers who were not part of the participating sample. A cronbach alpha test was utilized to check for and ensure the reliability of the instrument.

Ethical considerations: Permission was sought from and granted by participants' prior data collection. The first author administered informed consent forms which detailed the purpose of the study and to which all participants signed an agreement to participate.

Data analysis: This article used a constant comparison technique to data analysis, which is consistent with qualitative research [32]. In this approach, data was reviewed and reread as it was collected, and the authors identified emergent patterns through a process of inductive reasoning. Then, as new data was gathered, social phenomena were categorized and their attributes noted, and instances were compared.

5. Findings

5.1 Teachers' understanding of e-learning and how it can be implemented within the classroom

The study revealed that teachers do not have any knowledge ofs e-learning, and how it is being implemented. The findings support Dagada and Chigona [6] that most teachers do not make use of digital tools because they lack the understanding of the complex relationships between content, pedagogy, and the technology to be integrated into the curriculum delivery. However, the findings are contrary to Kaur and Abas [10] that teachers' readiness for e-learning helps their schools to design e-learning strategies comprehensively and to implement its technology goals effectively. Instead, this finding shows that there is a need for schools to assist teachers to improve their technological pedagogical content knowledge if the institutions are to successfully domesticate e-learning platforms. When the teachers do not possess the needed understanding for the successful implementation of e-learning it means the goals associated with e-learning cannot be achieved. Kiilu & Muema [7] opine that e-learning understanding and implementation are powerful enabling tools for educational change and reform and many of the productivity gains in the developed world economies over the past decade to a great extent can be attributed to the impact of technology. The findings connect with De Villiers [18] observation that lack of critical non-technical skills are among the things that need to be addressed in the teaching of education. These findings is agreeing with Hare [22] who observe that in many African countries there is a deficiency of a determined strategy for online use within the schooling zone despite acknowledging technology as an enabler in improving access and quality of schooling. Furthermore, one of the challenges facing online teaching is the insufficiency of perception, coupled with a shortage of qualified teachers within information communication technology knowledge, which has resulted in the deficiency of interest and seeming lethargy related to adopting ICT in the classroom. However, Davis et al. [27] assert that technological systems do not serve their purpose of improving organizations if they are not utilized and the potential benefits of technological systems are often not realized because of the intended users' lack of will to utilize them. Further highlighted that, users shy away from using systems because they either do not believe they will help improve their jobs or believe they are difficult to use and this is what is being confirmed by the study.

6. Classrooms condition

The study revealed that even if teaching and learning are expected to make use of technology within the classroom, the reality is that classrooms do not support any technology learning. This is contrary to the findings of Kiilu & Muesma [7] that e-learning is the feature of the 21st century and all institutions worldwide are looking for innovative and more effective ways to deliver education and to connect more broadly learners and other stakeholders. However, this finding is supporting Glenda [3] e-learning effectiveness relies on a stable network with specific software, a repository for managing the delivery of content, and a good social environment created by the online interaction among learners. The finding is supported by Skhephe and Caga [29] that COVID-19 has disrupted how teaching is delivered as a result the impact of COVID-19 has gained critical importance, with the hope of drawing scientific driven solution to this predicament online teaching is an uncompromising option. This finding is also noted by De Villiers [18] that, lack of critical non-technical skills are among the things that need to be addressed in the teaching of in education.

7. Conclusion

Delivering quality education is the primary goal of any nation-building. During and after the COVID-19 pandemic e-learning serve as a powerful tool that provides an opportunity for both learners and teachers in their schools to improve their technological skills so that they can meet the needs of the 21st century. However, the implementation of e-learning needs to be done with great care. This study explored teachers' readiness for e-learning during the COVID-19 pandemic, South Africa. This study focuses on teachers' readiness for e-learning during COVID-19 pandemic. In this study, the researcher concludes that for teachers to be ready for e-learning, the implementation of it needs to be monitored by educational officials.

Furthermore, the researcher concludes that there is a need to form e-learning policies to be implemented across all schools and infrastructure needs to be made available across all schools in order to support e-learning.

8. Recommendations

Before the outbreak of the COVID-19 pandemic, the teaching and learning process has been taking place within the classroom with physical contact. The researchers recommend that; education officials need to organize continuous e-learning workshops for teachers. The researcher further recommends that classrooms need to be redesigned in order to promote e-learning since it is a feature of the 21st century. The researcher further recommends that teaching requires relevant content and strategies for e-learning, which is a feature of the 21st century that needs to be made compulsory. Lastly, for teachers to master these aspects, they need proper exposure to all the processes involved before they can enter their classroom.

Author details

Melikhaya Skhephe
North West University, South Africa

*Address all correspondence to: sikepemk@gmail.com

References

[1] Rosen D. From Chalkboards to Chatboards: What Will e-Learning Look Like in 2075? 2014. Available from: http://elearningindustry.com/elearning-futurewhat-will-elearning-looklike-2075 [Accessed: 20 June 2019]

[2] Raines PM, Clark CD. Rethinking Pedagogy for a Digital Age: Designing and Delivering E-Learning. Oxford: Routledge; 2019

[3] Glenda D. Digital Activism in the Social Media Era. Springer Nature; 2016. pp. 1-12

[4] Hammond M. Introducing information communications technology in schools in England: Rationale and consequences. British Journal of Educational Technology. 2013;**45**(2):191-201. DOI: 10.1111/bjet.12033

[5] Mncube V, Olewale B, Hendricks W. Exploring teachers' readiness for e-learning: On par with the fourth industrial revolution? International Journal of Knowledge Innovation and Entrepreneurship. 2019;**7**(2):5-20

[6] Dagada D, Chigona A. Integration of E-learning into curriculum delivery at university level in South Africa. International Journal of Online Pedagogy and Course Design. 2013;**3**(1):53-65

[7] Kiilu R, Muema E. An e-learning approach to secondary school education: E-readiness implications in Kenya. Journal of Education and Practice. 2012;**3**(16):142-148

[8] Cloete A. Technology and education: Challenges and opportunities. Theological Studies. 2017;**73**(4):5-20

[9] Njagi LW. Teacher factors influencing students academic achievement in secondary schools in Nyandarua County, Kenya. International Journal of Education and Research. 2013;**3**(1):145-158

[10] Kaur K, Abas Z. An Assessment of e-Learning Readiness at Open University Malaysia. Malaysia: Faculty of Education, Arts and Social Sciences Open University Malaysia; 2018

[11] Amir Z, Krish P. Mobile learning readiness among Malaysia students at higher learning institutes. Asian Social Science. 2012;**8**(12):5-20

[12] Hung ML. Teachers readiness for online learning: Scale development and teacher perceptions. Computers & Education. 2016;**94**(2016):120-133. DOI: 10.1016/j.compedu.2015.11.012

[13] Bruggeman M. An online Engagement Framework for Higher Education. Online Learning. John Wiley & Sons Inc.; 2020

[14] Scherer R, Sarah K, Howard R. Profilling teachers' readiness for online teaching and learning in higher education: Who's ready? Computers in Human Behavior. 2021;**118**:106675. DOI: 10.1016/j.chb.2020.106675

[15] Carril C. Pedagogical roles and competencies of university teachers practicing in the e-learning environment. The International Review of Research in Open and Distributed Learning. 2013;**14**(3):462-487

[16] Shea W. Technological Changes in Shea Butter Production in Ghana: A Case Study of Shea Butter Production in the Yendi District of the Northern Region of Ghana. London: SAGE Publications; 2007

[17] Martin F, Budhrani K, Wang C. Examining faculty perception of their readiness to teach online. Online Learning Journal. 2019;**23**(3):97-119. DOI: 10.24059/olj.v23i3.1555

[18] Villiers D. Planning to use ICT in schools. Journal of Education. 2010; **29**(1):1-17

[19] Kassim CKHCK, Nasir NEM, Ahmad S. Academic dishonesty of accounting students at higher learning institutions. Mediterranean Journal of Social Sciences. 2015;**6**(2):702-707

[20] Kozma R. National policies that connect ICT-based education reform to economic and social development. Human Technology. 2005;**5**(4):358-367

[21] Were E, Rubagiza J, Denley P, Sutherland R. The Use of ICT to Support Basic Education in Disadvantaged Schools and Communities: A Review of Literature. Rwanda: EdQual RPC; 2007

[22] Hare H. Survey of ICT in Education in Tanzania. Washington, DC: World Bank; 2007

[23] Mangesi K. Survey of ICT in Education in the Gambia. Washington, DC: World Bank; 2007

[24] Farrell G. Survey of ICT in Education in Rwanda. Washington, DC: World Bank; 2007

[25] Teo T. Modelling technology acceptance in education: A study of pre-service teachers. Computers & Educations. 2009;**52**(2):302-312

[26] Park SY. An analysis of the Technology Acceptance Model in Understanding University Students' Behavioral Intention to use e-learning. Educational Technology & Society. 2009;**12**(3):150-162

[27] Davis FD, Bagozzi RP, Warshaw PR. Perceived usefulness, perceived ease of use and user acceptance of information technology. MIS Quarterly. 1989;**13**(10):318-333

[28] Reed P. Awareness, attitudes and participation of teaching- staff towards the open content movement in one university. Research in Learning Technology. 2012;**21**(2012):1-14

[29] Skhephe M, Caga NP. Dynamic factors affecting technology integration in accounting classrooms: A literature review. In: 12th International Conference on Education and New Learning Technologies. Valencia, Spain; pp. 8907-8913. ISBN: 978-84-09-17979-4. ISSN: 2340-1117. DOI: 10.21125/edulearn.2020.0052 2020

[30] Leavy P. Research Design Quantitative, Qualitative, Mixed Methods, Arts Based and Community Based Participatory Research Approaches. New York: Gilford Press; 2017

[31] Bogdan RC, Biklen SK. Qualitative Research of Education: An Introduction to Theories and Methods. Boston, MA: Allyn & Bacon; 2015

[32] Gray A. Effective Differentiation: A Training Guide to Empower Teachers and Enable Learners With SEND and Specific Learning Difficulties. Texas: Routledge; 2018

Section 2

MOOC for Lifelong Learning, Equity and Inclusion

Chapter 8

MOOCS for Lifelong Learning, Equity, and Liberation

Ebba Ossiannilsson

Abstract

Quality education for all is both a human right based on social justice and liberation and a force for sustainable development and peace. The goal of education for all is stated in United Nations UNESCO Sustainability Goal 4, 2030 Agenda, which aims to ensure inclusive and equitable quality education and promote lifelong learning opportunities for all. This chapter is based on a systematic literature review. In this chapter, the focus is on global initiatives in education as a global common. The findings support that knowledge is a universal entity constructed by individuals, and it belongs to anyone anywhere and at any time. The year 2012 was dubbed the Year of the MOOC, but because of the COVID-19 pandemic, 2020 marked another milestone. MOOCs have dramatically changed the way people learn, and how to access knowledge. MOOCs offer an affordable, flexible way to learn new skills, advance a career, and deliver quality educational experiences. MOOCs have the potential to help individuals enjoy learning and acquire knowledge in a variety of ways. In the changing learning landscapes and the futures of learning, MOOCs can play a variety of roles, such as stand-alone courses in informal and non-formal learning and modules integrated into formal education. It is time to develop and offer more agile, seamless, rhizomatic learning opportunities that promote human rights equity and liberation.

Keywords: equity, human rights, liberation, lifelong learning, MOOC, OER, open educational resources, open learning, open movement, self-determined learning, social justice

1. Introduction

Education is both a human right and a force for sustainable development and peace [1]. Every goal of the 2030 Agenda requires education to equip people with the knowledge, skills, and values they need to live with dignity, build their lives, and contribute to their societies [1–4].

The novel coronavirus disease (COVID-19) is the most significant public health emergency in the 21st century to date. In higher education institutions, teaching practices have been profoundly disrupted by the closure of their physical campuses, and the crisis has highlighted the urgent need for policymakers and institutional leaders to adapt their educational and policy models accordingly [5]. The ongoing pandemic has thus increased the interest in online education, as many educational institutions, such as schools and campuses, as well as societies, in most countries around the world have been on lockdown since March 2020. Consequently, the largest massive open online course (MOOC) providers have experienced dramatic growth since the onset of the pandemic [6, 7].

The year 2012 was coined the year of the MOOC [8]. However, 2020 marked another milestone for MOOCs because of the COVID-19 pandemic. Millions of people around the world are now using MOOCs to learn for a variety of reasons, such as professional development, career transition, college preparation, supplemental learning, lifelong learning, and corporate e-learning and training.

MOOCs are free online courses in which anyone can enroll. MOOCs offer an affordable and flexible way to learn new skills, advance careers, and deliver quality educational experiences at scale. MOOCs have dramatically changed the way the world learns. According to Mooc.org [6]. traditional classrooms can only serve a limited number of students, but millions of people around the world want—and need—a quality education.

The United Nations Educational Science and Cultural Organization (UNESCO) considers that open education and the open movement, such as Open Educational Resources (OER), MOOCs, Open Science, and Open Access, are the most efficient ways to achieve the United Nations UNESCO Sustainability Goals (SDG), particularly SDG4 on education, as well as to promote resilience and sustainability in quality education for all, equity, lifelong learning, and well-being [9]. The use of the term "global commons" underscores the universality of education and the collective global responsibility for education. Education, particularly open education, is a global common goal in achieving equity, social justice, and human rights. Another initiative of UNESCO, which goes beyond the SDGs and aims at empowering individuals to achieve their personal goals, is the global initiative Futures of Education: Learning to Become [2]. This initiative serves as a catalyst for reimagining how knowledge and learning can shape the future of humanity and the planet. The most coherent means of giving shape to this vision of regenerative education is through the principle of education as a global common, which was initially outlined in the 2015 UNESCO report Rethinking Education [10]. In this context, education, knowledge, and their importance for a prosperous future are among the most important global commons, which include water, the atmosphere, and biodiversity.

In this chapter, the focus is on global initiatives in education as a global common. MOOCs are highlighted in relation to the goal of achieving human rights, equality, lifelong learning, liberation, and social justice. Issues of quality are also addressed in this context.

2. Method

This chapter was conducted as part of a systematic review of the literature, including official reports. The purpose of a literature review is to provide an overview of the current state of knowledge in a defined area. Previous research is analyzed to determine what is known from the past, and any inadequacies or gaps in knowledge are [11–13]. The review is conducted systematically using a structured approach to examine each document's process of information gathering, evaluating, and data analysis.

In addition, the chapter is based on the mixed methods approach [11–13], and moreover the chapter is based on the author's own research, experience, and perspectives in a period of almost 20 years. The author has selected examples from the ongoing discourse and debate on the challenges and opportunities of MOOCs in lifelong learning and the future of education, mainly based on official sources, such as the Commonwealth of Learning (COL), the European Commission (EC), UNESCO, the Organization for Economic Cooperation and Development (OECD), and the World

Economic Forum (WEF). In addition, research and information from the largest and most well-known MOOC providers were used as sources. However, these sources do not always represent the official view.

2.1 Issues, controversies, and problems

This chapter does not claim to provide a comprehensive overview of international developments on MOOCs in the field and in the world. Instead, it highlights key international developments. The chapter focuses on the challenges and opportunities related to MOOCs regarding lifelong learning, equity, and liberation.

3. Results

In this section, MOOCs are described according to typology, definitions, and numbers. The largest MOOCs providers are then reviewed. The initiatives by the largest global organizations on open education and lifelong learning and the case for education as a human right, equity and liberation are reviewed. The chapter ends with a discussion of the findings, a conclusion based on them, and recommendations for further research.

3.1 Massive open online courses

Massive open online courses (MOOC) are free online courses in which anyone can enroll. MOOCs offer an affordable and flexible way to learn new skills, advance careers, and deliver high-quality educational experiences at scale [6, 7].

In response to an open online course designed and led by George Siemens at Athabasca University and Stephen Downes at the National Research Council, Dave Cormier at the University of Prince Edward Island and Bryan Alexander at the National Institute for Technology in Liberal Education coined the term MOOC in 2008 [14]. Downes [14, 15] later argued that every letter in the abbreviation MOOC could be negotiated (**Figure 1**), and the concept has evolved over time.

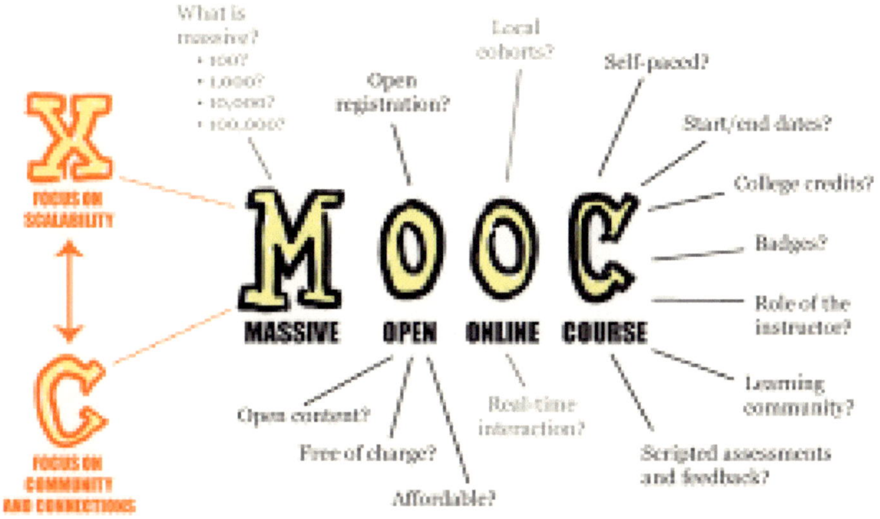

Figure 1.
MOOC (see [14, 15], Mathieu Plourde (Mathplourde on Flickr)).

The first successful MOOC was Sebastian Thrun and Peter Norvig's course, "Artificial Intelligence," at Stanford University in the fall of 2011. More than 160,000 people around the world enrolled to learn together, which was the first time in history that a course had attracted so many participants [6].

MOOCs have dramatically changed the way the world learns. According to Mooc.org [6] traditional classrooms can only serve a limited number of students, but millions of people around the world want–and need–a quality education.

3.2 MOOCs, typology, and definitions: cMOOC and xMOOC

The phenomenon of MOOCs stems from connectivism theory. Siemens [16] defined connectivism as a theory of learning that describes the process of learning through the establishment of online connections between people. While each MOOC has a unique structure and style, MOOCs in general can be divided into two categories: cMOOCs and xMOOCs. According to George Siemens [17].

> *...cMOOCs focus on the creation and generation of knowledge, while xMOOCs focus on the duplication of knowledge.*

The original MOOC was a cMOOC. The terms "cMOOC" and "xMOOC" were coined by Stephen Downes, the co-creator of the first cMOOC that was published on the Internet. Launched in 2008, the course was called "Connectivism and Connective Knowledge" (CCK08) and attracted 2,200 enrolled participants. cMOOCs are based on the learning theory of connectivism. Connectivism was first introduced in a blog post in 2004, which was later published in an article by Siemens (16). It was later extended in two publications in 2005: Siemens' Connectivism: Learning as Network Creation and Downes' An Introduction to Connective Knowledge [15, 18].

The theory of connectivism emphasizes the power of networking with other individuals, gathering diverse opinions, and focusing on end goals as the basis of learning. Connectivism is a learning theory aimed at understanding learning in the digital age. Connectivism explains how Internet technologies have created new ways for people to learn and share information over the World Wide Web and with each other. It emphasizes how Internet technologies, such as web browsers, search engines, email, wikis, social networks, online discussion forums, YouTube, and any other tool that allows users to learn and share information with other people, have contributed to new ways of learning. Technologies have enabled people to learn and share information on the World Wide Web and with each other in ways that were not possible before the digital age [15, 18]. Learning occurs not only within an individual, but also within and across networks. A key feature of connectivism is that much of the learning can take place through peer networks that occur online. In connectivism learning, a teacher guides students to information and answers important questions when they arise to help students learn and share independently. Students are also encouraged to search for information online and express what they find. A networked community often develops around such shared information.

Connectivism is based on the idea that learning occurs in networks [14, 16] and that some networks can "support [learners'] agency and cognition" [15, p. 117]. Furthermore, "knowledge is distributed across a network of connections, and therefore learning consists of the ability to construct and traverse these networks" [15]. According to Siemens [16, n.p.], the principles of connectivism include the following:

- *Learning and knowledge rests in diversity of opinions.*
- *Learning is a process of connecting specialized nodes or information sources.*
- *Learning may reside in non-human appliances.*
- *Capacity to know more is more critical than what is currently known.*
- *Nurturing and maintaining connections is needed to facilitate continual learning.*
- *Ability to see connections between fields, ideas, and concepts is a core skill.*
- *Currency (accurate, up-to-date knowledge) is the intent of all connectivism learning activities.*
- *Decision-making is itself a learning process. Choosing what to learn and the meaning of incoming information is seen through the lens of a shifting reality. While there is a right answer now, it may be wrong tomorrow due to alterations in the information climate affecting the decision.*

Connectivism views learning as a process of creating connections and expanding or increasing network complexity. Connections can have different directions and strengths [19]. Siemens, argued that cMOOCs are:

> *... based on the idea that learning takes place in a network where learners use digital platforms such as blogs, wikis, and social media platforms to make connections with content, learning communities, and other learners to create and construct knowledge. [17, n.p.].*

A connective MOOC (i.e., cMOOC) is open to anyone. Courses are online for a specific period and according to a specific syllabus. The web with its open systems and software is used to facilitate learning, but also to share information and knowledge. Participants in a cMOOC are responsible for what they learn and what and how they share it. As the course progresses, the networking among the learners helps to shape and form the course content in a rhizome-like and agile manner as it moves along. The teacher serves only as a facilitator.

In a cMOOC, participants take on many roles, both as learners, teachers, and facilitators. All are responsible as peer learners, sharing information and engaging in collaborative experiences and discussions. Haber [8] argues that cMOOC reflects the open vision of the web itself, namely that content continuously is generated by the online community and shared with others in an open manner.

Some top universities, such as Harvard, MIT, and Stanford, have begun offering MOOCs in a slightly different format called xMOOC (extended MOOCs). xMOOCs are built around professors and are more oriented toward a traditional classroom structure, rather than the structure as an open online community of learners based on connectivism theory. xMOOCs mostly mirror classroom instruction by combining a pre-recorded video lecture with quizzes, tests, or other assessments. The xMOOCs landscape is expanding daily and now covers an increasing number of topics in all disciplines. The largest providers today are Coursera [20], edX [21], FutureLearn [22], SWAYAM [23], Udacity [24], and ClassPert (a free search engine for online courses).

Although cMOOCs and xMOOCs share the common goal of providing open and free (or relatively low-cost) education to the public, they have distinctly different modalities, structures, and qualities. The learning environment set up for each of the MOOC forms is suitable for different learners and different methods of knowledge acquisition.

3.3 MOOCs statistics

In the years before 2020, the growth of MOOC providers had stagnated, garnering a similar number of learners each year. However, in 2020, providers collectively gained over 60 million new learners. Coursera alone accounted for half that number, gaining almost as many users in one year as its closest competitor edX had garnered since it was founded. By the end of 2020, 16.3 million MOOCs had been announced or launched by some 950 universities worldwide. Around 2.8 million courses were added in 2020 alone (**Figure 2**) [7].

Boosted by the pandemic, MOOCs garnered 180 million learners in their ninth year (**Figure 3**) [21].

One-third of learners who had ever registered on a MOOC platform did so in 2020. The pandemic brought many people into online education. MOOC providers

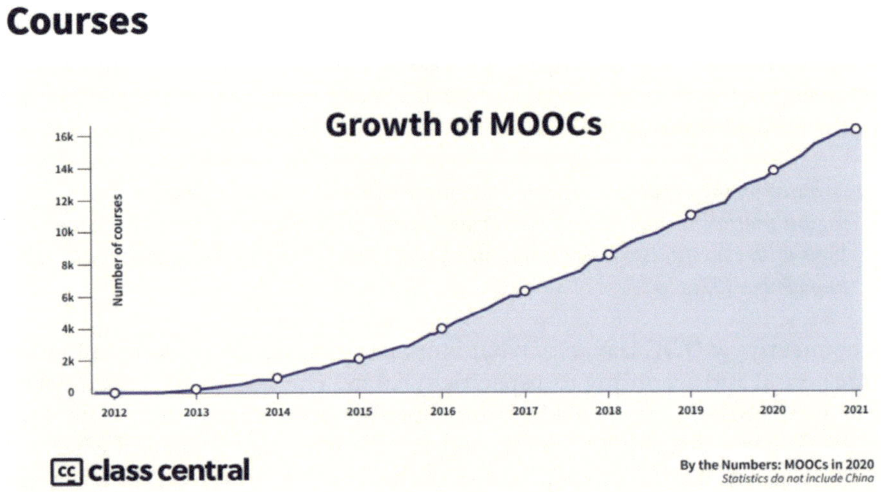

Figure 2.
Growth in MOOCs (see [21]).

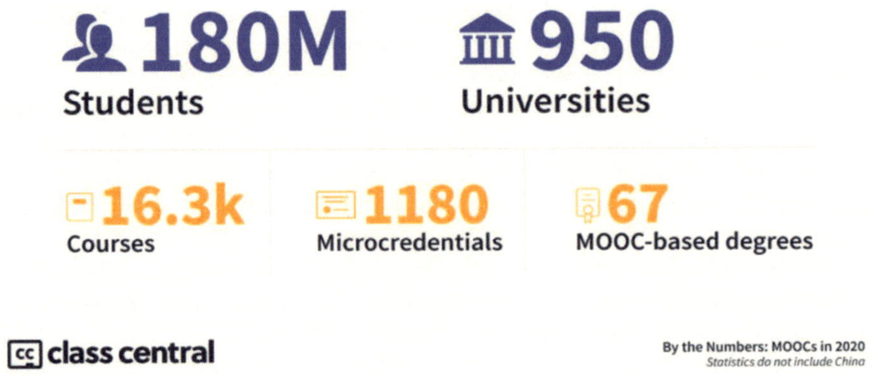

Figure 3.
MOOCs according to number (see [7]).

	Learners	Courses	Microcredentials	Degrees
Coursera	76 million	4,600[3]	610	25
edX	35 million	3,100	385	13
FutureLearn[2,4]	14 million	1,160	86	28
Swayam[2]	16 million	1,130	0	0

Figure 4.
The largest MOOC providers in numbers (see [7]).

benefited immensely by attracting many learners to register in free online courses from top universities. Class Central was no exception. Of all people who had used Class Central, 40% did so for the first time in 2020. Now in its nineth year, the modern MOOC movement has surpassed 180 million learners, excluding China. In 2020, providers launched over 2,800 courses, 19 online degrees, and 360 micro-credentials. **Figure 4** shows the top MOOC providers in terms of users and offerings.

3.4 The largest MOOC providers

Currently, the largest MOOC providers are Coursera [20], edX [21], FutureLearn [22], and SWAYAM [23], and Udacity [24], which are described in brief in alphabetic order in the following subsections.

3.4.1 Coursera

Based on a vision to create life-changing learning experiences for learners around the world, Daphne Koller and Andrew Ng founded Coursera in 2012. In partnership with the world's leading universities and companies, Coursera provides access to high-quality online courses and degrees for anyone, anywhere, to bring the best learning opportunities to every corner of the world. Today, Coursera partners with more than 200 leading universities and companies. More than 82 million learners, over 100 Fortune 500 companies, and more than 6,000 colleges, businesses, and governments use Coursera to access world-class learning. In February 2021, Coursera received B-Corp certification, so they not only have a legal obligation to their shareholders, but also positively impact the broader community as they continue their efforts to lower the barriers to world-class education for all. Anytime, anywhere. Coursera's most important core belief is that learning is the source of human progress, and that learning is considered a human right. They believe that education and knowledge have the power to change the world by transforming disease into health, poverty into prosperity, and conflict into peace. They also argue that education has the power to transform lives, families, communities, and societies. Regardless of who the learners are and where they live, learning empowers everyone to change and grow and redefine what is possible. That's why access to the best learning is a right, not a privilege - it's Coursera's mission. Everyone everywhere has the power to change their lives through learning [20].

3.4.2 edX

The story of edX began as an experiment and expanded to a global movement [21]. Spearheaded by edX, the concept began as a way for organizations to offer free online courses to millions of students around the world. While the Internet enabled innovation on a massive scale across a wide range of industries, higher education reached only a tiny fraction of the world's curious minds. One afternoon in a lab at Massachusetts Institute of Technology (MIT), Professor Anant Agarwal and his colleagues at MIT and Harvard outlined a far-reaching experiment: a platform that would offer their courses online and freely available to anyone who wanted to take the challenge. In February 2012, Professor Agarwal's course at MIT, Circuits and Electronics, was launched, and edX.org was born (edX, 2021). By opening the classroom through MOOCs, edX brings the best courses from the best schools to millions of learners around the world. The edX platform is designed to enable educators to deliver education at a scale that is equal to or better than on-site learning.

MOOC providers have changed education in many ways and continue to do so. edX, for example, has developed innovative modular degrees - MicroMasters® programs and Professional Certificate, which provide flexible and affordable educational opportunities that learners at all levels can use to succeed in an increasingly complex and technologically advanced world, in addition to their full online master's degrees.

In connection with its MicroMasters™ program, other educational programs, and related services, edX regularly works with many types of organizations from around the world: academic institutions (e.g., major research universities, technical colleges, and liberal arts colleges), nonprofit organizations, national governments, nongovernmental organizations (NGOs), and multinational corporations.

An institution that strongly aligns with edX's mission and offers the opportunity to contribute strategically, content-wise, and/or financially to the consortium is very welcome to collaborate with edX and discuss where it is today and where it wants to go with online/blended learning and MOOCs. In return, edX provides a range of technical, marketing, and educational services (e.g., training, onboarding, high-level program management, learner technical assistance, course strategy, design, build, delivery, and repeat consultations that include data analytics, etc.) to its members who participate in the MicroMasters program and other educational programs. edX offers the highest quality online courses from institutions that share the commitment to excellence in teaching and learning. More than 34 million learners worldwide are enrolled in 100 million enrollments in 2,800 edX courses in subjects such as the humanities, math, and computer science [21].

In 2012, edX realized that it was time for a seismic shift in education from the tried and true to the new and from "for some" to "for all." By opening up the classroom through online learning, edX has empowered millions of learners to unlock their potential and become changemakers [21].

edX offers opportunities to learn from more than 160 member universities. It has made three commitments to the world. From the beginning, they have stayed true to these commitments:

- Increase access to quality education for everyone everywhere.
- Improve teaching and learning on campus and online.
- Advance teaching and learning through research.

Figure 5 shows the statistics for edX in 2020.

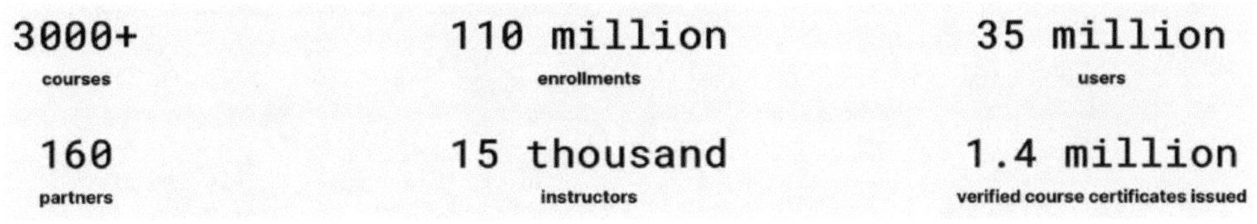

Figure 5.
EdX statistics in 2020 (see [21]).

3.4.3 FutureLearn

FutureLearn is a private company jointly owned by the Open University United Kingdom and the SEEK Group [22]. The Open University has over 50 years of experience in distance learning and online education. SEEK is a diverse group of companies with the common goal of helping people lead more fulfilling and productive work lives and helping organizations succeed.

FutureLearn launched its first courses in September 2013. Since then, millions of people have registered in its courses. FutureLearn offers a wide range of courses from leading universities and cultural institutions around the world. Courses are delivered step-by-step, and they are accessible via mobile devices, tablets, and desktops, which allows students to integrate learning into their lives [22].

FutureLearn works with several internationally renowned organizations of professional associations, such as the Association of Chartered Certified Accountants (ACCA) and the Institution of Engineering and Technology (IET), businesses such as the BBC and Marks & Spencer, and the UK Government. With over hundreds of partners around the world, including many of the best UK and international universities as well as institutions with vast archives of cultural and educational material, such as the British Council, the British Library, the British Museum and the National Film and Television School [22] is one of the world's leading providers of MOOCs.

FutureLearn believes that learning should be an enjoyable social experience. Their courses offer the opportunity to discuss what students are learning with others, which helps in making discoveries and developing new ideas. FutureLearns' (2021) values are based on three pillars: learning everything, learning together, and learning with experts [22]:

Learn anything: Whether you want to advance your career or discover a new hobby, there is an online course for it. With online programs and degree programs, you can even expand your knowledge.

Learn together: Join millions of people from around the world who are learning together. Online learning is as easy and natural as chatting with a group of friends.

*Learn with ex*perts: Meet educators from top universities and cultural institutions.

3.4.4 SWAYAM

In 2014, the Ministry of Human Rights Development (MHRD) in India announced Study Webs of Active Learning for Young Aspiring Minds (SWAYAM) as the national platform for MOOCs under its National Mission on Education through Information and Communication Technology (NME-ICT) [23].

3.4.5 Udacity

In February 2012, Thrun founded the Udacity company, which began developing and offering MOOCs for free. Udacity is where lifelong learners come to learn

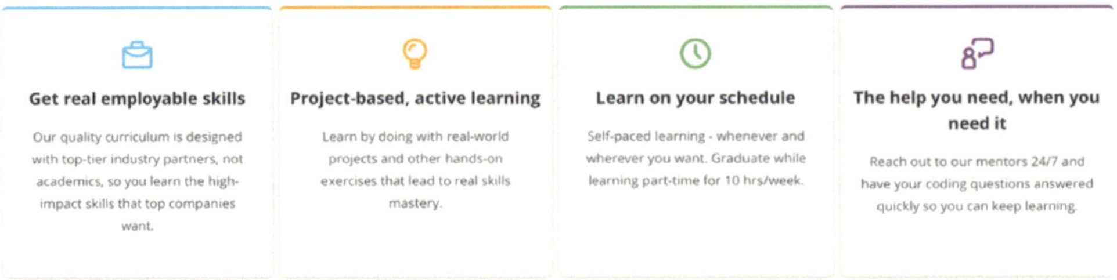

Figure 6.
Udacity services and offers (see [24]).

the skills, they need to get the jobs they want and to build the lives they deserve. Udacity reaches out to individuals, governments, and businesses. Their mission is to train the world's workforce for the jobs of the future. They partner with leading tech companies to learn how technology is changing industries and to teach the critical technological skills that companies require in their workforce. Udacity's Nanodegree programs are developed in partnership with the world's most innovative tech companies and taught by industry leaders Udacity [24].

Udacity students are a community of global learners who share the common goals of progress and change. Their unique learning model allows for unprecedented levels of engagement with students, and students are accompanied through their learning journey from the first moment a member of the marketing team answers a question on Facebook to the penultimate moment when a member of the careers team receives news that a graduate has landed a new job. Udacity's mantra is "Students First," which is the guiding light as the company continues its mission to provide the highest quality learning possible for as many students as possible [24].

Udacity [24] has claimed that their powerful and flexible digital education platform can prepare even the hardest working learners to take on the most in-demand tech roles. They also have claimed that their active learning offerings have the critical factors required to deliver real results and teach real, employable skills that are project-based. Moreover, students can learn on their own schedules and get help whenever they need it, as shown in **Figure 6**.

3.5 UNESCO initiatives in open education

3.5.1 UNESCO's SDGs

Every goal of the 2030 Agenda requires education to equip people with the knowledge, skills, and values they need to live with dignity, shape their lives and contribute to their societies [1, 10]. Education is both a human right and a force for sustainable development and peace.

The educational goals are stated in SDG 4 of the 2030 Agenda, which aims to ensure inclusive and equitable quality education by 2030 and promote lifelong learning opportunities for all. It requires political will, global and regional collaboration, and commitment from all governments, civil society, the private sector, youth, the UN, and other multilateral organizations to address education challenges and build systems that are inclusive, equitable, and relevant for all learners. Open education is probably the only way to achieve these goals. The first cMOOC was based on OER, which played a crucial role, as all the materials in the course were in the Creative Commons (CC). The MOOC movement and OER movement are related and strongly connected. The OER movement subsequently resulted in the UNESCO OER Recommendation in 2019 [9]. The UNESCO OER Recommendation outlined five areas of action:

(i) building the capacity of stakeholders to create, access, re-use, adapt and redistribute OER; (ii) developing supportive policy for OER; (iii) encouraging inclusive and equitable quality OER; (iv) nurturing the creation of sustainability models for OER; and (v) promoting and reinforcing international cooperation in OER [9, n.p.].

3.5.2 UNESCO's the futures of education: learning to become

In 2019, the International Commission on the Futures of Education was launched by UNESCO to reconsider how knowledge and learning could shape the future of humanity and the planet [2]. The Global Futures of Education initiative of UNESCO, Learning to Become, aims to rethink education and shape the future. The initiative, which involves broad public and professional engagement, aims to stimulate a global debate on how to reimagine knowledge, education, and learning in an increasingly complex, uncertain, and precarious world.

Although the Futures of Education initiative was animated by the recognition that the world's uncertainty, complexity, and fragility were rapidly increasing, it could not have foreseen the global health pandemic in only a few months, which was a reminder that dramatic changes can occur more suddenly and unexpectedly than anyone expects. On one hand, the pandemic has exposed many weaknesses and vulnerabilities, including increased inequalities, risks associated with the privatization of education, and the lack of preparation for the massive shift to digital and distance learning. On the other hand, some positive aspects have also become increasingly visible in society. It is evident that the answer to the challenges facing many societies involves solidarity and strong resilience. There is increased attention to the common good. The same is true of the ingenuity, commitment, and creativity of the many teachers, families, and students who have created remarkable learning experiences.

The pandemic has forced a massive shift away from learning and teaching in traditional settings that depend on physical interaction. The COVID-19 pandemic has compromised public education and increased the risk of fragmentation and disintegration. There has been an increased awareness of the multiple roles that schools play in addition to academic learning, such as child and adolescent well-being, health, and nutrition. The increased awareness and appreciation could serve as the basis for a new way forward in public education.

3.5.3 UNESCO: lifelong learning - a key competence

The Lifelong Learning Initiative of UNESCO [3, 4], which rethinks lifelong learning beyond the conceptual boundaries of education, emphasizes the possible reconnection of learning to larger social–emotional domains. This expands thinking about the "future of education" to include new perspectives on strategic areas such as the role of institutions, the use of technology, sources of knowledge and well-being, and people's access to learning and education.

Even in the richest economies, millions of people face financial and other barriers that exclude them from learning and prevent them from reaching their potential. The multidimensionality and complexity of the challenges people face require the implementation of a holistic vision and an ecosystem of lifelong learning. Moreover, the Fourth Industrial Revolution (4IR) combined with the dislocations caused by climate change, demographic change and the transformation of the labor market have implications for education. Therefore, the education policy agenda must prioritize lifelong learning beyond education and labor market policies [3, 4].

UNESCO has thus argued that the challenges facing humanity, not to mention those posed by the pandemic COVID-19 and the inequalities it exacerbates, requires people who identify as learners throughout their lives, in a society that is a learning society. Achieving this requires a needs-based, learner-centered approach to education that empowers individuals of all ages and backgrounds to dynamically profile and use every learning process and its outcomes to reach their full potential, so that they can become what they want to become. Learning must be a collective process that recognizes the value of peer and intergenerational learning. This social-ethical dimension emphasizes learning to care for one another, foster diverse communities, and ensure the well-being of the planet. A collectively built global learning ecosystem should fluidly integrate formal, non-formal and informal learning, as well as different learning modalities, both online and offline. Such an ecosystem enables planned or spontaneous, individual, or collective learning in all domains throughout the life course and beyond. Legal foundations and mechanisms that recognize lifelong learning as a human right, social justice and liberation must not only ensure the recognition, validation and accreditation of learning outcomes acquired in different contexts. It also requires the democratization of the negotiation of individual and social emotions in learning. It builds on the free availability of educational resources as an 'educational commons' while strengthening learning opportunities through transformed educational institutions, reinvented (public) spaces for learning and revitalized learning in the workplace.

The UN Lifelong Learning Initiative is based on the argument that generating a global culture of lifelong learning is key to addressing the challenges fronting humanity, such as the climate crisis, technological and demographic change, the challenges posed by the pandemic COVID -19 and the inequalities it has exacerbated [3, 4]. Therefore, there is an urgent need to create a culture of lifelong learning. Ten action points are emphasized by UNESCO: (i) recognize the holistic character of lifelong learning; (ii) promote transdisciplinary research and intersectoral collaboration for lifelong learning; (iii) place vulnerable groups at the core of the lifelong learning policy agenda; (iv) establish lifelong learning and equitable access to learning technology for the common and the public good; (vi) transform schools and universities into lifelong learning institutions, and transform pedagogies to be open to the community; (vii) recognize and promote the collective dimension of learning; (viii) encourage and support local lifelong learning initiatives, including learning cities; (ix) reengineer and revitalize workplace learning; and (x) recognize that lifelong learning is a human right.

Learning to learn thus represents a key competence in lifelong learning, and it is a prerequisite for acquiring and improving skills, knowledge, and attitudes. It is a key resource of personal development and active citizenship. It is seen as a skill that can be developed by all, which could ultimately promote the development of democracy. Briefly, learning to learn is defined as giving the learner responsibility for the activity of learning and orchestrating their own learning [3, 4].

Learning to learn concerns the ability to absorb and continue learning, to organize learning individually or collectively, and to make the best use of time, information, and learning opportunities. It includes the ability to set goals, identify the means of and obstacles to achieving these goals according to an individual learning strategy, and effectively monitor and evaluate one's learning process.

This competence means acquiring, processing, and assimilating new knowledge and skills, as well as seeking and using guidance. In learning to learn, the learner builds on previous learning and life experiences to use and apply knowledge and skills in a variety of contexts: personal, professional, and social. Identifying opportunities to increase one's motivation and confidence is critical to learning to learn. Learners and trainers function as motivators and facilitators of participants' learning in their educational work, with the aim of developing positive attitudes toward learning throughout the life course.

3.6 OECD

The OECD initiative The Future of Education and Skills 2030 [5] aims to help education systems determine the knowledge, skills, attitudes, and values that students need to succeed and shape their futures. The initiative aims to create a shared understanding of the knowledge, skills, attitudes, and values that learners will need in the 21st century [25, 26].

3.7 WEF

The World Economic Forum (WEF) is the International Organization for Public–Private Cooperation. The Forum brings together political, business, cultural, and other leaders in society to shape global, regional, and industrial agendas [27].

It is critical that individuals take an active attitude toward their own lifelong learning, according to Schwab, the founder, and Executive Chairman of WEF. The Future of Jobs 2018 report points out that businesses and governments need to dynamically encourage workforces to learn and develop skills. Artificial intelligence, robotization, and automation will create new jobs and wealth for millions of people. In addition, people worldwide will need to change, upskill, re-skill, and un-skill their work and careers during their lifespan, and throughout the transition. In all sectors the world needs people with talents and diversity in every way, but especially those who can offer a unique perspective. Fortunately, the digital world has given us new opportunities to reinvent ourselves, continue to learn, and be competitive. To take advantage of these opportunities and participate in the digital workplace, a lifelong learning plan is imperative.

4. Discussion

Quality education for all is a human right, and it aims at achieving social justice and liberation. All global organizations, such as the Commonwealth of Learning (COL), the European Commission (EC), OECD, UNESCO, and WEF, therefore have emphasized the urgent need to implement an open approach to education to achieve the global goals of quality education and the SDG 4 of accessibility, equity, equality, lifelong learning, inclusiveness, and democracy. During the COVID-19 pandemic, the education system was challenged, and the limitations became highly visible, especially the difficulties faced by vulnerable groups. Lifelong learning, equality, and liberation were key issues dealt with by societies to ease tensions between inside and outside organizations and enable boundaryless thinking and seamless learning [28]. Seamless learning involves the integration of learning experiences across different dimensions, including formal and informal learning contexts, individual and social learning, and the physical world and cyberspace.

During the pandemic, all MOOC providers confirmed the increased interest in MOOCs by both education institutions and users [7, 20–24]. There was a new peak in the MOOC year of 2020, which was called the second year of the MOOC field. The first one was in 2012. However, it was argued that MOOCs were limited because enrollment was low at about 10%. However, MOOCs are a different type of learning opportunity, and they are usually aimed at a very different audience: lifelong learners and learners who want to take control of and design their own learning journey [25, 26]. Most MOOC learners are self-directed learners [25, 26, 29, 30] and they often choose to learn through MOOCs for the joy of learning, up-skilling, or reskilling. Sometimes, learners just have the goal of networking in a rhizome way.

Rhizomatic learning, according to Gilles and Guattari [31–33], is a variety of pedagogical practices recently identified as a methodology for network-based education [33]. Rhizomatic theory emphasizes that learning is most effective when it allows learners to respond to evolving circumstances, fluidly and seemingly effortlessly, in a kind of serendipity. Cormier argued that in this way "the community is the curriculum" and the focus is on the flow and engagement of learners [32, 33].

It is crucial to understand this form of learning pathway, which can be formal, informal, and non-formal in nature. Furthermore, it is therefore crucial to understand the theories and practices of the theories that underlie MOOCs, as it has already become clear that the first MOOC, Siemens, and Downs' cMOOC, was based on connectivism. Connectivism pedagogies, such as connectivism and rhizomatic learning, propose giving learners responsibility and agency in online learning ecologies so that they can tailor learning experiences to their learning needs using all means, including time, space, mode, path, and media. According to networked learning theories, networked online spaces provide multiple entry points [34–37], and learners in these spaces should take the lead in their own lifelong learning journey [25] and in learning from their experiences.

MOOC learners are usually self-directed. Self-directed learning builds on heutagogy [37]. Like connectivism and rhizomatic learning, self-directed learning is based on a networked theory of learning that promotes learner agency while further expanding other aspects of learning and the role of the learner as an agent of learning. The theory builds on established learner-centered learning theories, such as constructivism, humanism, reflection, and transformational learning [38]. Central to heutagogy is the concept of the learner as the primary agent in their learning [39]. The learner makes decisions about learning based on what is learned and how and whether and to what extent learning has been achieved (e.g., self-assessment). Also central to the theory are the following principles: (i) self-efficacy, which is the learner's belief in their own abilities; and (ii) capability, which is the learner's ability to demonstrate an acquired competency or skill in new and unique settings. The resulting experience of both has the potential to create transformative learning. In addition, reflection, and critical thinking about what has been learned and the learning process in the form of double-loop learning (metacognition) is another principle of heutagogy. Finally, self-directed learning is characterized by non-linear learning, in which the learning path is learner-driven and not predefined or sequential, as the learner determines what to learn and how to learn it. As a result, this path can often be chaotic and divergent, like learning in a connectivism and rhizomatic learning environment [39].

It is important to understand the role that MOOCs play in individual learning in terms of self-directed and rhizome learning pathways. This role is paramount in understanding the bigger picture of open learning, the role of MOOCs in this context, and how they contribute to the lifelong learning, equity, and liberation of individuals, communities, and societies.

5. Conclusion and recommendations

This chapter is based on the argument that knowledge is a universal entity and that it is constructed by individuals and belongs to anyone who asks for it wherever they need it. The theories of connected learning and learner-centered learning support the view that learning should be designed to enhance learners' agency by harnessing and nurturing learners' intrinsic motivation to learn. Learner agency through heutagogy and online learning ecologies provides sustainable learning experiences, as autonomy is given to the learner, which is highlighted in connectivism and rhizomatic learning. Rather than being constrained by predefined goals or objectives, learning is defined by the needs of learners. It is meaningful if it meets these needs and involves learners in deciding what and how to learn. This approach, which is already characteristic of informal learning, can help establish learner agency as the standard for learning, develop learner self-efficacy and skills as a pathway to active, meaningful, and satisfying learning, and promote critical thinking and reflection in formal learning environments.

Before the advent of MOOCs and OER, quality education was a preserve of the privileged few. Therefore, the MOOC raise in 2012, the COVID-19 pandemic [40], and the UNESCO OER recommendation for implementation of its five areas have made a dramatic change in the educational landscape. The direction of education has shifted toward the fulfillment of human rights, quality education for all, equity, and liberation. Every person has the potential to create change, whether in their own lives, in their communities, or in the world. The transformative power of education can unlock this potential. In this regard, the UNESCO initiative on the future of learning, Learning to Become, is crucial in liberating learners to fulfill their self-goals and assume responsibility as global citizens. MOOCs play a critical role in this liberation because well-educated citizens are more likely to be healthy, responsible, and happy. Well-being and education are strongly linked, which the pandemic has demonstrated to the world.

MOOCs have the potential to help individuals enjoy learning, acquire knowledge in diverse ways, and be part of a learning society. In changing "learning landscapes" and the future of learning, MOOCs can play a variety of roles, such as stand-alone courses in informal and non-formal learning and as modules integrated into formal education. The advantages of MOOCs include the possibilities of upscaling and thus offering all global citizens high-quality learning opportunities [41–45]. In addition, the potential of micro-credentials is promising, which is another departure from the elitist education system that has been predominant for the past several centuries. It is time for agile, seamless, rhizomatic learning opportunities and a learning curriculum for individuals' personal choices in the global learning landscape, which must be open to everyone across the globe to achieve lifelong learning, equity, and liberation. MOOCs can play a key role in the achievement of these goals.

Conflict of interest

The authors declare no conflict of interest.

Author details

Ebba Ossiannilsson
Swedish Association for Distance Education, International Council for Open and Distance Education, International Council on Badges and Credentilals, Lund, Sweden

*Address all correspondence to: ebba.ossiannilsson@gmail.com; info@i4quality.se

References

[1] UNESCO. Leading SDG 4 - Education 2030. 2021. Available from: https://en.unesco.org/themes/education2030-sdg4

[2] UNESCO. Futures of education, learning to become. 2019. Available from: https://en.unesco.org/futuresofeducation/

[3] UNESCO Institute for Lifelong Learning; 2020. Available from: https://unesdoc.unesco.org/ark:/48223/pf0000374112

[4] UNESCO. Embracing a Culture of Lifelong Learning: Contribution to the Futures of Education Initiative: Report – a Transdisciplinary Expert Consultation. Hamburg: UNESCO.

[5] OECD. The state of higher education. One year into the COVID-19 pandemic. 2021. Available from: https://www.oecd-ilibrary.org/education/the-state-of-higher-education_83c41957-en?_ga=2.239633280.248329523.1625384020-423207501.1625147232

[6] Mooc.org. About MOOCs. 2021. Available from: https://www.mooc.org/about-moocs

[7] Shah D. By the Numbers: MOOCs in 2020. Class Central. 2020. Available from: https://www.classcentral.com/report/mooc-stats-2020/

[8] Haber J. MOOCs. The MIT Press Essential Knowledge Series. 2014. Available from https://mitpress.mit.edu/books/moocs

[9] UNESCO. Recommendation on open educational resources (OER). 2019a. Available from: http://portal.unesco.org/en/ev.php-URL_ID=49556&URL_DO=DO_TOPIC&URL_SECTION=201.html

[10] UNESCO. Rethinking Education. 2015.Towards a global Common Good. 2015. Paris: UNESCO. Available from https://unevoc.unesco.org/e-forum/RethinkingEducation.pdf

[11] Creswell JW. Research Design Qualitative, Quantitative, and Mixed Methods Approaches. 4th edition. London: SAGE Publications; 2013.

[12] Creswell JW. Research Design: Qualitative, Quantitative and Mixed Methods Approaches. 4th edition. Thousand Oaks, CA: SAGE: 2014.

[13] Creswell, JW, Creswell JD. Research Design: Qualitative, Quantitative, and Mixed Methods Approaches. Thousand Oaks, CA: Sage Publications; 2018.

[14] Downes S. New technology supporting informal learning. Journal of Emerging Technologies in Web Intelligence. 2010;2(1): 27-33.

[15] Downes S. Recent work in connectivism. European Journal of Open, Distance and E-learning. 2019;22(2): 112-131. Available from: https://edtechbooks.org/-NvTV

[16] Siemens G. Connectivism: A learning theory for the digital age. Elearnspace [blogpost]. 2004 December 12. Available from: https://edtechbooks.org/-zKa

[17] Siemens, G. Massive open online courses: Innovation in education. In McGreal, R., Kinuthia W., & Marshall S, editors. Open educational resources: Innovation, research, and practice Vancouver: Commonwealth of Learning and Athabasca University; (2013). (pp. 5-16).

[18] Siemens G. Connectivism: A learning theory for the digital age. International Journal of Instructional Technology and Distance Learning. 2005;2: 1-9.

[19] AlDahdouh AA., Osório, AJ, Caires S. Understanding knowledge network, learning and connectivism. International Journal of Instructional Technology and Distance Learning. 2015;12(10): 3-21.

[20] Coursera. 2021. About Coursera. Mountain View: Coursera; 2021. Available from https://about.coursera.org

[21] edX. About us, transformation through education. Cambridge US: edX; 2021. Available from https://www.edx.org/about-us

[22] FutureLearn. About FutureLearn, our story. London: FutureLearn; 2021. Available from https://www.futurelearn.com/about-futurelearn

[23] SWAYAM. About SWAYAM. New Delhi: SWAYAM; 2021. Available from SWAYAM. https://tools.kib.ki.se/referensguide/vancouver/#webb-webbsi

[24] Udacity. The latest digital skills, within reach. 2021. Available from: https://www.udacity.com

[25] Ossiannilsson E. Let the learners yake the lead for their lifelong learning Jjourney. In: Keengwe J, Keengwe G., Onchwari, editors. Handbook of Research on Learner-Centered Pedagogy in Teacher Education and Professional Development. p. 159-180. Hershey: IGI Global; 2017.

[26] Ossiannilsson E. Promoting active and meaningful learning for digital learners. In: Keengwe, J, editor. Handbook of research on mobile technology, constructivism, and meaningful learning. Hershey: IGI Global; 2017.

[27] WEF. On the agenda. 2021. Available from: https://www.weforum.org/agenda/archive

[28] Hambrock H, de Villiers F, Rusman E, MacCallum K, Arrieya Arrifin S. Seamless learning in higher education: Perspectives of international educators on its Ccurriculum and implementation potential. Global research project International Association for Mobile Learning; 2020. Pressbook.

[29] Ossiannilsson E, Altinay F, Altinay Z. Analysis of MOOCs practice from learner experiences and quality cultures. Educational Media International. 2015;4: 272-283.

[30] Ossiannilsson E, Altinay Z, Altinay F. Towards fostering quality in open online education through OER and MOOC practices. In: Jemni M, Kinchuk M, Khribi K, editors. Open Education: From OERs to MOOCs (Lecture Notes in Educational Technology). New York City: Springer; 2017.

[31] Deleuze G, Guattari F. A Thousand Plateaus: Capitalism and Schizophrenia. Minnesota: University of Minnesota Press; 1987.

[32] Ossiannilsson E. Benchmarking e-learning in higher education: Lessons learned from international projects [doctoral dissertation]. Finland: Oulu University; 2012.

[33] Cormier D. Rhizomatic education: community as curriculum. Innovate: Journal of Online Education. 2008;4(5): 1-8.

[34] Siemens, G. Knowing Knowledge. Vancouver: Lulu Press; 2006.

[35] Siemens G. Connectivism: A learning theory for the digital age. International Journal of Instructional Technology and Distance Learning. 2005;2(1):3-10.

[36] Siemens G. (2007). Connectivism: Creating a learning ecology in

distributed environments. In: Hug T, editor. Didactics of Microlearning. Concepts, Discourses, and Examples. Munster: Waxmann Verlag; 2007. p. 53-68.

[37] Mbati L. Creating awareness around rhizomatic principles in mLearning: A means to improving practice. International Journal of Mobile and Blended Learning (IJMBL). 2017;9(2): 74-87.

[38] Hase S, Kenyon C. From andragogy to heutagogy. 2000; Ultibase Articles, 5, 1-10. Available from: https:// edtechbooks.org/-Ibt

[39] Blaschke LM, Bozkurt A, Cormier D. (2021). Learner agency and the learner-centered theories for online networked learning and learning ecologies. In: Hase S, L. M. Blaschke LM, editors. Unleashing the Power of Learner Agency. EdTech Books, 2021. Chapter 4.

[40] Bozkurt A, Jung, I., Xiao, J., Vladimirschi, V., Schuwer, R., Egorov, G. et al. A global outlook to the interruption of education due to COVID-19 pandemic: Navigating in a time of uncertainty and crisis. Asian Journal of Distance Education. 2020;15(1):1-128.

[41] Creelman A, Ehlers UD, Ossiannilsson E. Perspectives on MOOC quality: an account of the EFQUEL MOOC Quality Project. INNOQUAL - International Journal for Innovation and Quality in Learning, 2014;2(3): 78-87.

[42] Ossiannilsson E. Quality Models for Open Online Learning (OOL), Open Educational Resources (OER) and Massive Open Online Courses (MOOCS). Brussels: European Commission ET Working Group on Open and Distance Learning (ODL); 2016. (Unpublished).

[43] Ossiannilsson E. Quality models for open, flexible, and online learning. Journal of Computer Science Research; 2020;2(4): no pages.

[44] Stracke, M, Trisolini, G. A Systematic Literature Review on the Quality of MOOCs," Sustainability, 2021; 13(11): 1-26,

[45] EADTU. OpenUpEd. 2021. Available from https://www.openuped.eu

Chapter 9

Equality, Diversity and Inclusion – A MOOC for Academic Purposes

Rita Bencivenga, Cinzia Leone and Anna Siri

Abstract

Since its fifth framework programme (1998–2002), the European Union has promoted gender equality and equal opportunities in the higher education sector and science and technological development. In its current framework programme for research and innovation, Horizon Europe (2021–2027), the EU requires scientists to systematically integrate the concepts of sex, gender and intersectionality into their research paths and to promote equality, diversity and inclusion (EDI) in their working environments. However, for historical reasons, following the EU requirements is challenging, particularly for scientists in STEM disciplines. The University of Genoa is planning a MOOC suited to a large research institution audience to address this problem. The MOOC's targets are researchers, scholars, administrative personnel and students interested in advancing EDI practices in the scientific fields. It enables them to understand the basic principles underlying the gender mainstreaming adopted by the EU and integrate methods and strategies related to sex, gender and intersectionality to progress towards an EDI-sensitive institution. Supported by a learner-centred instructional strategy, this chapter explores the choices related to EDI-sensitive methods and strategies adopted to develop and implement an online education path. Theoretical and practical implications are also discussed.

Keywords: equality, diversity and inclusion, EDI-sensitive university, gender equality, higher education, MOOC

1. Introduction

It is widely believed that research performing and financing organisations (RPOs and RFOs) should be sensitive to Equality, Diversity, and Inclusion (EDI). The European Union (EU), its Member States and national funding organisations have been taking action to help higher education institutions (HEIs) apply for research funding to include sex/gender, intersectionality, diversity and inclusion analyses in their research and throughout their activities, enabling them to promote EDI within their organisations and in the scientific fields.

However, promoting an EDI-informed learning path and research activities requires the introduction of formal, organisation-focused knowledge and knowledge of cross-cutting topics. The idea of the MOOC originated from a search for EDI-focused online courses that did not reveal resources useful to achieving the learning aims described above. The chapter describes the path towards the creation of the MOOC.

In the following pages, we will begin by outlining the state of the art on the course content (EDI) and the chosen format (MOOC). The following paragraph will briefly outline the theoretical framework relating to the transition from lifelong learning to heutagogy. We will then detail the structure and contents of the course and conclude with a reflection on the relevance of the content chosen for HEIs that intend to continue on the EDI path.

2. State of the art

2.1 Equality, diversity and inclusion in academia

EDI is a strategic topic for the higher education sector. It impacts institutional culture, research and learning and teaching. In planning and designing the MOOC on EDI, we focused on the most up-to-date documents and strategies, in order to provide the learners with a helpful roadmap in devising policies for higher education and research and in implementing or supporting ideas and actions in their daily activities, as professionals or students.

The creation of the MOOC has been inspired by the favourable moment in equality, diversity and inclusion strategies and policies at EU level and in the academic sector. The EU Gender Equality Strategy 2020–2025[1], the Strategy for the Rights of Persons with Disabilities 2021–2030[2], the LGBTIQ Equality Strategy 2020–2025[3] and the EU Roma strategic framework for equality, inclusion and participation for 2020–2030[4] are all part of a Union of Equality to which the European Commission has committed itself, in order to accelerate the process towards equality, diversity and inclusion in Europe.

These documents follow a political path whose main steps are represented by the commitment, in 2015, of EU ministers to promote social inclusion and cultural diversity and foster the education of disadvantaged young people by ensuring that education systems address their needs[5]. A similar commitment, focused this time on the higher education system, was declared by higher education ministers at the Ministerial Meeting of the Bologna Process in 2015, where they agreed to make higher education systems more inclusive[6]. This was reiterated by the European Commission in its 2017 renewed agenda for higher education.

At the academic level, clear indications have been issued by reports and position papers [1–3] that define the best practices and the approaches to follow to progress rapidly and steadily towards more inclusive academia, supporting institutional growth and capacity building to promote the progress and innovation of European

[1] https://eur-lex.europa.eu/legal-content/EN/TXT/PDF/?uri=CELEX:52020DC0152&from=EN. Last visited on 15 August 2021

[2] https://ec.europa.eu/commission/presscorner/detail/en/ip_21_810. Last visited on 15 August 2021

[3] https://ec.europa.eu/info/sites/default/files/lgbtiq_strategy_2020-2025_en.pdf. Last visited on 15 August 2021

[4] https://ec.europa.eu/info/sites/default/files/eu_roma_strategic_framework_for_equality_inclusion_and_participation_for_2020_-_2030_0.pdf. Last visited on 15 August 2021

[5] Informal Meeting of European Union Education Ministers, 2015, 'Declaration on Promoting citizenship and the common values of freedom, tolerance and non-discrimination through education', Paris, France, 17 March 2015. Retrieved on 15 August 2021 from http://ec.europa.eu/dgs/education_culture/repository/education/news/2015/documents/citizenship-education-declaration_en.pdf

[6] Education Ministers of EHEA member countries, 2015, 'Yerevan Communiqué', EHEA ministerial meeting 2015, Yerevan, Armenia, 14–15 May 2015. Retrieved on 15 August 2021 from http://www.ehea.info/media.ehea.info/file/2015_Yerevan/70/7/YerevanCommuniqueFinal_613707.pdf

society. More recently, in a book promoted by the Council of Europe, it is reaffirmed that, in order to be persuasive, institutional leaders need to understand how to adapt their arguments for diversity and inclusion to different audiences and contexts [4].

Inclusiveness is therefore a strategic question for the higher education sector. It impacts institutional culture, research and learning and teaching. HEIs aim to be more open and inclusive and find new ways to enable people from traditionally less represented backgrounds to participate and progress in their working or learning careers, thus increasing diversity.

Diversity is a condition for excellence, and fairness in competition attracts talent at all levels. Non-diverse research environments are less creative and produce poorer results; diverse learning environments are more stimulating than homogenous ones. To support inclusiveness, HEIs may adopt strategies with high impact potential, such as equity in recruitment practices, mentorship and initiatives to ensure inclusive research and an inclusive work environment.

Since the early 1960s, diversity management has been commonly focused on historically disadvantaged groups such as women and minorities, but the concept of diversity has expanded over time, due to growing awareness about differences. For several years, the focus on gender equality has demonstrated, for example, the existence of a "leaky pipeline" [5] for people who identify as female in academia [6, 7]. The gap in academia is affected by ethnicity and intensifies when reaching senior academic roles [8]. Geographical factors may negatively influence a career path, hindering the publication process [9]. The myth that STEM disciplines represent spaces in which identity does not matter has been shattered by research focusing on lesbian, gay, bisexual, trans and sexually/gender diverse (LGBTQ+) individuals [10].

Currently, sexual and gender diversity, age and other grounds for potential discrimination have become more visible. The grounds for potential discrimination recognised by EU legislation, in the EU Charter for fundamental rights[7], are sex, race, colour, ethnic or social origin, genetic features, language, religion or beliefs, political or any other opinion, membership of a national minority, property, birth, disability, age or sexual orientation. The challenge is now to monitor these grounds at the academic level to promote EDI. The challenge is facilitated by the focus placed by the European Commission on addressing equality diversity and inclusion in an intersectional [11] perspective, stimulating the progress towards inclusive organisational practices that foster equity across multiple intersecting identities [12].

HEIs are becoming increasingly aware of the fact that "[k]nowledge production and research at universities and research-performing institutions are not as inclusive as they could be." ([1], p. 19). Current research deals with challenges, climate change, poverty, sustainable food production, which could benefit from broader perspectives, promoting excellence and innovation.

Likewise, global challenges such as climate change adaptation, poverty reduction, sustainable food production and, more recently, the COVID pandemic, will be more effectively addressed with an inclusive agenda in mind, since this expands the range of perspectives brought to bear on these problems. The same thinking can and should be applied to the teaching curriculum at research-intensive HEIs, by making the reading materials and the research used as references more inclusive.

The League of European Research Universities (LERU) has identified five opportunities for universities wishing to promote equality, diversity and inclusion (EDI) to become institutions where anyone with potential can thrive: better reflect and connect local and global challenges; discover and include the most outstanding

---

[7] https://fra.europa.eu/en/eu-charter/title/title-iii-equality. Consulted on 10 August 2021.

talents by reconsidering the definitions of excellence and success in the academic community; fully realise the potential in all staff and students; enhance wellbeing across the institution to the benefit of recruitment, retention and performance, and increase the validity and quality of research results and knowledge production and transfer [1].

2.2 Massive online open courses (MOOC)

Massive Open Online Courses (MOOCs) have developed rapidly and now play a leading role in achieving a "universal" model of education [13–15]. Dave Cormier, University of Prince Edward Island, coined the term Massive Open Online Courses (MOOCs) in 2008, following an early experiment in activating an online course entitled "Connectivism and Connective Knowledge", taught by Professors George Siemens and Stephen Downes [16].

According to Bates [17] and Hayes [18], a MOOC (Massive Online Open Course) can be defined as a product for teaching:

- Capable of providing a structured learning path that includes a syllabus and explicit learning objectives, materials and activities to support learning, an assessment system based on quizzes, exercises or projects, a certification process.

- Accessible through an online platform.

- Designed and managed to be enjoyed by many people [19].

- Built for free participation, i.e., without binding prerequisites and without requiring membership of a particular institution or costs for participation [20].

These characteristics imply that a MOOC should not be a repository of Open Educational Resources (OER), or a so-called blended course (although a blended course may also make use of a MOOC), or even a pathway that has a limited number of enrollees or prohibited access to specific categories of people [21].

Those who benefit most from this new model of education are mainly those who, for various reasons, have difficulty following traditional models of education.

Over the years, web platforms providing distance learning through MOOCs have multiplied, and the number and type of content creators have also increased, gradually including important international academic institutions [22, 23].

In the beginning, the first MOOCs had a solid and deep collaborative philosophy (cMOOCs), with a constructivist-connectivist slant, in which participants played an active and predominant role over that of the teacher, who became a facilitator [24].

This philosophy then evolved into a commercial model (xMOOCs) with a delivery-instructionist slant, more widespread and implemented by large institutions (mainly major US universities such as MIT, Harvard, Stanford), carrying on a more traditional model of education, based on video-recorded lectures [25].

However, more recent research has shown that this distinction is no longer feasible, due to the increasing overlap between these two extremes [26, 27].

In Italy, use of MOOCs has been spreading at an increasing rate, driven by the simultaneous growth of the phenomenon of so-called "telematic universities" [28] and the creation of EUDOPEN, a platform for the delivery of defined courses by a network of Italian universities and bodies/associations/networks of scientific and cultural importance **Figure 1**.

Figure 1.
EduOpen platform.

However, it must be highlighted that, while indicated as a resource capable of increasing access to quality education [29], certain aspects of MOOCs have been criticised, especially the difficulties associated with assessment based predominantly on multiple-choice questionnaires [30, 31], poor interaction with participants [32, 33], failure to meet instructional design criteria [30, 34] and use of technology that is not accessible or user-friendly [30].

It is therefore crucial to incorporate pedagogical, didactic, organisational, communicative and technological features that - in the perception of participants and teachers or through the analysis of best practices - result in a "high-quality" MOOC "[35–39].

The literature on the topic is extensive [40].

Learning design for MOOCs seems to follow specific approaches, given that the audience for which they are intended requires a different instructional design than one that works for a defined number of students. Indeed, since anyone with an internet connection can sign up for a MOOC, faculty staff cannot offer personalised support to every student. Consequently, the instructional design of a type of learning that must necessarily be self-regulated is a topic that must be considered carefully.

In creating the MOOC, we will follow the guidelines and reflections for evaluation proposed by the Conference of Italian University Rectors [39], as well as the checklist for verifying the quality of the MOOC case study, divided into the following six macro-environments:

1. MOOC STRUCTURE AND SYLLABUS.

2. TEACHING MATERIALS.

3. ONLINE LEARNING ACTIVITIES.

   a. Asynchronous/synchronous peer-to-peer online learning activities.

   b. Asynchronous/synchronous online teaching activities with staff/faculty.

   c. Non assessed online learning activities.

4. ASSESSMENT OF LEARNING.

   a. Quizzes.

   b. Assignments.

5. TUTORING, MONITORING AND COMMUNICATION.

6. LEARNING MANAGEMENT SYSTEM (LMS) FEATURES.

Concerning the recognition of CFUs, reference is made to the Guidelines in force in Italy according to Art. 4, paragraph 4, of Ministerial Decree no. 47 of 30 January 2013 (as amended), promoted and adopted by ANVUR (National Agency for the Evaluation of the University System and Research).

To calculate the CFUs deliverable through a MOOC, CRUI [41] points out that:

- Each recognised CFU corresponds with at least six hours of online teaching activity (e.g., actual duration of multimedia materials + Interactive learning activity).

- The online teaching activity can be calculated based on the actual duration of the video/interactive materials multiplied by two, adding the estimated duration of the planned online activities.

- The calculation does not include study materials (e.g., textbooks, articles, web resources and others), which are instead considered as part of the student's study time, with at least nineteen hours per CFU.

The forced digitization we are experiencing due to the COVID19 pandemic has pushed academic institutions around the world to focus on MOOCs (Massive open online courses) to strengthen their educational offer and encompass inclusion, quality and sustainability **Figure 2**.

The success of the formula success, at least quantitatively speaking, is confirmed by the numbers: over 180 million enrolled students and 950 universities at the beginning of 2021 (almost double the number of a year earlier), over 16 thousand free online courses on the leading international platforms.

The main trends in the development of MOOCs today can be grouped into the following three: the institutionalisation of degrees based on MOOC offerings, the concentration in oligopolies of MOOC distribution platforms, and the development of professionalising forms of accreditation for the lifelong market. This paper focuses precisely on this third point.

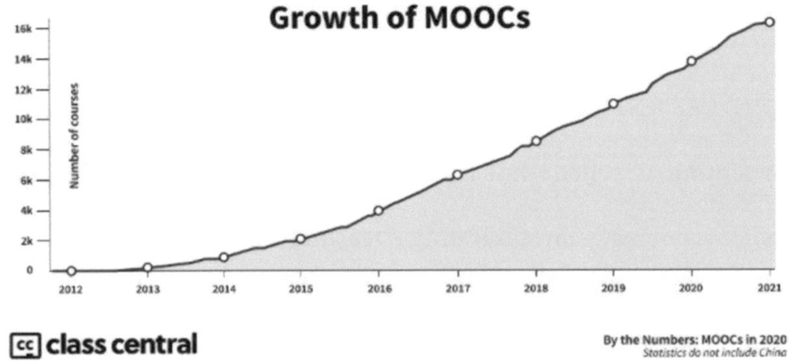

Figure 2.
By the numbers: MOOCs in 2020 (Source: Class Central: https://www.classcentral.com/report/mooc-stats-2020).

3. Theoretical framework: lifelong learning and heutagogy

Lifelong learning is considered a crucial element for individual growth and human development, a valuable opportunity to develop and maintain one's skills [42]. The emergence of this subjective right to lifelong learning implies a rethinking of training processes to enhance skills, abilities and knowledge (cognitive, experiential, relational, technical) related to a life project [43]. Following Dewey [44], education and training are located within a "hidden" process of formation that stimulates permanent attitudes and interests, i.e., lasting mental and emotional habits. In this sense, education is a process of construction, identification and enhancement of different identities that continues throughout a lifetime (lifelong learning). It takes place in different environments of training and experience (lifelong learning). It acquires the value of deep learning (life-deep learning) when it is cognitively and emotionally consolidated, allowing us to communicate with ourselves and with others, regardless of different values (cultural, moral, ethical, social, religious, etc.).

Putting everyone in a position to have equal rights and opportunities for lifelong learning, regardless of their social, cultural and geographic background, is a challenge that enables everyone to participate effectively and with information as citizens in social and political life.

The turning point can come about if training does not focus solely on the acquisition of skills functional to the profession but also addresses the typical tasks of an adult in the various social contexts. An educational policy based solely on a traditional educational model no longer has any meaning or usefulness today. Learning today means living a plurality of experiences, in which everyone recognises themselves and takes direct responsibility for learning, deciding what, how, where and when to learn.

To address the many unprecedented challenges in the cultural, social and professional lives of individuals and modern societies, a new approach to human development must be promoted, a "progression from pedagogy to andragogy to self-regulation, with learners likewise progressing in maturity and autonomy" [45].

The shift from andragogy to heutagogy expands on the self-directed learning practices of andragogy and involves trainees taking an active role in developing their own learning skills to meet their own needs [46–48]. The core of heutagogy is the principle of learner agency [49], and two additional principles are self-efficacy (learner's perception of their understanding of concepts and ability to apply and carry out specific tasks) and capability (develop their capacity to perform these tasks in new and unique environments).

Heutagogy builds on previous theories such as self-directed learning, humanism, capability, constructivism and self-regulation and self-determination [50–52].

It encourages the development of skills of autonomy and exploration, reflection and critical thinking, and innovation and entrepreneurship. It provides opportunities to develop students' self-directed, self-determined and lifelong learning skills, which are critical skills in online learning contexts, and the possibilities of theory align closely with those offered by technology [50–55].

Learners choose their training path by reflecting on their own strengths and weaknesses and exploring new strategies that fit their learning style. Such a process of self-reflection allows for double-loop learning, where the learner is put in a position to evaluate the effectiveness of their problem-solving strategies, evaluate alternative learning resources to activate [56] and their actions along with the beliefs acted upon [57].

Heutagogy has been found to be effective in blended and online learning [52, 55, 57–60]. It is a net-centric theory [61–63], and its intersection with technology is likely to stimulate the definition of one's own learning path, the ability to create one's own content, the ability to seek and explore sources of knowledge, to connect and collaborate with others, to reflect on new information and knowledge and to share one's work [54, 64].

The availability and accessibility of technology solutions enable and facilitate access to educational resources, learning communities and global knowledge exchange. Examples include OERs, Open CourseWare and MOOCs [65].

In addition, social media [52, 57], community-based learning [57], the use of e-portfolios [64] and mobile learning [66] are other technology-supported learning contexts that meet the heutagogical approach.

In this framework, the meaning of training processes is reformulated to integrate certain trends aimed at effectively fostering:

- access to personalised paths based on prior knowledge and objectives to be achieved (Personalised Learning).

- socially-based interactive learning that stimulates the sedimentation of knowledge, while providing an open and flexible pathway, supported by online technologies (Interactive/Social Learning) [47, 49, 67].

- access to experiences concerning one's personal and professional learning and updating needs (Self-regulated learning and employability).

The possibilities offered by new technologies allow for the enhancement of the heutagogical perspective, as they allow for student-generated content and promote active engagement in the learning process through collaboration and self-reflection, engaging in double-loop learning [68].

Within this framework, heutagogy aligns with lifelong learning, as highlighted in the European Framework for Personal, Social and Learning to Learn Key Competence (LifeComp) [69] and the European Framework for the Digital Competence of Educators (DigCompEdu) [70], meaning that this approach is capable of developing competences for continuous learning.

4. Developing the MOOC: equality of opportunities, diversity of representation: towards an equality, diversity and inclusion (EDI) sensitive university

4.1 The wider context

The MOOC is being created within a Horizon 2020 project entitled GenderEX: Gender for Excellence in Research. GenderEx is coordinated by the Kadir Has University Gender and Women's Studies Research Center. The project aims at exchanging knowledge and engaging best practices to stimulate the integration of the Sex and Gender Dimension in Research Content. Three leading international educational institutions are members of the GenderEX partnership: University of Lund (Sweden), University of Genoa (Italy) and Technological University Dublin (Ireland). The overall aim of GenderEX is to further the adoption of a sex/gender dimension in all areas of research and across multiple scientific disciplines in Turkey by enhancing the capacity of GWSRC-KHAS for training and engaging more researchers into this field, with a primary focus on Early-Stage Researchers (ESRs).

Since the Horizon Europe framework programme adopted an intersectional approach to research and innovation, GenderEX has added this aspect in its activities, in order to equip the participants with the most updated scientific perspectives. The perspective of the MOOC is therefore widened to encompass an EDI approach.

4.2 Methodology and architecture

Creation of the MOOC was divided into three phases: secondary and primary research, followed by synthesis and implementation.

Secondary data were collected through several activities, summarised in **Table 1**. A specific search for MOOCs promoting EDI was not limited to the EU. No MOOCs specifically addressing how to promote EDI in academia were found. The team involved in creating the MOOC learning content was formed of experts in gender and EDI-related issues, science and technology. The FIAGES project, focusing on promoting gender equality in STEM academic disciplines and ICT companies, provided a review of the existing learning resources produced by public and private organisations involved in EU projects in the 7th and 8th framework programmes (FPs). The FIAGES project has contributed to the creation of an online course [71], the content of which has been used as a model for the parts of the MOOCs relating to gender issues.

The primary research activities consisted of discussions within the MOOC working group during weekly partners' online meetings (due to the restrictions imposed by the COVID pandemic).

The total duration of the meetings and the selection process was thirty-five hours. Five meetings with the local team (from two to two and a half hours each) made it possible gradually to include secondary research data and search for new or different information to fill in the gaps.

Secondary and primary data enabled the team to draft the MOOC contents and learning experiences (summarised in **Table 1**). The MOOC team held weekly review meetings to consider the emerging secondary and primary research results, reframe content, where necessary, and avoid repeating information that could be sourced elsewhere. The main task was to bear in mind constantly that the information is aimed at higher education staff and students with no previous knowledge or experience in gender studies or EDI theory and practices. The theoretical aspects were therefore kept to a minimum and links to external sources were used to allow those interested to explore theoretical aspects. Over five such meetings, the MOOC team developed and refined a first draft of the MOOC modules. This draft was circulated to UNIGE staff, GenderEX partners and external experts, selected for their critical views of gender equality, diversity and inclusion studies.

4.3 Target groups and learning objectives

The course is aimed at researchers and students in academic and other research institutions. In addition, it should be of particular interest to Gender Equality

Primary research	Secondary research
Discussions within GenderEX partnership	Literature review
Meetings with external experts	EU reports and legislation
Team meetings	Examples and models
Internal testing	Comparable examples from other sectors

Table 1.
Methods used to select and organise the contents.

Plan (GEP) and EDI team members and Gender equality/EDI equality/diversity officers / focal persons.

The course is particularly suitable for middle managers aiming to start the path towards institutional change and for administrative personnel.

In fact, the MOOC aims to bridge the gap between gender experts and human resources officers, in order to pursue synergies and improve the integration of EDI tools and considerations into decision-making processes.

4.4 Course highlights, learning objectives and outcomes

The MOOC guides participants in becoming more EDI-sensitive in their working and learning activities in an HEI context. EDI is still often interpreted as a mere numerical balance of research participants, but cultural transformation leading to structural change is necessary to achieve gender equality, respect for diversity and inclusion.

Structural change needs to involve EDI-sensitive institutional processes and strategies and requires a vision of equality at individual and organisational levels that crosses disciplinary boundaries and engages with a variety of theoretical perspectives. Institutional and structural interventions challenging behaviour, attitudes and cultures are pivotal in achieving EDI in a broad sense.

The MOOC is based on an inventory and review of existing content provided by the EU and by international organisations, the results of previous projects focused on equal opportunities, gender equality, diversity and inclusion, a review of the scientific literature and the professional experience of the team members.

The introduction and the three modules include videos, texts and quizzes, and the learner is asked to perform tasks that apply the content to real cases. Other resources include links to external websites, videos, podcasts, reports and scientific resources.

The learning objectives of the MOOC, in terms of demonstrable skills and knowledge that will be acquired by the participants, are:

- Knowledge of university policies and infrastructure on EDI, as promoted by the EU and by its European Universities Initiative

- Familiarisation with Gender Equality Plans, Equality Committees (Comitati Unici di Garanzia - CUG) and Positive Action Plans (Piani di Azione Positivi – PAP)

- Understanding and learning to apply key achievements and indicators of EDI policies and actions

- Awareness of the importance of an “EDI-sensitive” academia

- Familiarisation with EU-funded gender equality, diversity and inclusion projects and their potential impact on students’ careers

- Awareness of the critical problems regarding gender in Research and Innovation

- Knowledge of the main EU policy frameworks and priorities to promote gender equality in research and innovation and of the new requirements introduced by Horizon Europe

At the end of the course, participants will have acquired the skills to strengthen EDI engagement in the governance of their institution or in their working or learning activities.

Through a deep immersion in the extensive learning material, at the conclusion of all the activities, the participants will receive a certificate of completion from the university sponsoring the course if they complete the online lessons, pass the module quizzes, view all course lectures and complete the course survey.

4.5 Format and organisation

The MOOC materials are based on an inventory and review of documents issued by the EU, the results of EU gender equality and diversity projects, the scientific literature in the field and the professional experience of the team members. It focuses on the more relevant topics to promote participants' awareness and knowledge of EDI in academia.

The online course hosted by the EduOpen platform (https://www.eduopen.org/), the first Italian portal of free university courses open to all [72], consists of four content modules. Firstly, the Introduction module will provide an explanation of the key issues and concepts of an EDI-sensitive academia. It offers the theoretical background and the EU support to higher education and research institutions. The participants will understand the links among EDI, the EU Union Equality concept and strategy and Sustainable Development Goal (SDG) no. 5, "Achieve gender equality and empower all women and girls" of the 2030 United Nations Agenda.

The first module, *Highlights of university policies and infrastructure on EDI as promoted by the EU and by its European Universities Initiative*, will explore reports and documents issued at institutional level. Gender equality is mentioned as early as 1957 in the founding Treaty of the European Economic Community (EEC). It is important to become familiar with the steps leading to the current perspectives and expectations about EDI. The module stimulates the debate on the scientific literature that has analysed the opportunities created and the obstacles faced in implementing them and uses illustrative case studies.

In the second module, Equality Committees (Comitati Unici di Garanzia - CUG) and Positive Action Plans (Piani di Azione Positivi – PAP), Gender Equality Plans, participants will learn about the different approaches to EDI at in different countries. While GEPs are mandatory by law in some, a softer approach allows universities to progress at individual level in others. The impact of the new Horizon Europe requirement for public organisations applying for funding to have a formal GEP will be discussed. The strategies adopted to satisfy this requirement and the risks of turning this into a box-ticking exercise will be analysed.

Lastly, the module on *Policies on EDI, their key features, relevance for students* highlights the key achievements and indicators of EDI policies and explains the connections between gender and the UNIGE Ulysseus, Milieu and GenderEX projects and their potential impact on UNIGE, its staff and students. More specifically, through this module, the participant will learn to interpret an EU-funded project addressing EDI topics and understand the strategies applied to adopt an overarching approach and to embed it in the complex set of follow-up activities, ranging from communication to dissemination, exploitation and evaluation. The participants will also learn how to contribute to the progress towards EDI through their individual role in the academic community.

The first edition of the EDI-focused MOOC course equips the participants with a set of multimedia learning tools.

For each module, 10-minute video-lectures, reports and scientific resources, key messages slides, reading materials, support through "Frequently Asked Questions clinics" and quizzes and assignments to monitor progress (multiple choice) are available. These can be taken in the participants' own time once they have registered for the MOOC.

Each module takes an average of two to three hours to complete and the course is based around a calendar of activities normally lasting four weeks.

The MOOC contents will be in English; some parts of the MOOC will, however, also be available in Italian, to assist participants who do not speak English. Where documents or reports are available in numerous languages (as is the case for many EU documents), links will be available to the multilingual repositories.

The participants are invited to submit questions through the course website. The most relevant questions will be answered by the team in the three virtual clinics. The FAQs and answers will thus become part of the MOOC and will be useful to future participants.

The material will be updated once a year or upon notification of broken links, new relevant documents and other important changes.

After completing the course, all participants will receive a certificate of attendance. The MOOC will be online by the end of 2021, and only formal assessment will enable us to understand its user-friendliness and effectiveness, through self-assessment and e-assessment.

5. Conclusion

The purpose of this case study was to describe the underlying strategies and choices for the design and implementation of the MOOC.

The current coronavirus pandemic sets several new challenges for the entire international community, and there is a growing need for MOOC curricula to be interdisciplinary. At the same time, the role of MOOCs in education, particularly non-formal and informal education, is growing in these turbulent times, due to the current heavy reliance on online communication and learning.

They represent the learning format that seems to best meet the expectations of education (formal, non-formal and informal) as they are inclusive, accessible and equitable.

The broader context of the MOOC is the GenderEX project co-financed by the EU, in which four partners activate a robust exchange of information to promote the integration of the sex and gender dimension into research and to engage in best practices together with international partners.

At the basis of the MOOC planning, there is the awareness that policies aimed at promoting equality, diversity and inclusion (EDI) in academia lead to improved personnel and students' retention and satisfaction, as well as discovery, integration, application and dissemination of knowledge.

Academic excellence cannot be pursued without providing support to everyone involved, irrespective of gender, race, ethnicity, religion, age, social class and other factors, allowing them to embrace a diverse range of interests, abilities and life experiences that will enhance the exploration of ideas vital to the academic mission.

Integrating the gender equality, diversity and inclusion (EDI) dimensions into academia contributes to more inclusive scientific and innovation processes and ensures people from underrepresented groups are included, remain visible and feel supported and valued.

In recent years, thanks also to the initiatives organised by the European Union, HEIs have established diversity guidelines and policies underlined by the commitment to academic excellence and inclusiveness and equal opportunities.

The MOOC described in this chapter aims to share best practices in EDI, and equality policies and strategies implemented at the academic level in Europe, allowing the participants to understand the roles they may have in benefiting from these policies in their professional activities and in promoting their implementation and progress actively.

The study responds to the need to train all those working or studying in the higher education sector on EDI and gender mainstreaming, – for which there is scattered online information requiring a significant amount of time to understand the process involved. The difficulty in identifying and using sound sources discourages people interested in learning about EDI-related issues: they are confronted with concepts outside of their academic learning paths and with the multidisciplinary nature of the gender studies field. The MOOC enables learners to follow a clear path, guiding them in applying EDI principles to all aspects of their research, from the initial idea to the dissemination and exploitation phase, and in achieving better gender equality in their working environments.

Acknowledgements

The GenderEX project has received funding from the European Union's Horizon 2020 research and innovation programme under grant agreement No. 952432. The opinions expressed in this chapter reflect only the authors' view and in no way reflect the European Commission's opinions. The European Commission is not responsible for any use that may be made of the information it contains.

Conflict of interest

The authors declare that they have no conflict of interest.

Author details

Rita Bencivenga[1*], Cinzia Leone[1] and Anna Siri[2]

1 University of Genoa, Italy

2 UNESCO Chair in Anthropology of Health, Biosphere and Healing Systems, University of Genoa, Italy

*Address all correspondence to: rita.bencivenga@unige.it

References

[1] Buitendijk S, Curry S, Maes K. Equality, diversity and inclusion at universities: the power of a systemic approach. LERU position paper. Leuven; 2019

[2] Claeys-Kulik A-L, Ekman JT. Universities' Strategies and Approaches towards Diversity, Equity and Inclusion. Examples from across Europe. Brussels; 2018

[3] laeys-Kulik A.-L. C, Jørgensen T. E., and Stöber, H. Diversity, Equity and Inclusion in European Higher Education Institutions: Results from the INVITED Project. Brussels; 2019

[4] Bergan S. and Harkavy I., Eds., Higher education for diversity, social inclusion and community, no. 22. Strasbourg, 2018.

[5] Berryman S., "Who Will Do Science? Trends, and Their Causes in Minority and Female Representation among Holders of Advanced Degrees in Science and Mathematics. A Special Report," A Spec. Rep. Rockefeller Found., p. 148, 1983, [Online]. Available: http://files.eric.ed.gov/fulltext/ED245052.pdf.

[6] Martinez ED et al. Falling off the academic bandwagon. Women are more likely to quit at the postdoc to principal investigator transition. EMBO Rep. 2007;**8**(11):977-981. DOI: 10.1038/sj.embor.7401110

[7] European Commission. She Figures 2018. Luxembourg: Publications Office of the European Union; 2019

[8] Bhopal K. Gender, ethnicity and career progression in UK higher education: a case study analysis. Res. Pap. Educ. 2020;**35**(6):706-721. DOI: 10.1080/02671522.2019.1615118

[9] Thaler K et al. Inadequate use and regulation of interventions against publication bias decreases their effectiveness: A systematic review. J. Clin. Epidemiol. 2015;**68**(7):792-802. DOI: 10.1016/j.jclinepi.2015.01.008

[10] Boustani K, Taylor K. Navigating LGBTQ+ discrimination in academia: where do we go from here? Biochem. (Lond). 2020;**42**(3):16-20. DOI: 10.1042/BIO20200024

[11] Crenshaw K., "Demarginalizing the Intersection of Race and Sex: A Black Feminist Critique of Antidiscrimination Doctrine, Feminist Theory and Antiracist Politics," Univ. Chic. Leg. Forum, vol. 1989, no. 1, 1989, [Online]. Available: http://chicagounbound.uchicago.edu/uclf/vol1989/iss1/8.

[12] Carbado DW, Gulati M. The intersectional fifth black woman. Du Bois Rev. Soc. Sci. Res. Race. 2013;**10**(2):527-540

[13] UNESCO. Forum on the Impact of Open Courseware for Higher Education in Developing Countries: Final Report; UNESCO (CI-2002/CONF.803/CLD.1): Paris, France, 2002. http://unesdoc.unesco.org/images/0012/001285/128515e.pd

[14] UNESCO. 2012 Paris OER Declaration; UNESCO: Paris, France, 2012; Available online: www.unesco.org/new/fileadmin/MULTIMEDIA/HQ/CI/CI/pdf/Events/Paris%20OER%20Declaration_01.pdf.

[15] Lorrie Schmid, Kim Manturuk, Ian Simpkins, Molly Goldwasser & Keith E. Whitfield (2015) Fulfilling the promise: do MOOCs reach the educationally underserved?, Educational Media International, 52:2, 116-128, DOI: 10.1080/09523987.2015.1053288

[16] Cormier, D., Siemens, G. (2010). The open course: Through the open door--open courses as re-search,

learning, and engagement. Educause Review, 45(4), 30 (2010).

[17] Bates, T. (2014), Teaching in the Digital Age. https://opentextbc.ca/teachinginadigitalage/

[18] Hayes, S. MOOCs and Quality: A Review of the Recent Literature; QAA: Gloucester, UK, 2015; Available online: http://publications.aston.ac.uk/26604/1/MOOCs_and_quality_a_review_of_the_recent_literature.pdf.

[19] Chapman SA, Goodman S, Jawitz J, Deacon A. A strategy for monitoring and evaluating massive open online courses. Evaluation and Program Planning. 2016;**57**:55-63

[20] DeBoer, J., Ho, A. D., Stump, G. S., & Breslow, L. (2014). Changing "course": Reconceptualizing educational variables for massive open online courses. Educational Researcher, 43(2), 74-84.

[21] Stracke CM, Downes S, Conole G, Burgos D, Nascimbeni F. Are MOOCs Open Educational Resources? A literature review on history, definitions and typologies of OER and MOOCs. Open Prax. 2020;**11**:331-341

[22] Chatti, M. A., Yousef, M. F., Schroeder, U., Wosnitza, M. (2014), What Drives a Successful MOOC? An Empirical Examination of Criteria to Assure Design Quality of MOOCs, in Proceedings of 2014 IEEE 14th International Conference on Advanced Learning Technologies.

[23] Peters, G., Seruga, J. A supply sided analysis of leading MOOC platforms and universities. Knowledge Management & E-Learning:An International Journal, 8(1), 158-181 (2016).

[24] Wang Z, Anderson T, Chen L, Barberà E. Interaction pattern analysis in cMOOCs based on the connectivist interaction and engagement framework. Br. J. Educ. Technol. 2017;**48**:683-699

[25] Stracke CM, Downes S, Conole G, Burgos D, Nascimbeni F. Are MOOCs Open Educational Resources? A literature review on history, definitions and typologies of OER and MOOCs. Open Prax. 2020;**11**:331-341

[26] Veletsianos G, Shepherdson P. A systematic analysis and synthesis of the empirical MOOC literature published in 2013-2015. Int. Rev. Res. Open Distrib. Learn. 2016;**17**:198-221

[27] Zawacki-Richter O, Bozkurt A, Alturki U, Aldraiweesh A. What research says about MOOCs—An explorative content analysis. Int. Rev. Res. Open Distrib. Learn. 2018;**19**:242-259

[28] Pozzi, F., Conole, G. Quale futuro per i MOOC in Italia? TD Tecnologie Didattiche, 22(3), 173-182. (2014).

[29] Clair RS, Winer L, Finkelstein A, Wald S, Finkelstein A, Fuentes-steeves A. Big Hat and No Cattle? The implications of MOOCs for the adult learning landscape. The Canadian Journal for the Study of Adult Education. 2015;**27**(3):65-82

[30] Lowenthal P & and Hodges C: International Review of Research in Open and Distance Learning, 16 (5) (2015), pp. 1-8.

[31] Kursun, E. (2016). Does Formal Credit Work for MOOC-Like Learning Environments? The International Review of Research in Open and Distributed Learning, 17 (3), 75-91. http://dx.doi.org/10.19173/irrodl.v16i5.2222

[32] Walker L. and B. Loch INNOQUAL-International Journal for Innovation and Quality in Learning, 2 (3) (2014), pp. 53-63.

[33] Chapman, Sarah & Goodman, Suki & Jawitz, Jeff & Deacon, Andrew.

(2016). A strategy for monitoring and evaluating massive open online courses. Evaluation and Program Planning. 57. 55-63. 10.1016/j. evalprogplan.2016.04.006.

[34] Margaryan, A., Bianco, M., & Littlejohn, A. (2015). Instructional quality of massive open online courses (MOOCs). Computers & Education, 80, 77-83. https://doi.org/10.1016/j. compedu.2014.08.005

[35] Wright C.R., Criteria for evaluating the Quality of Online Courses, Alberta Distance Education and Training Association, 2003.

[36] Ehlers, U.-D. (2004). Quality in e-Learning from a Learner's Perspective. European Journal of Open, Distance and E-Learning (EURODL), 7 (1).

[37] Ehlers, U.-D. 2012.Quality Assurance Policies and Guidelines in European Distance, and E-learningIn I Jung & C. Latchem (Eds.), Quality assurance and accreditation in distance education and e-learning, pp. 79 -90. New York: Routledge.

[38] Ehlers U-D. Open Learning Cultures. A Guide to Quality, Evaluation, and Assessment for Future Learning. Berlin, Heidelberg: Springer; 2013

[39] Conole, G. (2013), MOOCs as disruptive technologies: strategies for enhancing the learner experience and quality of MOOCs, Revista de Educación a Distancia, vol 39, pp 1-17, available at: www.um.es/ead/red/39/ conole.pdf

[40] Stracke, Christian M., and Giada Trisolini. 2021. "A Systematic Literature Review on the Quality of MOOCs" Sustainability 13, no. 11: 5817. https:// doi.org/10.3390/su13115817.

[41] Conferenza dei Rettori delle Università italiane - CRUI (2017). Progetto MOOCs Italia. Linee guida nazionali per la predisposizione di MOOCs di qualità erogati dalle Università italiane. Available at the webpage: https://www.crui.it/ images/1-_LineeGuidaMOOCsItalia_ aprile2017.pdf.

[42] Ehlers U-D, Kellermann SA. Future skills: The future of learning and higher education. Results of the International Future Skills Delphi Survey: Baden-Wurttemberg Cooperative State University; 2019 https://bit.ly/2WogLKv

[43] Whiting, K. (2020). These are the top 10 job skills of tomorrow— And how long it takes to learn them. World Economic Forum. https://www. weforum.org/agenda/2020/10/ top-10-work-skills-of-tomorrow-how-long-it-takes-to-learn-them.

[44] Dewey J. Experience and education. New York: Macmillan; 1938

[45] Canning, N. (2010). Playing with heutagogy: Exploring strategies to empower mature learn- ers in higher education. Journal of Further and Higher Education, 34(1), 59-71.

[46] McAuliffe, M., Hargreaves, D., Winter, A., & Chadwick, G. (2008). Does pedagogy still rule? In Proceedings of the 2008 AAEE Conference, December 7-10, 2008. Yeppoon, Queensland. http://www. engineersmedia.com.au/journals/aaee/ pdf/AJEE_15_1_McAuliffe%20F2.pdf

[47] Hase, S. (2009). Heutagogy and e-learning in the workplace: Some challenges and opportunities. Impact: Journal of Applied Research in Workplace E-learning, 1(1), 43-52. DOI: 10.5043/impact.13

[48] Snowden M, Halsall JP. Self-determined approach to learning: A social science perspective. Cogent Education. 2016;3(1):1247608 https:// doi.org/10.1080/23311 86X.2016.1247608

[49] Hase, S., & Kenyon, C. (2000). From andragogy to heutagogy. In UltiBase Articles. http://ultibase.rmit.edu.au/Articles/dec00/hase2.htm

[50] Blaschke, L. M., & Hase, S. (2019). Heutagogy and digital media networks: Setting students on the path to lifelong learning. Pacific Journal of Technology Enhanced Learning, 1(1), 1– 14. https://doi.org/10.24135/ pjtel.v1i1.1

[51] McLoughlin, C., & Lee, M.J.W. (2010). Personalised and self regulated learning in the Web 2.0 era: International exemplars of innovative pedagogy using social software. Australasian Journal of Educational Technology, 26(1), 28-43. http://www.ascilite.org.au/ajet/ajet26/mcloughlin.pdf

[52] Blaschke, L. M. (2014). Using social media to engage and develop online learners in self- determined learning. Research in Learning Technology. http://www.researchinlearningtechnology.net/index.php/rlt/artic le/view/21635/ html

[53] Agonács, N., & Matos, J. F. (2019). Heutagogy and self- determined learning: A review of the published literature on the application and implementation of the theory. Open Learning: The Journal of Open, Distance and e-Learning, 34(3), 223– 240.

[54] Cochrane, T. (2020). Exploring #heutagogy. Exploring Educational Technology (Weblog). https://thomcochrane.wordpress.com/2020/10/14/exploring-heuta gogy/

[55] Lock J, Sakhal S, Cleveland-Innes M, Arancibia P, Dell D, De Silva N. The heutagogical bridge: Linking blended and online learning to technology-enabled lifelong learning. British Journal of Educational Technology. 2021

[56] Alkire S. Subjective Quantitative Measures of Human Agency. Social Indicators Research. 2005;**74**(1):217-260

[57] Narayan, V., Herrington, J., & Cochrane, T. (2019). Design principles for heutagogical learning: Implementing student- determined learning with mobile and social media tools. Australasian Journal of Educational Technology, 35(3), 86– 101. https://doi.org/10.14742/ ajet.3941

[58] Blaschke, L. M. (2012). Heutagogy and lifelong learning: A review of heutagogical practice and self-determined learning. The International Review of Research in Open and Distance Learning, 13(1), 56– 71. https://doi.org /10.19173/irrodl.v13i1.1076

[59] Cochrane, T., & Munn, J. (2020). Integrating educational design research and design thinking to enable creative pedagogies. Pacific Journal of Technology Enhanced Learning, 2(2), 1– 14. https://doi.org/10.24135/pjtel.v2i2.58

[60] Rivers, C., & Holland, A. (2020). Does blended learning change what learning is? (Weblog.) WonkHE. https://wonkhe.com/blogs/ does- blend ed-learn ing- chang e- what- learn ing- is/

[61] Anderson T. Theories for learning with emerging technologies. In: Veletsianos G, editor. Emerging technologies in distance education (pp. 35– 50). Athabasca University Press; 2010

[62] Dron J, Anderson T. Teaching crowds: Learning and social media. Athabasca University Press; 2014 https://www.aupress.ca/books/120235-teaching-crowds/

[63] Blaschke, L. M., & Hase, S. (2019). Heutagogy and digital media networks: Setting students on the path to lifelong learning. Pacific Journal of Technology Enhanced Learning, 1(1), 1– 14. https://doi.org/10.24135/pjtel.v1i1.1

[64] Blaschke, L. M., & Marin, V. I. (2020). Applications of heutagogy in

the educational use of e- portfolios. Revista de Educación a Distancia RED. https://revis tas.um.es/red/artic le/view/407831

[65] Thomas A, Campbell LM, Barker P, Hawskey M. Cetis publications. 2012. Into the wild: Technology for open educational resources URL: http://publications.cetis.org.uk/2012/601

[66] Cochrane, T., & Munn, J. (2020). Integrating educational design research and design thinking to enable creative pedagogies. Pacific Journal of Technology Enhanced Learning, 2(2), 1– 14. https://doi.org/10.24135pjtel.v2i2.58

[67] Kahle D. Designing open education technology. In: Iiyoshi T, Kumar MSV, editors. Opening up education: The collective advancement of education through open technology, open content and open knowledge. Cambridge: The MIT Press; 2010 http://mitpress.mit.edu/sites/default/files/titles/content/9780262515016_Open_Access_Edition.pdf

[68] Blaschke, L. M. (2021). The dynamic mix of heutagogy and technology: Preparing learners for lifelong learning. British Journal of Educational Technology, 52, 1629– 1645. https://doi.org/10.1111/bjet.13105

[69] Sala A, Punie Y, Garkov V, Cabrera Giraldez M. LifeComp: The European framework for personal, social and learning to learn key competence. In: EUR 30246 EN. Office of the European Union: Publications; 2020 https://doi.org/10.2760/302967

[70] Redecker C. European framework for the digital competence of educators: DigCompEdu. In: Punie Y, editor. EUR 28775 EN. Luxembourg: Publications Office of the European Union; 2017 https://doi.org/10.2760/159770

[71] Bencivenga R, "Transferability of methods and strategies for advancing gender equality in academia and research: a case study of an online course aimed at academic and professionals," in Learning Technology for Education Challenges, 2021, pp. 90-100.

[72] Siri A, Rui M. (2017). The EduOpen Innovation. The University of Genova opens to MOOCs: A case study. EMEMItalia 2016, in Design the Future!, pp. 393-402.

Chapter 10

Massive Open Online Courses (MOOCs) in Sub-Saharan African Higher Education Landscape: A Bibliometric Review

Abdullahi Abubakar Yunusa, Irfan Naufal Umar and Brandford Bervell

Abstract

In this study, we examined articles focused on Massive Open Online Courses (MOOCs) implemented in the sub-Saharan African (SSA) Higher Education context that describes the different models of MOOCs enacted as an initiative to provide access and opportunity to acquire quality higher education across different disciplines within the sub-region. In addition, the review aims to identify those factors that facilitate or inhibit the success and growth of MOOCs in the SSA context to understand how MOOCs has fared between the time 2012 to 2021. Based on this premise, 30 articles were included in the review in accordance with the authors' set criteria. Results revealed that there are very few collaborations, linkages, and relations between MOOCs researchers in SSA, similarly there is a slow growth of MOOCs production, Narrative, Conceptual and Discourse analysis are the dominant analytical methods, while the perennial challenges of poor internet connectivity, lack of policy framework, poor bandwidth and electricity and lack of personnel with the requisite competences were the major hinderances to MOOCs growth in SSA. The inferences, implications and future directions were discussed.

Keywords: MOOCS, production, relations, Challenges, sub-Saharan Africa, Higher Education, Bibliometric Review

1. Introduction

Massive Open Online Courses (MOOCs) have emerged as a disruptive technological innovation in the educational sphere and has stoked conversations among critical stakeholders in education [1, 2]. MOOCs are educational offerings that have broken the barriers of distance, time and space and provided opportunity for diverse population of learners to access quality and affordable education. However, there is an indication that the number of paid MOOCs users are on the increase with a corresponding decrease in the number of MOOCs enrollees in the broader global context. According to Shah [3], over the period of seven years, the number of new MOOC users are shrinking while more and more people are paying for MOOCs with corresponding rise in the number of MOOCs degrees. Nevertheless, over 100 million people have enrolled in MOOCs in about 900 universities that offer more than 11,000 MOOC courses since its inception in 2008 [3].

Over the years, MOOCs has evoked different interests among researchers, institutional managers and media organizations such as The New York Times, blog posts and other information dissemination platforms [4] and this is viewed as a reflection of its acceptance and recognition of its vast potentials for promoting equity, individualized learning, flexibility, and the massification of the learning process [1, 5]. ... MOOC was coined by David Cormier [6] to describe a course with a very large enrolment and open to diverse range of students. Openness in terms of content, design, accessibility and diverse criteria for completion or success following the successful launch of Connectivism and Connective Knowledge (CCK08) course in 2008. MOOCs may vary based on pedagogical interactions, participants experience and learning outcome [7].

In recent times, MOOCs have evolved into different formats: the connectivist MOOCs also known as cMOOCs, is a form of MOOCs in which users engage in learning through social engagement and interaction, wherein they create, co-create and share knowledge and learning experiences. Bates [8] described the key features of cMOOCs as based on networked learning, because learning develops through connections and discussions among participants in social media space without standard technology platform. In contrast, the xMOOC is designed in the form of the traditional model of teaching (also refered to as transmission model) Zhao, Wu, and Huang, [9] referred to xMOOCs as the 'teacher-centric' MOOC model. A recent addition is the Hybrid MOOC which is an agglomeration of the cMOOCs and xMOOCs. The range of MOOCs affordances for opening up to a large number of willing learners of diverse background, eliminating geographical, and resource constraints, flexibility, scalability, and affordability in terms of cost when compared to traditional education systems and the ability to be enrolled in both formal and informal offerings [10] makes it a good fit for sub-Saharan Africa and for learners in resource constrained regions [11, 12]. Nevertheless, MOOCs are bedeviled by issues of contextual relevance, attrition, poor completion rates, issues around credentialling and credit values [1, 13, 14]. Also, despite its popularity MOOCs are still nascent in sub-Saharan Africa as it is more popular in developed countries [14, 15]. A quick search on the Scopus database show that none of the prolific authors of MOOCs literature are in the sub-Saharan African context and the authors in SSA are seemingly not connecting (see **Figure 1**). This scenario makes it plausible to investigate the growth and research trends in order to understand the MOOCs phenomenon in the SSA [16].

Given that, there are conflicting positions regarding the low patronage of MOOCs in SSA. Some authors argued that "MOOCs offered on Cousera platforms

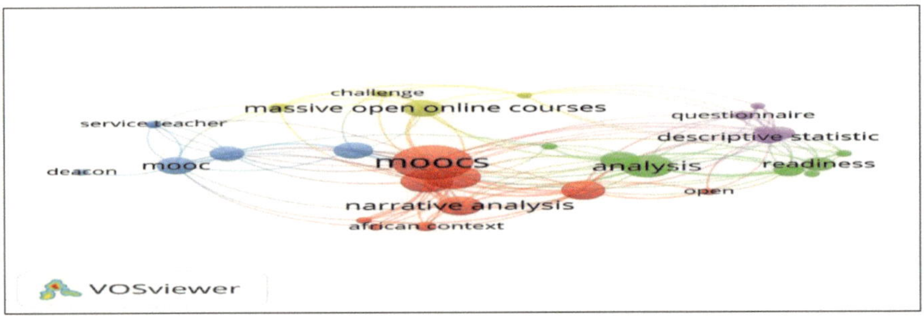

Figure 1.
Network visualization of most occurring keyword terms in MOOCs articles in SSA.

were more successful among the young, male, well-educated and employed students in developed contexts [17, 18].Whereas, Ngimwa and Wilson, [11] reported that low technological level in Africa do not impede the adoption of educational technology, contrary to previous research studies [19–21]. Therefore, it is important to dig further to shed more light on the evolution of a disruptive technology such as MOOCs.

This chapter adopts a systematic bibliometric review approach to identify, collect, analyze, and synthesize articles focused on MOOCs applications in sub-Saharan Africa higher education in order to highlight the MOOCs growth landscape within the scope of authors occurrence and links strength, contexts of publication, adoption trends, research design strategies and the factors inhibiting the growth of MOOCs in the region across different disciplinary contexts. Bibliometric review is a technique that is used to highlight the activities of recorded knowledge and identifies the patterns, forms, and shape of the phenomenon of interest [22] Accordingly, bibliometric analysis is relevant in identifying, mapping, and visualizing the pattern of MOOCs authorship, adoption, implementation, and opportunities in the SSA higher education context based on publication trends. The review of literature shows a resurgence of Bibliometric studies across different scientific field. However, we align with the recommendation by Veletsianos & Shepherdson, [23] to the extent that more research is needed to clearly understand whether MOOCs literature are biased towards countries, or regions [24] as well as the growth of the technology within the SSA context. **Figure 1** illustrates the most recurring keyword terms within the corpus on MOOCs in SSA.

There are several studies that have focused on MOOCs across time periods, research objectives, outcomes, using diverse theories and methodological approaches. For instance, Liyanagunawardena et al., [4] conducted a systematic review article on MOOCs between 2008 and 2012; Albelbisi, Yusop, Kalsum, and Salleh [25] Mapped the factors promoting MOOCs, while, Yunusa and Umar [26] reviewed articles on MOOCs adoption, awareness, and barriers in sub-saharan Africa. In that work, forty articles were identified and analyzed to shed light on MOOCs trajectory in sub-Saharan Africa. Since then, more MOOCs platforms have emerged without clarity on the MOOCs trends in SSA. Moreover, the need for MOOCs in underserved communities has been made more stronger with the outbreak of the Corona virus disease (COVID-19) which had upset the norms, stunted and negatively impacted on academic activities in most parts of SSA [27] Hence, this study is Plausible. Moreover, identifying these factors will provide further empirical evidence for reference, guide and inform decisions on policy, curriculum design as well as learning design for MOOCs in the sub-Saharan African region. Moreover, de Waard et al., [28] noted that "more research needed to be undertaken into the realities, benefits, and challenges of MOOCs in order to properly map their dynamics" (P.112). Against this backdrop, this study seeks to achieve the following objectives:

i. To identify and collate articles on MOOCs in sub-Saharan African (SSA) higher education published in peer reviewed Journals, Conference proceedings and prominent academic databases.

ii. To identify the publication trends, different contexts, samples, and subject areas /disciplinary contexts of the studies as well as the research designs within the literature.

iii. To identify the different MOOC models enacted and the main challenges highlighted in the literature. And

iv. To draw on the information gathered to make inferences on the implications of the findings to higher education in sub-Saharan Africla.

Consequently, the paper responded to the following research questions:

1. What are the MOOCs articles published in peer reviewed journals, conference proceedings, academic databases focused on sub-Saharan Africa (SSA)?

2. What are the different contexts in the subregion, subjects, samples, disciplines, and research designs adopted in the identified articles?

3. What are the different models of implementation and the inhibiting factors highlighted in the studies on MOOCs in SSA?

4. What are the recommendations that could be advanced for policy and practice based on the information gathered from the Bibliometric review?

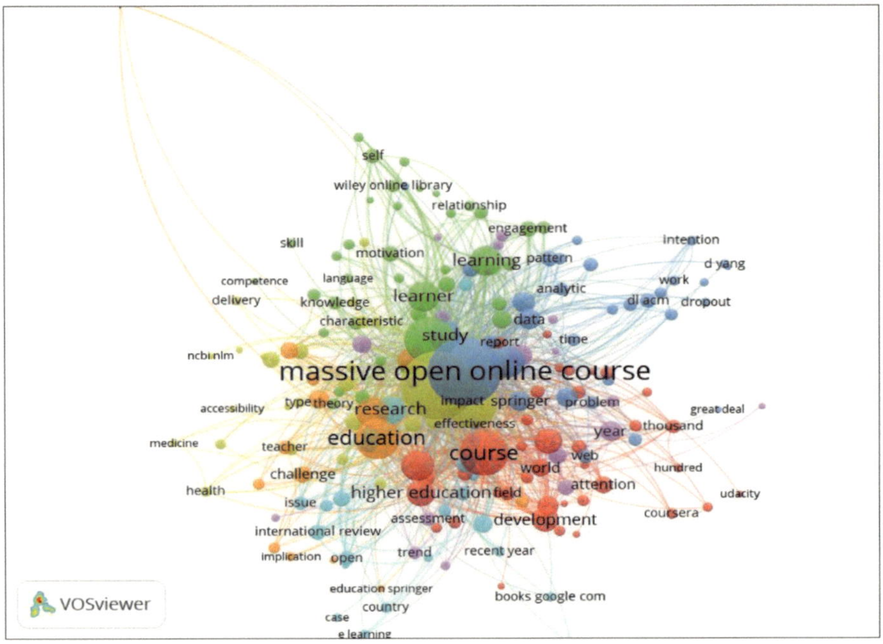

Figure 2.
Network visualization of the co-occurrence of keyword terms on Scopus database.

From **Figure 2**, the most recurring terms within the search strings on Scopus database was massive open online courses, followed by course, education, research, higher education, learning, learner, and development. The size of the circle represents the weight of the term relative to other terms while the lines represent the relationships between the terms.

Figure 3 depicts the authors in the articles on MOOCs in SSA, indicating their relations and occurrences. The size of the circle around an author represents the weight and the co-occurrence of the author within the literature in the review. The absence of line strings as connections/links suggests that not much of collaboration and references to the different MOOCs projects has been made by the authors. The authors with the most occurrences are Czerniewicz, Deacon Small, Walji, [29] with

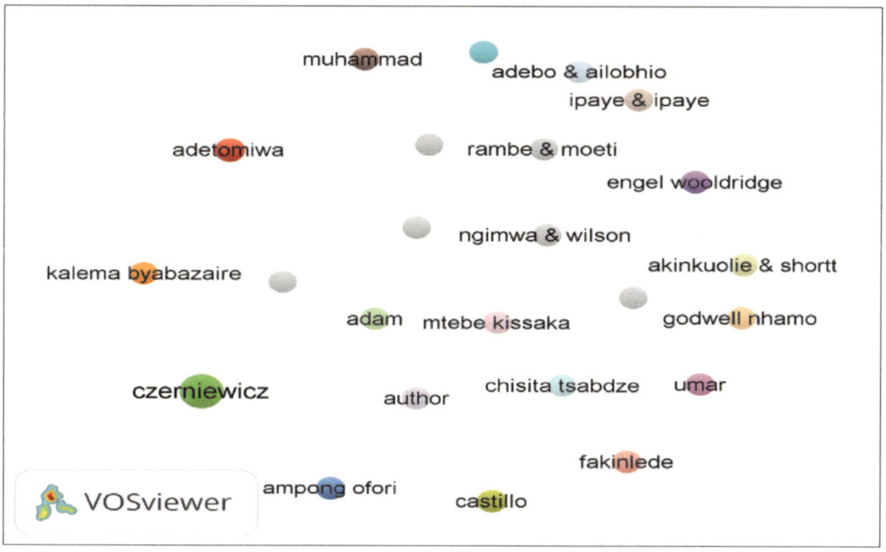

Figure 3.
Network visualization of authors occurrence in MOOCs articles landscape in SSA.

a total of 30 link strengths and 29 links. Two occurrences within the 42 items, while authors such as Kalema and Bybazaire, Adetomiwa, Ampong and Ofori, Mtebe and Kissaka, Umar and Muhammad all have only one occurrence, one link strength and in most cases no links and total links strengths.

2. Methodology

2.1 Method and design

This study adopted the bibliometric review approach by mining data from databases Scopus, and the Harzing, Publish or Perish software [30] for literature management. We developed a set of article inclusion and exclusion criteria and followed the Preferred Reporting Items for Systematic Reviews and Meta-Analyses (PRISMA) protocol by Moher, Liberati, Tetzlaff and Altman [31]. The PRISMA protocol is a sequential process to search, identify, collect, analyze, synthesize and report findings from the published articles. We searched databases for articles focused on "MOOCs" in sub-Saharan Africa, we used search terms such as (TITLE-ABS-KEY ('massive AND open AND online AND courses' OR 'mooc') AND TITLE-ABS KEY ('higher AND education' OR 'higher AND education AND institutions') AND TITLE-ABS-KEY KEY ('moocs') AND TITLE-ABS ('sub-saharan AND africa')) AND PUBYEAR >2011-2021.We also used Boolean functions to search the databases.The reference pages of retrieved articles were also chain searched (snowballing technique) for relevant articles. The articles were then sorted and organized based on the predetermined criteria, **Table 1** showcases the criteria for inclusion and exclusion of the articles, whereas **Figure 4** depicts the review process. Next we used the VOSviewer clustering and visualization software [32, 33] to cluster and map the authors identified within the review based on co-occurrence and the citation network. **Figures 1** and **2** shows the Network Visualization of authors of the articles on MOOCs in SSA and the Keyword strings within the bibliometric review.

Inclusion Criteria

- Articles published in the English Language.
- Articles focused on MOOCs in sub-Saharan African context.
- Articles published between 2012 and 2019
- Articles that are focused on MOOCs in Higher Educational Institutions and Universities in sub-Saharan Africa.

Exclusion criteria

- Articles published in language other than English.
- Articles that focused on e-Learning as broad concept
- Articles on MOOCs published earlier than 2012.
- Articles that focused on MOOCs in second circle institutions (secondary schools)

Table 1.
Article selection criteria for the systematic review of MOOCs awareness, adoption and barriers in SSA.

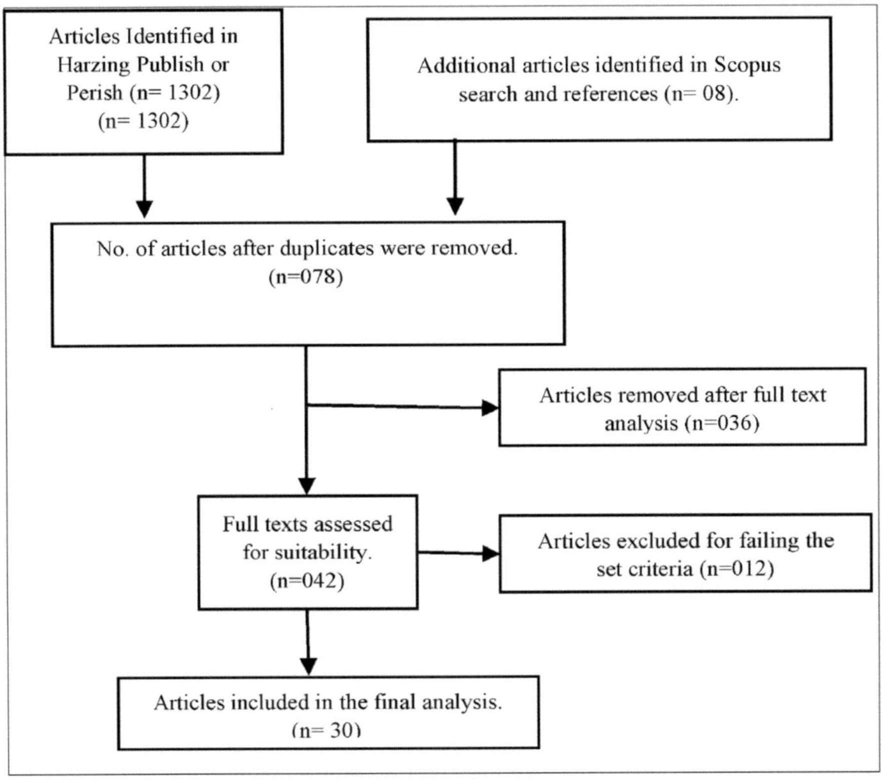

Figure 4.
Literature inclusion and exclusion process adapted from PRISMA Moher, Liberati, Tetzlaff and Altman [31].

3. Results and analysis

To properly sort the articles, they were coded based on contexts, research design, subjects and sample size, disciplinary contexts, MOOCs model of implementation, and the inhibitions to the success of the MOOCs projects.

i. Contexts: refer to the location where the study was conducted and geographical region

ii. Research Design: The bibliometric review was based on the classification of research methodology by Creswell [34] which included Qualitative, Quantitative and /or Mixed method research, Narrative analysis/ Conceptual analysis papers published in reputable journals were also included.

iii. Subjects and Sample: Refer to the respondents, their affiliations and the number involved in the studies. Consequently, the sample size of subjects are grouped into; small, medium, & large and coded as (≤ 150 = small sample); ($> 150 \leq 250$ = medium sample) and (>250 = Large sample).

iv. Subject/Disciplinary Context: refers to the discipline under which the MOOC was implemented.

v. Implementation Models: The review identified the different framework adopted / used in the MOOCs implementation in sub-Saharan Africa.

vi. Milestones / Achievements refers to the milestones attained within the identified studies for reference as well as.

vii. Barriers towards the adoption and implementation of the MOOCs models highlighted in the reviewed articles.

In line with the above-mentioned measures, 30 articles were found relevant to the focus of the systematic bibliometric review. However, three articles: *Applying MOOCocracy learning culture themes to improve digital course design and online learner engagement* by Akinkulie & Shortt (2020) *Digital neo-colonialism and massive open online courses (MOOCs): colonial pasts and neoliberal futures,* by Adam Taskeen [35] and *A Kenyan Cloud School: Massive Open Online & Ongoing courses for blended and lifelong learning* by Jobe [36] despite its focus on Secondary school education level because it appears to be one of the first of its kind in SSA and offers interesting insights in to the development and testing of MOOCs at that level. They were also included despite their broad focus on MOOCs and its fundamental goals and contributes to the understanding of MOOCs from historical, philosophical, and pragmatic principles of implementation, and make the case for MOOCs based on the unique context of underserved communities rather than on neoliberal philosophical world view of openness and accessibility.

3.1 Contexts and yearly article production trends

The distribution of articles based on the context or location of MOOCs adoption and implementation studies is illustrated in **Figure 5**.

Figure 5 illustrates the scientific production trends of MOOCs articles based on contexts. Nigeria tops the chart with nine articles followed by South Africa with five, Articles focused on the broader African context have four articles Kenya three, Uganda two while Ghana, Tanzania, Zimbabwe, and Eswatini (Swaziland) produced one article each. The publication trends show a significant growth between 2012 and 2014 from one article to four in 2013 and five in 2014, and three each for 2015 and 2016, another rising wave was observed in 2017 with five articles which appeared to be the "plateau of production" then began the downward slide from 2018 with four and two each in 2019, 2020 and one in 2021. There are prospects for additional literature in 2021 going forward given the increase in E-learning research spurred by the impacts of the COVID-19 pandemic (Yunusa, Ismaila, Dada,

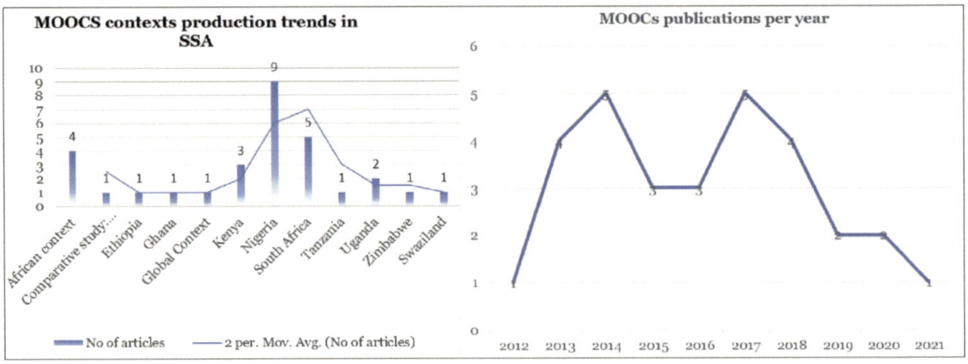

Figure 5.
Spread of MOOCs articles in SSA context.

Solomon & Agbo, [27] which provided varied options for technology mediated engagements in the form of MOOCs, emergency remote teaching, and online learning models.

3.2 Subjects and sample size

The subjects and samples sizes featured in the reviewed articles are presented in **Figure 6**.

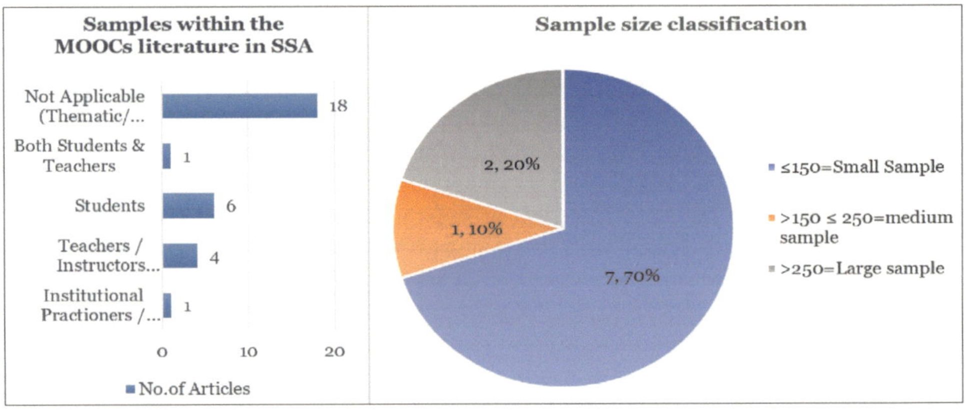

Figure 6.
Research sample characteristics and sample size classification within the review.

From **Figure 6**, the distribution of the articles by types of sample characteristics shows that Thematic, discuss, narrative analysis is the most dominant research techniques within the SSA literature 56% (n = 18 articles), followed by articles with students as respondents 25% (n = 6), articles with teacher, instructors or facilitators as respondents 16% (n = 4) while the least form of samples are institutional leaders and both teachers and students each with one article (4%).

3.3 Disciplinary contexts of the MOOCs literature in SSA

What are the different subjects/course or disciplines within which MOOCs were adopted/ implemented in SSA?

Table 2 shows that the MOOCs articles within SSA were focused on only seven disciplinary/ subject contexts, spread across the period under the review. The

Subjects/Discipline/MOOC's Context	Author(s)
Archives and Records Management Computer Science	Chisita & Tsabedze [37] Mtebe & Kissaka [38]
Digital Skills / Green Economy	Godwell & Nhamo [39]; Oyo et al., [17]
Capacity building/ Continous Professional Development (CPD)	Jobe, [36]; Boga & McGreal, [21];Wambugu [40]; Czerniewicz et al., [41]; Mapitsa [42]
Mathematics	Reju & Jita [43]
MOOCs Readiness, Adoption and differentiated MOOCs contexts and Evaluation	Fakinlede et al. [44]; Oyo & Kalema [45]; Rambe & Moeti [46]; Van Stam [47]; Odebero [48]; Mapitsa [42]; Waldegiyorgis [49] Czerniewicz et al. [29] Muhammad et al. [50]; Fiannu Blewett et al. [51, 52]; Kpolovie et al., [53]; Ngimwa et al. [11]; Yunusa & Umar [26]; Adam, T. [35]; Akinkuolie & Shortt [54].
Systematic Review of MOOCs Literature	Safana & Nat [55]

Table 2.
Disciplinary contexts of MOOCs literature within the study.

subject areas covered are presented in a chronological order for ease of reference. They include, Archives and records management, Computer science, Digital skills and Economy, continued professional development (CPD) MOOCs, Mathematics, Readiness factors, differentiated as well as Systematic review. Despite the low production the spread depicted MOOCs as a multidisciplinary avenue (**Table 3**).

3.4 Research design and methods utilized in MOOCs studies in SSA

The different research approaches used within the reviewed articles are illustrated in the **Figure 7**.

From **Figure 7**, the statistics on the research design and instruments are presented. The design groupings were classified based on the recommendation by Creswell [34]. Conceptual narrative discourse was the most prominent in the literature (n = 14) followed by quantitative research design (n = 8), Mixed methods (n = 4), and qualitative research design (n = 3), The least recurring of the designs was the experimental design (n = 1).while the most used instrument/ analytical technique was narrative and discourse analysis, followed by survey questionnaire, combinations of survey questionnaire, interview and observations, systematic reviews, and the least was experimental testing approach.

3.5 Disparate forms of MOOCs implementation models in SSA

The review of the MOOCs articles revealed that the MOOCs implementation models in SSA are based on two fundamental models. The connectivist MOOCs (cMOOCs) and teacher centric MOOCs (xMOOCs) (Bates [8]; Gaebels [60] as cited in [39]), particularly the teacher guided models that mimic the traditional teaching method where the learning experiences are guided by the teacher as the second predominant model/approach. On the other hand, 50% of the articles were based on narrative/thematic/discourse analysis and anecdotes wherein the authors draw on their experiences and evolution of MOOCs in other contexts to propose indigenous / contextualized formats for the African continent. For instance, Rambe & Moeti [46] enunciated the potentials of MOOCs to disrupt the educational landscape in Africa.

However, the authors argued that for that to happen, the MOOCs curriculum must be designed within the context of the needs of the African environment not as an extension of the elitist models from established institutions (such as MIT,

SN/Paper title	Author(s)/ date	SSA context (s)	Disciplinary context	Research design	Subjects/samples	Statistical tools	Journal
1. Enhancing the Quality of Computer Science Education with MOOCS in Sub-Saharan Africa	Mtebe, & Kissaka, [38]	Tanzania (But focused on Africa)	Computer Science	Not Applicable Narrative/Conceptual discuss	NA	NA	*Handbook on research on Active Learning* IGI Global Book Chapter
2. Massive Open Online Courses (MOOCs) and Green Economy Transition: Feasibility Assessment for African Higher Education	Godwell Nhamo [39]	South Africa	Green Economy Transition Courses (Sustainability) Focused on Africa	Narrative/Exploratory Analysis (Feasibility assessment for Higher Education)	Not Applicable	Not Applicable	Journal of Higher Education in Africa (JSTOR)
3. MOOCs for in-service Teachers: The case of Uganda and lessons for Africa	[17]	Uganda	Digital literacy & Lifelong Learning within Uganda's Teachers E-learning Portal (TEP)	Quantitative Research design (Evaluation of Teachers Completion of digital literacy course on MOOCs (using end of course examination report)	In-service teachers in Uganda = **120** in-service-teachers	Simple descriptive statistics	Revista Espanola de Pedagogia
4. An empirical investigation of the emergent issues around OER adoption in Sub-Saharan Africa	Ngimwa & Wilson, [11]	Comparative study of Kenya, Uganda & South Africa	Adoption of OERs	Qualitative Research design	Institutional practioners in Higher Education Institutions in SSA (Teacher Education in sub-Saharan Africa (10 TESSA participants and 9 non-TESSA participants) 19 were interviewed	Descriptive Stats analysis using Nvivo version 8 for Thematic analysis	Learning, Media and Technology
5. Massive Open Online Courses (MOOCs) for Professional Teacher and Teacher Educator Development: A Case of TESSA MOOC in Kenya	Wambugu, [40]	Kenya	TESSA MOOC E-Learning portal for teacher professional development in SSA	Mixed method research combining Questionnaire with Focused group discussion	Teachers, Teacher Educators and Other stakeholders/interested parties -participants were drawn from University 16, Secondary school 12	Descriptive Statistics, Frequency & Percentages and Narrative analysis	Universal Journal of Educational Research

SN/Paper title	Author(s)/ date	SSA context (s)	Disciplinary context	Research design	Subjects/samples	Statistical tools	Journal
					and Primary School 5 and educators 23 = **56** registered (47completed)		
6. Readiness for MOOCs: Learners' inequity in Nigeria	Kpolovie & Iderima, [53]	Nigeria	Readiness for MOOCs Evaluation	Quantitative Research Design (Comparative ex-post facto Research design) Using questionnaire	University Undergraduate & Postgraduate student from 4 different universities **1200**	Descriptive analysis, Frequency, mean, and Standard Deviation	EPRA International Journal of Economic and Business Review
7. Readiness for Online Learning in Higher Education: A Mixed Methods Assessment of Students at a Nigerian University	Fakinlede, Yusuf, & Mejabi, [44]	Nigeria	Students Readiness for MOOCs in Nigeria	Concurrent Mixed Method Study(Survey & Pen and Paper Interview	University Undergraduate student **119**	Descriptive Statistics using frequencies and percentages	Malaysian Journal of Distance Education
8. Systematic Review on Massive Open Online Courses Based on Primary/Meta-Analysis	Safana & Nat, [55]	Nigeria	Systematic Review of MOOCs across different contexts	Quantitative Research method	Peer reviewed articles on MOOCs in Africa **40**	Descriptive Stats	International Journal of Scientific & Technology Research
9. Opportunities and Challenges for Open Educational Resources and Massive Open Online Courses: The Case of Nigeria.	Ipaye & Ipaye, [56]	Nigeria	Higher Educational Institution and readiness to adopt OERs	Quantitative Narrative/ Conceptual Analysis (Anecdotal)	Not Applicable	Descriptive Analysis (textual)	Commonwealth of Learning Educo-Health Project Ilorin Nigeria
10. Students' experiences with distance and online learning of university-level undergraduate mathematics in Nigeria	Reju & Jita, [43]	Nigeria	Mathematics	Mixed-Method Research Design with Narrative Content Analysis	Undergraduate students **60**, while 10 students were interviewed for the qualitative data	Descriptive Statistics and Non-parametric Binomial Analysis	International Review of Research in Open and Distributed Learning

SN/Paper title	Author(s)/ date	SSA context (s)	Disciplinary context	Research design	Subjects/samples	Statistical tools	Journal
11. A Kenyan Cloud School. Massive Open Online & Ongoing courses for blended and lifelong learning	Jobe, [36]	Kenya	English Language and Kiswahili (Secondary School Subjects taught in Kenya)	Iterative Design Research approach (Design, Development, and Implementation)	Exploratory research NOT Applicable	Narrative and Situational Analysis	Open-Praxis
12. Introducing MOOCs to Africa New Economy Skills for Africa Program-ICT	Boga & McGreal, [21]	African Context	Capacity Building on ICT skills (NESAP-ICT) Using the Coursera Platform	Narrative/ Thematic / Discuss analysis based on author's world view	Not Applicable	Narrative analysis and presentation	Commonwealth of Learning auspace.athabascau.ca
13. Boosting Higher Education in Africa through Shared Massive Open Online Courses (MOOCs)	Escher, Noukakis, & Aebischer, [57]	African Context	Assessment of MOOCs program in Africa and Identifying the potential for its growth	Narrative/ Conceptual presentation	Not Applicable	Narrative analysis	*Education, learning, training: Critical issues for development. https://library.oapen.org/*
14. MOOCs for Development: Trends, Challenges, and Opportunities	Castillo, Lee, Zahra, & Wagner, [52]	African Context	MOOCs4development Conference in African Context (Focused on underserved regions of the world)	Descriptive content analysis	Not Applicable	Descriptive & Narrative analysis	Conference Report (Informational Technologies & International Development) www.moocs4d.org
15. Factors Affecting MOOC usage by students in selected Ghanaian universities	Fianu, Blewett, Ampong, & Ofori, [51]	Ghana	Generic evaluation of MOOCs as learning medium/ Not disciplinary specific	Quantitative Research design? Questionnaire	Undergraduate students **207**	PLS-SEM	Education Sciences
16. Can Massive Open Online Courses Fill African Evaluation Capacity Gaps?	Mapitsa, Khumalo, Engel, & Wooldridge, [42]	South Africa	Evaluation Capacity development (Theory of Change for development)	Narrative Content Analysis drawn from course data	Not Applicable	Descriptive Narrative analysis	African Evaluation Journal (http://www.aejonline.org)

DOI: http://dx.doi.org/10.5772/intechopen.99041

SN/Paper title	Author(s)/ date	SSA context (s)	Disciplinary context	Research design	Subjects/samples	Statistical tools	Journal
17. Massive Open Online Courses (MOOCs) and the 'revolution' in higher education: Implications for Africa	Woldegiyorgis & Carvalho, [49]	Ethiopia	MOOCs potential in Higher Education Context	Narrative Analysis (Conceptual Paper)	Not Applicable	Descriptive Narrative analysis	Proceedings of the 13th international conference on African private higher education
18. The Place of MOOCs in Africa's Higher Education	Odebero [48]	Kenya	MOOCs in African Higher Education (Multi-access learning theory)	Descriptive Survey Research of Published articles on MOOCs	Not Applicable (Online artifices, Newspapers, Magazines & blogs)	Thematic Narrative Analysis	Chapter in A book-IGI Global
19. Developing world MOOCs: A curriculum view of the MOOC landscape	Czerniewicz, Deacon, Small, & Walji, [58]	South Africa (African Context)	MOOCs in African Higher Education, prospects for contextualized offerings	Thematic Narrative Analysis	Not Applicable	Thematic Narrative analysis	Journal of Global Literacies, Technologies, and Emerging Pedagogies
20. Massive Open Online Courses: awareness, adoption, benefits and challenges in Sub-Saharan Africa	Muhammad, Mustapha, & Haruna, [50]	Nigeria	MOOCs in University Contexts	Quantitative Research Design (Questionnaire)	Undergraduate students in two universities in Nigeria **(300)**	Descriptive Statistics, Multiple linear regression analysis	International Journal of ICT and Management
21. Massive Open Online Courses awareness and adoption by Nigeria university students: A Case Study	Adebo & Ailobhio, [59]	Nigeria	MOOCs in the university context	Quantitative Research design (Questionnaire)	Undergraduate students **(126)**	Descriptive statistics using frequency counts and Analysis of variance	International Journal of Computer Engineering and Information Technology
22. eLearning in Africa and the Opportunity for Innovative Credentialing	van Stam, [47]	Zimbabwe	Credentialing	Thematic Narrative Analysis	Not Applicable	Thematic/ Narrative Analysis	Conference paper
23. MOOC - Making and Open Educational Practices	Czerniewicz, Deacon,	South Africa	MOOC Educators Open Practices	Mixed-Method Research design using Semi-structured Interviews,	University Educators using MOOCs **(22)**	Thematic/ Narrative analysis	Journal of Computing in Higher Education

SN/Paper title	Author(s)/ date	SSA context (s)	Disciplinary context	Research design	Subjects/samples	Statistical tools	Journal
	Glover, & Walji, [41]			Focus Group and artifacts			
24. Disrupting and democratizing higher education provision or entrenching academic elitism: towards a model of MOOCs adoption at African universities	Rambe & Moeti, [46]	South Africa	MOOCs in higher Education context: A comparative narrative between Africa and America	Thematic Narrative analysis underpinned by Disruptive Innovation Theory	Not Applicable (Mainstream literature review)	Thematic Analysis	Educational Technology Research and Development
25. Massive pen online courses for Africa by Africa	Oyo & Kalema, [45]	South Africa	MOOCs implementation strategies	Thematic, Narrative Analysis	Not Applicable literature review	Thematic/ Narrative Analysis	The International Review of Research in Open and Distributed Learning.
26. Adoption of massive open online courses (MOOC) for librarians' professional development in Africa	Fagbohun et al., (2018)	Nigeria	Advancing the course for the adoption of MOOCs for librarians' continuing professional development	Conceptual/Narrative Analysis	Not Applicable	Not Applicable	Library and Information Science in the Age of MOOCs (pp. 37-65). IGI Global.
27. Applying MOOCocracy learning culture themes to improve digital course design and online learner engagement	Akinkuolie & Shortt [54]	International/ Global context	Culture / Adaptive / Bespoke MOOC	Thematic/ Content Analysis & Synthesis	Not Applicable	Thematic analysis	Education Technology Research and Development
28. Leveraging Massive Open Online Courses (MOOCs) for Increased Access and Quality Education in Nigeria.	Yunusa, Umar, & Ussher [12].	Nigeria	The paper advocated for the adoption of MOOCs as a panacea to the challenges of limited opportunities for	Conceptual / Narrative analysis	Not Applicable	Exploratory narrative analysis	Proceedings of the Asian Conference on Education and International Development (ACEID 2020). Tokyo, Japan.

SN/Paper title	Author(s)/ date	SSA context (s)	Disciplinary context	Research design	Subjects/samples	Statistical tools	Journal
			acquiring university education in Nigeria				
29. Digital neocolonialism and massive open online courses (MOOCs): colonial pasts and neoliberal futures,	Adam,T. [35]	South Africa	The paper was a holistic evaluation of the MOOCs platforms to understand their epistemologies and relevance to different socio-cultural contexts particularly sub-Saharan Africa.	Conceptual/ Narrative discourse analysis	Not Applicable	Narrative discourse analysis	Learning, Media, and Technology
30. Massive open online courses (MOOCs): a tool for intercontinental collaboration in archives and records management education in Eswatini	Chisita & Tsabedze [37]	Eswatini (Swaziland)	The article explored the views of archives and records management (ARMS) professionals about MOOCS as an open platform to advance the growth of the discipline/ profession	Qualitative research design using interpretative technique drawn from interview texts	Students and Lecturers **(n = 60)**	Interpretative analysis	Archives and records management education

Table 3.
Summary of the reviewed MOOCS articles in SSA context.

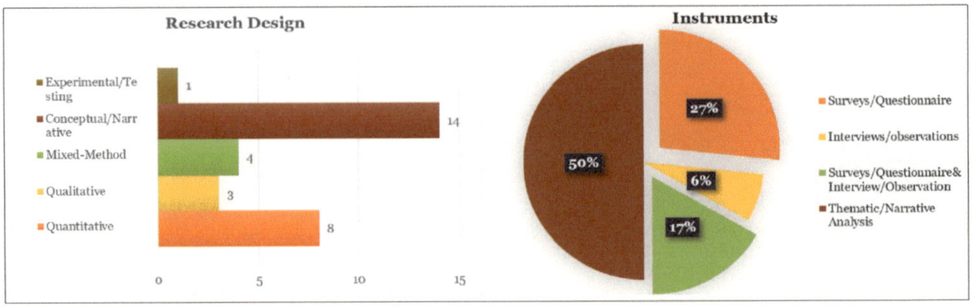

Figure 7.
Research designs and relevant instruments within MOOCs articles on SSA.

Harvard, Stanford etc.,). Similarly, Mtebe and Kissaka [38] dwelled on the potentials of MOOCs to enhance the quality of Computer Science Education in Tanzania, Similarly, Nhamo, [39] examined the feasibility of MOOCs for driving the transition to the development of green economy in Africa. furthermore, Boga & McGreal [21] reported their experience with how Cousera platform was used to provide opportunity for the enhancement and development of ICT skills in Sub-Saharan Africa to prepare them for the evolving knowledge economy. MOOCs as capacity building vehicles include the Teachers E-learning Portal (TEP) for enhancing the teacher's digital literacy and life-long learning capabilities in Uganda [17], The Teacher Education for Sub-Saharan Africa (TESSA), also known as TESSA MOOCs [40] which focused on Kenyan Teachers and Teacher Educators. The predominant themes for the narrative analyses also include opportunity for innovative credentialing [47]; MOOCs revolution implications for African Higher Education (Carvalho & Woldegiyorgis [49]; MOOCs for addressing African evaluation capacity [42]; Boosting African Higher Education through shared MOOCs [57] and the advocacy for a wholly African MOOCs (MOOCs for Africa by Africa [45]). Though an emerging phenomenon in the African context a few MOOCs adoption focused on the lower rung of the educational stream (Primary and Secondary education); The Kenyan Cloud School MOOCs for teaching foundational subjects [36].

3.6 The inhibiting factors within the MOOCs literature on SSA

A cluster of the inhibiting factors based on the reviewed literature was also created using the VOS viewer application. **Figure 8** presents the visualization of the

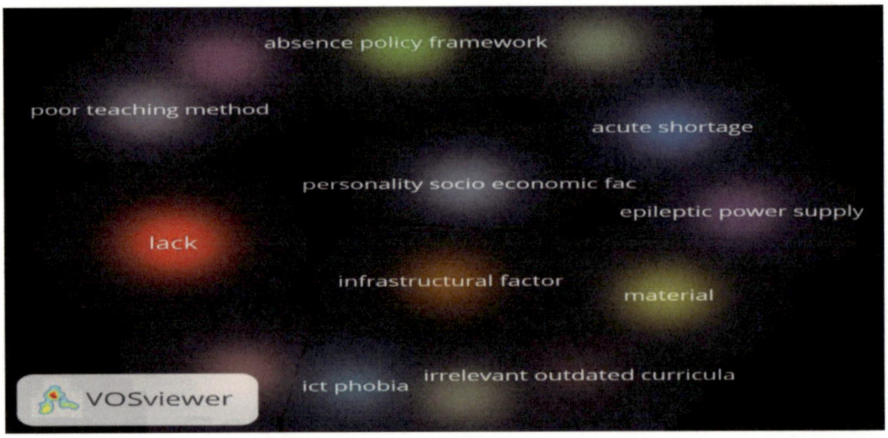

Figure 8.
Cluster density visualization of inhibitions to MOOCs growth in SSA.

text density visualization of the inhibiting factors of MOOCs in SSA. The most prominent are absence of policy framework to guide the adoption and implementation of the MOOCs platforms, poor teaching methods, acute shortage of expertise and personnel, Infrastructural factors, and irrelevant and outmoded curriculum across the SSA context.

4. Discussion

This paper aims to provide insights on the evolution of MOOCs in sub-Saharan Africa by searching, locating, and identifying articles on different *aspects of MOOCs* focused on sub-Saharan African contexts. Published between 2012 and 2021 *The Harzing publish or persish* literature search and management software along with the Scopus data base were used to identify 30 articles based on the authors' set criteria. The choice of the time period of the review was premised on the global evolution of the MOOCs phenomenon, given that MOOCs began to rise in 2013 [61] and was a Buzzword in 2012, [62]. The findings show a slow but steady production of articles on MOOCs in SSA domain, though with a bit of in consistencies. For instance, there was significant growth observed between 2012 to 2014, with a slight decline in 2015 and 2016, However, an increase was recorded in 2017 which appeared to be the highest since then. Though, from global perspectives MOOCs literature have been on the ascendancy, the probable reason for the slow pace of the scientific production of MOOCs in SSA may not be far from the myriads of challenges hindering its adoption in the sub-region. Nonetheless, significant publications have been recorded by the frontline countries in E-learning adoption and uptake such as Nigeria, South Africa, Kenya, and Tanzania.

These countries have recorded significant growth in internet penetration and usage including web based technologies such as the popular learning management systems, Moodle [19, 63]. According to a report by the international telecommunication union (ITU [64]) Kenya and Tanzania ranked 3rd and 4th behind Nigeria and South Africa as countries in Africa with the fastest growing mobile technology subscribers and internet users [63] given these statistics it can be concluded that the growth of MOOCs as reflected in the bibliometric review followed this trajectory even though these are not necessarily used for education purposes. Also, the low production may not be unconnected with the socio-economic status of the SSA countries as well as the doubts on its ability to impact positively given the disparity in the learning conditions between the environment where MOOCs was founded and the developing environment such as the SSA. Moreso that empirical evidence have shown that individuals who are already educated and have higher socio-economic status are more disposed to the MOOCS particularly in the developed contexts [65, 66] Notwithstanding, MOOCs has the potential to reduce inequities in education when contextualized and structured on the needs of the underserved communities [35, 67].

In terms of research design, the systematic bibliometric review revealed that the conceptual, narrative and discuss analysis was the most dominant within the reviewed literature. This is also not surprising given the scenario mentioned earlier. The contradictions around the conception of MOOCs as a technology that can facilitate the inclusion of underserved individuals is still raging within the SSA contexts. As [35, 46, 67] argued, until the issues around the contextualization and relevance of MOOCs to Africa is fully resolved, most discussions around the phenomenon would continue to be anecdotal and based on the experiences of the privilege few who are only opportune to experience MOOCs either through shear individual self-directedness and determination to achieve certain learning goals as in the case of the Rwandan citizens [68] or through interventions and partnerships as is the case with the TESSA MOOCs [40] which emphasized MOOCs based on partnership with global organizations and prominent MOOCs providers such as Cousera (www.cousera.org), edX(edx.org), Udemy (www.udemy.com), FutureLearn (futurelearn.com), Openlearning (www.openlearning.com) etc.

Regarding subject area, disciplinary contexts, and samples that were more pronounced in the MOOCs articles, the novelty of the MOOCs and it's slow pace stuck out. This is because the most prominent subject areas and the themes revolved around, readiness, willingness to adopt, and the researchers narration the relevance of MOOCs to some of the disciplinary contexts such as Evaluation management and Archives and records management practitioners [37, 42]. Thus, underscoring the explorative inclination of MOOCs research. It is however, encouraging to observe the widening of the scope of research based on discipline as it cut across the STEM, STEAM and Continued personal and professional development of individuals and collectives across the different fields within the review (covering, Archives and Records Management, Computer science, Green Economy, and Mathematics). The presence of computer science, mathematics and the arts and humanities resonate with the courses that recorded completions in prominent platforms [69], thus, reflecting the multidisciplinarity of the phenomenon. Similar reasons may be advanced for the sampling techniques and sample sizes expressed within the MOOCs literature in SSA.

The dominant model among the MOOCs within the empirical literature are the traditional MOOCs format (xMOOCs), which is a replication of the teacher dominated model, followed by the connectivist MOOCs (cMOOCs). This outcome may also be ascribed to the predominance of the conceptual or theoretical views of the MOOCS phenomenon aligning with the findings of [16] they found that conceptual model constituted the most employed in their review as more than half of the articles in the corpus used this approach. However, these researchers argued against viewing MOOCs from theoretical or conceptual perspectives as according to them there is no evidence of how this benefits the growth or otherwise of MOOCs [70].

In that sense, it may therefore be inferred that the predominance of conceptual approach to the MOOCs phenomenon signifies a limitation in the actual practice or adequate utilization of the MOOCs affordances or technology within the context of the study. In terms of research methodology, and instruments, the findings also corroborated previous literature but add to the body of evidence from SSA perspectives. Additionally, conceptual narratives and thematic discourse analysis outnumbered the use of survey, observation, or a combination of both. The survey instrument approach was the next most used, followed by qualitative method while the least was the experimental and/ or testing-based article. More investment in MOOCs through partnership and innovative conception of the technology in SSA will benefit from the exploration MOOCs vast potentials through empirical research. Regarding the milestones, the successes and the enthusiasm demonstrated in the few MOOCs within the SSA literature (e.g TESSA MOOCs in Kenya, E-learning Portal, Uganda) underscores the relevance of MOOCs in providing and facilitating accessibility and learning at scale. While the inhibitions are peculiar issues with developing countries, which needed to be solved through concerted efforts, conscious quality policy and legal framework for the implementation of MOOCs and more investment through partnerships with established institutions and MOOCs providers.

5. Conclusion

This paper sought to identify articles published on MOOCs focused on the technology in SSA between 2012 and 2021 to understand the growth and production trends of the phenomenon. 30 articles were found relevant and included in the bibliometric review. The review identified the most recurring keywords, the prolific authors, and their relations depicting a lack of collaborations among the experts within SSA. The low production of MOOCs articles signifies that despite the much-taunted disruptive potential of MOOCs to address the needs of underserved communities, the expectations are yet to be met. Perhaps due to the underlying challenges inherent in developing environments and the philosophy of being a neocolonial product and not fit for the SSA context. The predominant literature was based on anecdotes and expert opinions with a few empirical articles. Based on the findings we can conclude that more collaboration, networking, and partnership is required to develop a nuanced indigenous MOOC for SSA.

6. Limitations, future studies, and recommendation

This study's limitations may be drawn from the broader aspects of bibliometric studies and the method. Though, the paper sought to highlight the growth of MOOCs production, and drew a matrix that included the journals, the paper did not cover the metrics on the sources and document types, albeit due to space constraints therefore, future studies might want to consider the journals, journal citation metrics and their ranking based on MOOCs article publication to offer more interesting insights. In addition, the review did not capture the authors citation metrics. But rather presented only the link strengths and occurrences of the authors. Furthermore, the review was based on literature from Harzing publish or perish and Scopus, even though Harzing is an integrative platform, there may be literature in other databases that were not captured. The review was primarily focused on SSA therefore limiting extrapolation to Africa in general despite common characteristics across the continent. Future studies might want to consider comparative reviews between SSA and the rest of the region (North Africa).

Acknowledgements

We acknowledge the authors of all the articles that were used in the review and appreciate their insights and contributions that guided the focus of the paper. We also appreciate the anonymous reviewers for their insightful comments that help shaped the paper.

Conflict of interest

The authors hereby declare that they have no conflict of interests regarding this paper.

Availability of data

All the data related to this article are contained in the article matrix which can be found from this link https://drive.google.com/file/d/1NLY1yXDTN-DOPr0wPpZAJ0cXN2IaHtGys/view?usp=sharing.

Author details

Abdullahi Abubakar Yunusa[1*], Irfan Naufal Umar[2] and Brandford Bervell[3]

1 Department of Curriculum Studies and Educational Technology, Usmanu Danfodiyo University Sokoto, Nigeria

2 Center for Instructional Technology and Multimedia, Universiti Sains Malaysia, Malaysia

3 College of Distance Education, University of Cape Coast, Cape Coast, Ghana

*Address all correspondence to: abdullahi.yunusa@udusok.edu.ng

References

[1] T. Teo and H.M. Dai: "The role of time in the acceptance of MOOCs among Chinese university students." Interact. Learn. Environ. vol. 0, no. 0, pp. 1–14, 2019.

[2] J. Jacoby: "The disruptive potential of the Massive Open Online Course: A literature review." *J. Open, Flexible, Distance Learn.* vol. 18, no. 1, pp. 73–85, 2014.

[3] D. Shah: Year of MOOC-based degrees: A review of MOOC stats and trends in 2018. Retrieved from https://www.class-central.com/report/moocs-stats-and-trends-2018/2019, January 6.

[4] T.R. Liyanagunawardena, A.A. Adams, and S.A. Williams: "MOOCs: A systematic study of the published literature 2008-2012." *Int. Rev. Res. Open Distrib. Learn.* vol. 14, no. 3, pp. 202, 2013.

[5] K.S. Hone and G.R. El Said: "Exploring the factors affecting MOOC retention: A survey study." Comput. Educ. vol. 98, pp. 157–168, 2016.

[6] S. Downes: Places to go: Connectivism and connective knowledge. *Innovate Online* 5(1). Retrieved from https://www.academia.edu/2869475/Places_to_go_Connectivi sm and_connective_knowledge 2008.

[7] T. Phan, S.G. McNeil, and B.R. Robin: "Students' patterns of engagement and course performance in a Massive Open Online Course." Comput. Educ. vol. 95, pp. 36–44, 2016.

[8] Bates T. MOOCs: Getting to know you better. Distance Education. 145-8, 2014 May 4;35(2).

[9] M. Zhao, J. Wu, and X. Huang: "A Framework of Building Effective MOOCs." International Conference on Management,Education and Social Sciences (ICMESS 2017). pp. 31–34 (2017).

[10] D. Tao, P. Fu, Y. Wang, T. Zhang, and X. Qu: "Key characteristics in designing massive open online courses (MOOCs) for user acceptance: an application of the extended technology acceptance model." Interact. Learn. Environ. vol. 00, no. 00, pp. 1–15, 2019.

[11] P. Ngimwa and T. Wilson: "An empirical investigation of the emergent issues around OER adoption in Sub-Saharan Africa." Learn. Media Technol. vol. 37, no. 4, pp. 398–413, 2012.

[12] A.A. Yunusa, I.N. Umar, and James Ussher: "Leveraging Massive Open Online Courses (MOOCs) for Increased Access and Quality Education in Nigeria." The Asian Conference on Education & International Development 2020 Official Conference Proceedings. pp. 14, 2020.

[13] A.A. Economides and M.A. Perifanou: "MOOC Affordances Model." vol. 562, no. 2016, pp. 605–613, 2018.

[14] R.A. Rasheed, A. Kamsin, N.A. Abdullah, A. Zakari, and K. Haruna: "A Systematic Mapping Study of the Empirical MOOC Literature." IEEE Access. vol. 7, pp. 124809–124827, 2019.

[15] R. McGreal: "Special Report on the Role of Open Educational Resources in Supporting the Sustainable Development Goal : Quality Education Challenges and Opportunities Quality Education : Role / Contribution of OER." *Int. Rev. Res. Open Distrib. Learn.* vol. 18, no. 7, pp. 292–305, 2017.

[16] A. Bozkurt, E. Akgün-Özbek, and O. Zawacki-Richter: "Trends and patterns in Massive Open Online Courses: Review and content analysis of research on MOOCs (2008-2015)." Int. Rev. Res.

Open Distrib. Learn. vol. 18, no. 5, pp. 1–23, 2017a.

[17] B. Oyo, B.M. Kalema, and J. Byabazaire: "MOOCs for in-service teachers: The case of Uganda and lessons for Africa." Rev. Española Pedagog. vol. 75, no. 1, pp. 121–141, 2017.

[18] G. Christensen, A. Steinmetz, B. Alcorn, A. Bennett, D. Woods, and E.J. Emanuel: "The MOOC Phenomenon: Who Takes Massive Open Online Courses and Why?" *Ssrn*. 2014.

[19] J.S. Mtebe and C. Raphael: "Key factors in learners' satisfaction with the e-learning system at the University of Dar es Salaam, Tanzania." Australas. J. Educ. Technol. vol. 34, no. 4, pp. 107–122, 2018.

[20] A.A. Yunusa, I.N. Umar, and B. Bervell: "Octennial review (2010-2018) of literature on M-learning for promoting distributed-based medical education in sub-Saharan Africa." *Int. Rev. Res. Open Distance Learn.* vol. 20, no. 2, 2019.

[21] S. Boga and R. McGreal: "Introducing MOOCs to Africa: New economy skills for Africa program – ICT." *CoL Athabasca Univ.* vol. CC-BY-SA, no. January, pp. 1–10, 2014.

[22] F.S. Harouna and S. Lei: "Review of Literature on Social Media Use : A Bibliometric Analysis." Eur. Bus. Manag. vol. 4, no. 4, pp. 101–111, 2018.

[23] G. Veletsianos and P. Shepherdson: "Who studies MOOCs? Interdisciplinarity in MOOC research and its changes over time." ... *Rev. Res. Open* ... . 2015.

[24] R. Wahid, A. Ahmi, and A.S.A. Alam: "Growth and Collaboration in Massive Open Online Courses: A Bibliometric Analysis." *Int. Rev. Res. Open* ... . 2020.

[25] N. Albelbisi, F.D. Yusop, U. Kalsum, and M. Salleh: "Mapping the factors influencing success of Massive Open Online Courses (MOOC) in higher education." *EURASIA J. Math. Sci. Technol. Educ.* 2018.

[26] A. A. Yunusa, I.N. Umar: Massive Open Online Courses (MOOCS) in a global context: awareness, adoption and barriers in higher education institutions, the sub-Saharan African perspective. shmuhammad.com.

[27] A.A. Yunusa, I.T. Sanusi, A.O. Dada, S.S. Oyelere, and Joseph Friday Agbo: "Disruptions of Academic Activities in Nigeria: University Lecturers' Perceptions and Responses to the COVID-19." 2020XV Conferencia Latinoamericana de Technologias de Aprendizaje. pp. 1–6., Ecquardo (2021).

[28] I. de Waard, A. Koutropoulos, R.J. Hogue, S.C. Abajian, N.Ö. Keskin, C.O. Rodriguez, and M.S. Gallagher: "Merging MOOC and mLearning for increased learner interactions." Int. J. Mob. Blended Learn. vol. 4, no. 4, pp. 34–46, 2012.

[29] L. Czerniewicz, A. Deacon, J. Small, and S. Walji: "Developing world MOOCs: A curriculum view of the MOOC landscape." *J. Glob. Literacies, Technol. Emerg. Pedagog.* vol. 2, no. 3, pp. 122–139, 2014.

[30] A.W Harzing: Publish or Perish, available from https://harzing.com/resources/publish-or-perish. 2007.

[31] D. Moher, A. Liberati, J. Tetzlaff, D. G. Altman, D. Altman, G. Antes, D. Atkins, V. Barbour, N. Barrowman, J.A. Berlin, J. Clark, M. Clarke, D. Cook, R. D'Amico, J.J. Deeks, P.J. Devereaux, K. Dickersin, M. Egger, E. Ernst, P.C. Gøtzsche, J. Grimshaw, G. Guyatt, J. Higgins, J.P.A. Ioannidis, J. Kleijnen, T. Lang, N. Magrini, D. McNamee, L. Moja, C. Mulrow, M. Napoli, A. Oxman, B. Pham, D. Rennie, M. Sampson, K.F.

Schulz, P.G. Shekelle, D. Tovey, and P. Tugwell: "Preferred reporting items for systematic reviews and meta-analyses: The PRISMA statement." *PLoS Med.* vol. 6, no. 7, 2009.

[32] N.J. Van Eck and L. Waltman: "Citation-based clustering of publications using CitNetExplorer and VOSviewer." *arXiv*. pp. 1–25, 2017.

[33] N.J. Van Eck and L. Waltman: "VOSviewer Manual version 1.6.16." *CWTS Meaningful metrics*. no. September, 2020.

[34] J.W. Creswell: Qualitative, quantitative and mixed methods approaches. Sage; 2014.

[35] T. Adam: "Digital neocolonialism and massive open online courses (MOOCs): colonial pasts and neoliberal futures." *Learn. Media Technol.* 2019.

[36] W. Jobe: "A Kenyan Cloud School. Massive Open Online & Ongoing courses for blended and lifelong learning." Open Prax. vol. 5, no. 4, pp. 301–313, 2013.

[37] C.T. Chisita and V.W. Tsabedze: "Massive open online courses (MOOCs): a tool for intercontinental collaboration in archives and records management education in Eswatini." *Rec. Manag. J.* vol. ahead-of-p, no. ahead-of-print, 2021.

[38] J.S. Mtebe and M.M. Kissaka: "Enhancing the quality of computer science education with MOOCs in sub-Saharan Africa." Handbook of Research on Active Learning and the Flipped Classroom Model in the Digital Age 2015.

[39] G. Nhamo: "Massive Open Online Courses (MOOCs) and Green Economy Transition: Feasibility Assessment for African Higher Education." Jhea/Resa. vol. 1121, no. 1, pp. 101–119, 2013.

[40] P.W. Wambugu: "Massive Open Online Courses (MOOCs) for Professional Teacher and Teacher Educator Development : A Case of TESSA MOOC in Kenya." Univers. J. Educ. Res. vol. 6, no. 6, pp. 1153–1157, 2018.

[41] L. Czerniewicz, A. Deacon, M. Glover, and S. Walji: "MOOC - Making and Open Educational Practices." J. Comput. High. Educ. vol. 29, no. 1, pp. 81–97, 2017.

[42] C.B. Mapitsa, L. Khumalo, H. Engel, and D. Wooldridge: "Can massive open online courses fill African evaluation capacity gaps?" African Eval. J. vol. 7, no. 1, pp. 1–7, 2019.

[43] C.O. and Reju and L.C. Jita: "Students' experiences with distance and online learning of university-level undergraduate mathematics in Nigeria." vol. 19, no. 2, pp. 112–125, 2018.

[44] C.O. Fakinlede, M.O. Yusuf, and O. V Mejabi: "Readiness for Online Learning in Higher Education : A Mixed Methods Assessment of Students at a Nigerian University." Malaysian J. Distance Educ. 16(1),. vol. 16, no. 1, pp. 37–57, 2014.

[45] B. Oyo and B.M. Kalema: "Massive open online courses for Africa by Africa." *Int. Rev. Res. Open Distrib. Learn.* vol. 15, no. 6, 2014.

[46] P. Rambe and M. Moeti: "Disrupting and democratising higher education provision or entrenching academic elitism: towards a model of MOOCs adoption at African universities." Educ. Tech Res. Dev. vol. 65, pp. 631–651, 2017.

[47] G. van Stam: "eLearning in Africa and the Opportunity for Innovative Credentialing." Fifth International Conference on e-Infrastructure and e-Services for Developing Countries (Africomm 2013) (2013).

[48] S. Odebero: "The Place of MOOCs in Africa's Higher Education." Handbook of Research on Innovation Technology Integration in Higher Education. pp. 248–261. *IGI Global*, USA (2016).

[49] A.A. Woldegiyorgis and L. Carvalho: "Massive Open Online Courses (MOOCs) and the 'revolution' in higher education: Implications for Africa." *13th Int. Conf. African Priv. High. Educ.* pp. 321–341, 2015.

[50] S.H. Muhammad, A. Mustapha, and K. Haruna: "Massive Open Online Courses : awareness, adoption, benefits and challenges in Sub- Saharan Africa." Int. J. ICT Manag. vol. 4, no. 2, pp. 60–68, 2016.

[51] E. Fianu, C. Blewett, G. Ampong, and K. Ofori: "Factors Affecting MOOC Usage by Students in Selected Ghanaian Universities." *Educ. Sci.* vol. 8, no. 2, pp. 70, 2018.

[52] N.M. Castillo, J. Lee, F.T. Zahra, and D.A. Wagner: "MOOCs for Development: Trends, Challenges, and Opportunities." Inf. Technol. Int. Dev. vol. 11, no. 2, pp. 35–42, 2015.

[53] P.J. Kpolovie and E.C. Iderima: "Readiness for MOOCs: Learners' inequity in Nigeria." EPRA Int. J. Econ. Bus. Rev. vol. 4, no. 7, pp. 5–25, 2016.

[54] B. Akinkuolie and M. Shortt: "Applying MOOCocracy learning culture themes to improve digital course design and online learner engagement." *Educ. Technol. Res. Dev.* no. 0123456789, pp. 2–5, 2021.

[55] A. Safana and M. Nat: "Systematic Review On Massive Open Online Courses Based On Primary/Meta-Analysis." Int. J. Sci. Technol. Res. vol. 6, no. 01, pp. 212–219, 2017.

[56] B. Ipaye and C.B. Ipaye: "Opportunities and Challenges for Open Educational Resources and Massive Open Online Courses : The Case of Nigeria . Commonwealth of Learning." *Educo-Health Proj. Ilorin, Kwara Niger. Abstr.* 2013.

[57] G. Escher, D. Noukakis, and P. Aebischer: "Boosting Higher Education in Africa through Shared Massive Open Online Courses (MOOCs)." *Rev. Int. Polit. développement*. vol. 5, no. 1, 2014.

[58] L. Czerniewicz and Andrew Deacon Janet Small Sukaina Walji: "Developing world MOOCs: A curriculum view of the MOOC landscape." *J. Glob. Literacies, Technol. Emerg. Pedagog.* vol. 2, no. 3, pp. 122–139, 2014.

[59] T. Adebo and T. Ailobhio: "Massive Open Online Courses awareness and adoption by Nigeria university students: (A Case Study)." Int. J. Comput. Eng. Inf. Technol. vol. 9, no. 3, pp. 41–46, 2017.

[60] M. Gaebel: 'MOOCs: Massive Open Online Courses (EUA Occasional Paper)', Brussels: European University Association (EUA) 2013.

[61] A. Bozkurt, N. Ozdamar Keskin, and I. de Waard: "Research trends in Massive Open Online Course (MOOC) theses and dissertations: Surfing the tsunami wave." Open Prax. vol. 8, no. 3, pp. 203–221, 2016.

[62] L. Yuan and S. Powell: "MOOCs and open education: Implications for higher education." *Cetis*. pp. 19, 2014.

[63] R.R. Joel S. Mtebe: "Investigating students' behavioural intention to adopt and use mobile learning in higher education in East Africa." Int. J. Educ. Dev. Using Inf. Commun. Technol. vol. 10, no. 3, pp. 4–20, 2014.

[64] International Telecommunications Union (ITU): World Telecommunication / ICT Indicators

Database. Geneva: International Telecommunications Union (ITU) 2010.

[65] S. Lambert: "Do MOOCs contribute to student equity and social inclusion?: A systematic review 2014–18." *Comput. Educ.* vol. 145, no. 103693, 2020.

[66] R. Pollack Ichou: "Can MOOCs reduce global inequality in education?" Australas. Mark. J. vol. 26, no. 2, pp. 116–120, 2018.

[67] B. Nkuyubwatsi: "Positioning Extension Massive Open Online Courses (xMOOCs) within the Open Access and the Lifelong Learning Agendas in a Developing Setting." J. Learn. Dev. vol. 3, no. 1, pp. 14–36, 2016.

[68] B. Nkuyubwatsi: "Fostering collaborative investment in massive open online courses (MOOCs)." *leicester. figshare.com*, 2015.

[69] T.R. Liyanagunawardena, S. Williams, ..., P. Version, and O. Access: "The impact and reach of MOOCs: a developing countries' perspective." *eLearning Pap.* vol. 0, 2014.

[70] A. Bozkurt, E. Akgün-Özbek, and O. Zawacki-Richter: "Trends and patterns in Massive Open Online Courses: Review and content analysis of research on MOOCs (2008-2015)." Int. Rev. Res. Open Distrib. Learn. vol. 18, no. 5, pp. 1–23, 2017b.

Chapter 11

The Adoption of Massive Open Online Courses in Selected Sub-Saharan African Countries: The Experiences of Urban Learners

Vollan Ochieng', Maurice Mutisya and Caroline Thiong'o

Abstract

MOOCs is slowly gaining traction in the education provisioning in SSA. Much of this is attributed to governmental and institutional aim of providing quality and affordable universal education to all learners. This chapter explores how MOOCs is affecting access to learning in SSA, with particular bias to urban education context. Evidence adduced in this chapter was adduced from secondary sources, involving review of relevant literature available from internet sources. In the internet sources visited, key search terms that were used in obtaining the relevant resources included but not limited to: 'MOOCs and education', 'MOOCs in Africa', 'Education technologies AND MOOCs in Africa', 'MOOCs, OERs adoption and adaptability in Africa', and 'MOOCs' challenges in Africa' among others. It emerged that while MOOCs is gaining the needed traction in the SSA education space, the pace of its development is slow and calls for a more concerted effort from concerned education stakeholders.

Keywords: urban education, massive open online courses (MOOCs), distance learning solutions, learning and teaching

1. Introduction

The onset of COVID-19 has set the stage for the hitherto ignored learning approach – virtual/distance learning solutions. The approach (distance learning) could be observed as a blessing amidst a curse (pandemic). It is an approach that could be explored and expanded to promote learning for all as it has the capability of breaching the geographical and distance barriers in access to quality education. With the school closures due to COVID-19, most governments in SSA, like the rest of the world, adopted distance learning to ensure continued learning. In this chapter, we look at Cote d'Ivoire, Ghana, Kenya and Nigeria as case examples. Evidence from the foregoing in the education space – catalyzed by COVID-19, indicates that the future of education is digital and online, further re-emphasizing the central place of Massive Open Online Courses (MOOCs) in the attainment of SDG-4. The MOOCs place is the education sphere is thus validated. From the foregoing, it would be important to understand the place MOOCs in the African educational context.

IntechOpen

This chapter explores the place of MOOCs in selected sub-Saharan African countries – Cote d'Ivoire, Ghana, Kenya and Nigeria – in relation to the advancement of education in the countries' urban areas.

2. What is MOOCs?

Massive Open Online Courses (MOOCs) is an education platform that is gaining popularity in the field of education in the recent times. Like the name, MOOCs are synonymized by learning provision that is technology enabled, meaning that they are largely utilizable via the internet or online, and are open (meaning their potential users are not restricted on access). Also, they are 'massive' in the sense that the platform can accommodate a huge (massive) number of learners at any given time [1]. MOOCs can be traced from Dave Cormier lecture on connectivism in 2008 that was used to synonymize learning's development [2].

Today, varied definitions of MOOCs do exists, and this is to a large extent attributed to the existing divergent viewpoints on MOOCs as a median of learning by proponents and opponents, emergence of varied platforms, MOOC's wider scope, as well as its perceived futuristic feature, where opponents perceive it as a yet to mature learning approach/medium that cannot be scalable in the current context.

At its inception stage, MOOCs' definition was that it was a learning platform that encompassed the linkage of social networks, accessible by a renowned expert in a study discipline, and an assemblage of open internet-based learning materials. The platform was such that it could accommodate mass number of learners, organized according to their field or discipline of study interest and study goals [3, 4]. Laurillard [5], on the other hand offered a perceived easier definition which stated that MOOCs is an online/internet enabled learning that is created to support a huge number of learners. Chai's [6] definition is no different from that of McAuley et al. [4], as the former [Chai's definition] maintained that MOOCs are open learning platforms that are freely accessible to all learners, geographical location notwithstanding, provided that such learners has access to internet connectivity and education enabling technologies like computers, tablets, and smartphones among others. De-Waard [7] reinforces the above captured definitions by maintaining that MOOCs is an online learning platform in which learners gather to share experiences and knowledge either at the workplace or in schooling aspects and work in collaboration as well as individually to learn more using the available learning resources in MOOCs platforms.

3. How MOOCs work

In terms of form or appearance, MOOCs being online based platform where users access learning contents via the internet, it often take or come in the following formats that users utilize in enhancing their skills-set: learners interaction platforms through forums; recorded or filmed video lessons; exams and internet-based assessments; engaging educational modules; literacy; and sets of problems for users to solve [6]. Typically, for each MOOC, there is need for a course platform and a provider of the course. Examples of providers of course(s) are universities and colleges that avail lecturers or instructors as well as course(s) learning materials for learners/users' access and interaction in the existing platform [6, 8]. Among the widely existing and known platforms that offer the requisite technological structure for MOOCs' course modules include Coursera (Udacity), EdX and Canvas among others [6, 9].

Given the above MOOCs' definitions and features, it can argued that definitions of MOOCs is inspired by its acronyms 'MOOC' as it emphasizes shared involvement or participation as well as collaboration in learning. Despite the notable definitions advanced for MOOCs, it is still observed to be loosely defined since in whole, MOOCs can be observed in relation to the scalability of distance and open learning services that are available online [8]. Ordinarily, a MOOC may be either less structured or fashioned in a university or college like system. MOOCs' despite not according its users the much-sought certification, it has gained traction in the recent past due to its contribution to the furthering and enhancement of users' employment prospects [6].

From the foregoing, it is evident that key distinguishing features of MOOCs are: free access to MOOCs' learning resources; and, mass participation in learning via the MOOCs' platform. We thus explore MOOCs in this paper from the mentioned MOOCs' features.

4. MOOCs in Africa

Proponents of MOOCs within and outside the continent is rooted on the perception that that MOOCs presents a perfect avenue for providing affordable and quality education for learners in higher education institutions (HEIs) and individuals in pursuit of career development [10]. This is expressly due to the fact that MOOCs is largely appreciated by users falling in this category [learners in HEIs, and those seeking to advance their careers] [6].

Africa has over the years contended with perennially low enrolments to HEIs, specifically due to high costs of university education, high or excess number of learners seeking opportunities at HEIs against few slots in existing HEIs or low grades attained at secondary/high school level that restricts entry to HEIs to only high performers. Consequently, learners unable to secure slots at prestigious public HEIs have been forced to discontinue their education, forcing them to settle for casual or low level employments that require minimum/low level of skills-set.

The diminished opportunities at HEIs led to the enactment of laws that permit privatization of higher education learning in the 1990s for most African countries, to accommodate learners unable to secure opportunities in public universities. This practice led to deliberate random increase in private HEIs in the continent. This practice expanded opportunities for learners seeking university slots, and even provided varied and flexible learning time. HEIs learners thus have had the option of choosing among the varied learning times, the ones that best suited their programs [10]. For instance, one could opt for either distance learning module, day, weekend or evening classes.

The irony however, is that even with these developments, learners who attain the minimum required HEIs entry points still fail to join HEIs, even when they are selected to join them, due to abject poverty that such learners are subjected to [11, 12]. The prevailing poverty scenario in Africa has reduced the continent into a mere spectator in the ongoing MOOCs discourse and practice. This could be understood given the widespread poverty incidence across the country in comparison with the context of the developed countries [13].

However, due to the high cost of schooling, including those pertaining to learning materials like textbooks, the continent see MOOCs as an alternative affordable education platform. This is particularly due to the MOOCs' feature of free utility, which has made MOOCs to be more attractive to developing countries. As noted previously, MOOCs prevalence is more on HEIs level compared to primary and secondary level in the African continent and this could perhaps be explain by the fact that at the HEIs level, funding and or support for learning lower than for primary and secondary levels. This is because the cost of learning increases with level, implying that the higher one goes the education ladder, the higher the cost. This has led to the governments (in sub-Saharan Africa) to prioritize provision of funding for primary level compared to secondary and tertiary levels respectively. Moreover, primary level is cheaper and covers more learners, which is a contrary case for tertiary level where the costs are higher yet covering fewer students [14]. MOOCs at HEIs in Africa is thus seen as a deliberate effort to address the high cost of HEIs and keep majority of learners from vulnerable, poor and marginalized areas in HEIs and or support them in accessing quality learning materials. The MOOCs platform is perceived as a crosscutting skills' development vehicle that is keen on eliminating school dropouts post-secondary education level [10]. However, due to the COVID-19, varied levels of learning institutions (including primary and secondary) have adopted the MOOCs as the new alternative learning platform to keep learning ongoing during the school closure period [6].

Oyo and Kalema [10], offers a model (**Figure 1**) that depicts the entry and or access scenario into HEIs in the African continent where in the past, access to HEIs was limited to learners from the privileged settings, dubbed the society of the elite. This was followed by the present scenario where access to HEIs is characterized by privatization of learning in HEIs to maximize on access and or enrolments to HEIs [both public and private]. The paradox however, is even with the increased privatization of HEIs with the aim of increasing access to higher education (HE) learning, an equally higher number of learners seeking HE learning are unable to enroll to these institutions owing to the fact that enrolment to the private HEIs involve costs that learners from poor, and marginalized settings/households are unable to afford [11, 12].

The era of MOOC is thus perceived as the future of learning and deemed as a driving vehicle for equal access to learning owing to its relatively cheap cost – free access to learning contents and materials, provided an individual has access to enabling devices or infrastructure like laptops, tablets, internet, and electricity among others [15]. Despite being viewed as a future education equalizing vehicle, COVID-19 has brought forth the future owing to the mass use of MOOCs' components that include the open educational resources (OERs). It is however important to note that for a noteworthy uptake of MOOCs and related OERs features, it is imperative that sub-Saharan African (SSA) governments prioritize the need to

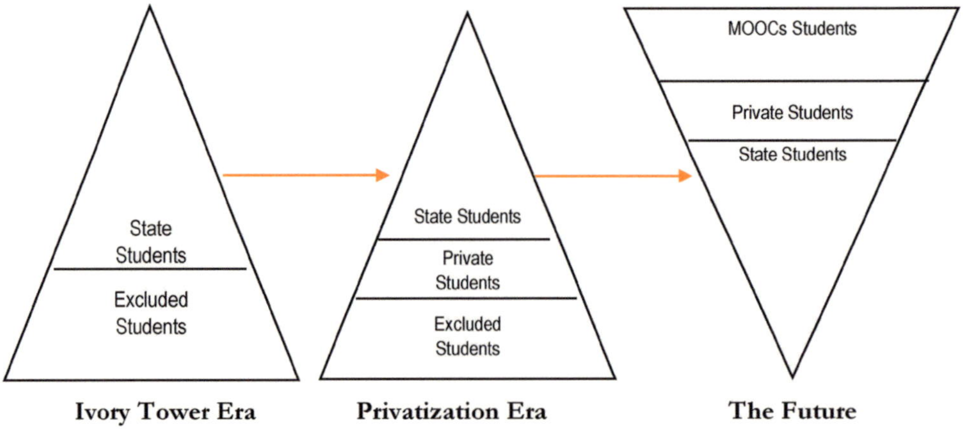

Figure 1.
HEIs' access viewpoints: The ivory tower era, the present [privatization era] and the future. Source: Adopted from Oyo and Kalema ([10], p. 4).

strengthen the HEIs' infrastructure and personnel. This include political good will towards MOOCs and OERs, strengthening HEIs' teaching/professional competencies, and providing free or cheap internet bandwidth to MOOCs users and potential users.

5. Effects of MOOCs on urban education in cote d'Ivoire, Kenya, Ghana, and Nigeria

The uptake of technology-enabled education in the African continent is on the rise, a situation that could be attributed to significant in-country investments in the provision of internet to its inhabitants, particularly through undersea fiber optic cables [16]. Users and or adopters of MOOCs in Africa, like in other global regions is to a large extent a preserve of higher learning institutions, with corporate bodies following in pursuit. This could be perhaps due to the fact that the genesis of MOOCs and related OERs was from top higher learning institutions that include Stanford, Massachusetts Institute of Technology (MIT), and Harvard, with the successes observed in these institutions' use and adoption of MOOCs believed to be replicable in other higher learning institutions.

Even with the observed internet provision efforts observed [16], Africa and in particular, sub-Saharan African (SSA) region, is still riddled with inadequate internet access, a situation which limits its participation and use in the global internet provided resources. For instance, the International Telecommunication Union (ITU) revealed that only about 16% of the region's (SSA) inhabitants (constituting some 140 million individuals) had access to internet as of 2014 [16]. Evidence [17, 18] indicate that the situation has not changed, as internet access in SSA has largely remained low. Equally, access at household level is even discouragingly low as households with internet access is below 20% [16, 17], with those in urban areas constituting the highest proportion of households with internet access [17]. This implies that the region's internet access gap is very high [19], thus reducing the region's capability in accessing and utilizing internet resources, among them MOOCs for learning and teaching [9, 20].

Online learning through various distance-learning solutions (education technologies – EdTechs) have been proven to reduce educational costs as well as promote access, quality and equitable learning [9, 16]. Considering that access to MOOCs and open educational resources (OERs) is to a large extent driven or enabled through internet, the SSA and the African continent at large remain underserved leading to diminished access to MOOCs' resources by learners and educators from this region. However, countries like Kenya, South Africa, Tanzania, and Uganda are making significant strides in the adoption and adaptation of online learning, by leveraging on existing enabling online-learning technology systems [21, 22].

Urban centers in SSA region are practically the areas that comparably to other regions in the continent (e.g. peri-urban, and rural areas), are enjoying internet coverage and access. It would therefore, imply that learning and teaching through MOOCs or OERs is more pronounced in urban areas than in rural or peri-urban areas [20]. However, this is not the case for a significant number of SSA countries. In Kenya, for instance, despite the country enjoying the use of undersea cable drawn all the way from the United Arabs Emirates (UAE) since 2009, a large swathe of the country is not accessing this service, resulting in over 70% of the population having no access to internet [18, 19]. This by extension has resulted in these underserved populations' inability to access interned-provided resources. In particular, education, which is a key user of internet for the development, sharing/distribution, revision, re/use of educational resources has been disadvantaged [23].

Even within the urban households, access to internet is limited to affordability and therefore I will not be surprising to find a high number of urban households not having access to internet. This has resulted in unequal access to internet and utilization of educational resources availed through internet-enabled platforms like MOOCs and OERs [9]. Against this background, MOOCs and OERs' utilization for learning and teaching in Kenya has not received the optimum user-threshold.

In Cote d'Ivoire, the predicament is same as that of Kenya, as there are inadequate infrastructure and systems that can support MOOCs and OERs for learning. In fact, limitations of internet access outside urban areas is considered a key impediment to the utilization of MOOCs and OERs, which if compounded by infrastructure and systems related limitations like inadequate learning institutions' staffing, ICT, and program design, worsens the situation [24, 25]. This however, could change if the country's recognition of the importance of distance learning solutions, through MOOCs and OERs, in provisioning of quality teaching and learning, especially at the higher education level is anything to go by (EdTech [25, 26]). The country sought to establish a MOOCs and OERs driven higher education institution – the Digital University of Ivory Coast – that was not only intended to promote distance learning for both urban and rural users, but also to modernize research and learning at higher education institution through the use of distance learning solutions (EdTechs) (**Figure 2**) [25, 27].

In Ghana, adoption and usage of MOOCs is likewise determined by the in/existence of enabling resources like MOOCs and OERs systemic quality, the system/platforms' performance, and learners and teachers computer knowledge [28]. While usage of MOOCs and OERs in Ghanaian urban areas would be expected to high,

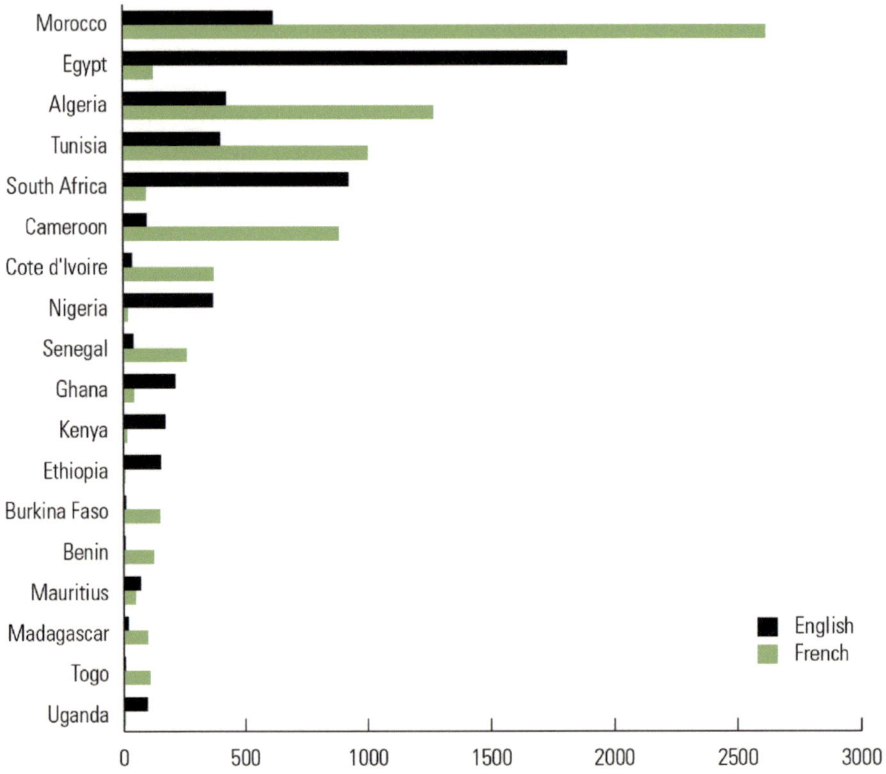

Figure 2.
African countries' participation in MOOCs, by instructional language. Source: Adopted from Gérard et al. [16].

considering the relative prevalence of internet in the country's urban areas, this is not the case due to the perceived and real lacking interest in MOOCs and their use among students [28, 29]. This is further exacerbated by the limited internet and enabling or assistive devices' [e.g. tablets, smartphones, computers etc.] access at the household level [30, 31], which limits usage of MOOCs and related OERs at urban household level. This situation has resulted in limited access to and usage of online learning and teaching resources for urban learners, further entrenching existing inequities in the provisioning of education and related resources at local and country level.

Nigerian context as pertains to MOOCs is a replica of the continent's investment in MOOCs. Notable MOOCs investments in Nigeria are premised in higher learning institutions given its flexibility and potentials [32]. Some of the universities in Nigeria that offer programs that mirror MOOCs include the University of Ibadan (UI), Kaduna State University (KASU), University of Portharcourt, Bayero University Kano (BUK), University of Lagos, the National Open University of Nigeria (NOUN), and Centres for Distance and Continuing Education at Ahmadu Bello University, Zaria (ABU) [33]. The biased adoption and adaptation of MOOCs in higher learning institutions in Nigeria points to a gap in adoption and utilization of the MOOCs platform in basic level (primary and secondary/high school levels), which are potentially key beneficiaries of MOOCs. Inadequate financial resources, lack of or inadequate enabling technological resources are some of the notable limiting factors that militate against development of education and related platforms in Nigeria [10, 21, 33]. While notable investments have been made that lends to positive trajectory in the adoption of MOOCs in Nigeria, they are to a large extent restricted or limited to higher learning institutions. Learners outside these institutions' environment are restricted in terms of access and use. Even those with access to the MOOCs platforms contend with the challenge of internet access among other technology aiding resources [32, 33]. This imply that urban learning and learners, though expected to benefit from MOOCs, also experience limitations in access and use of MOOCs, considering the inadequate enabling infrastructure.

6. Conclusion

African governments as well as educational institutions have recognized the central place of MOOCs and OERs in the advancement of quality and inexpensive education that meet the global or international standards. Against this background, there are noteworthy efforts, undertaken through a painstaking process, that can be witnessed in the continent's education providing institutions, particularly higher education institutions. A key effort in this context is the provision of learning programs in universities that imitate and mirror the MOOCs and OERs approaches, like online learning and teaching as well as provisioning of learning materials for learners' access freely. There are however, salient gaps that key education stakeholders could take into account, if efforts to promote and improve MOOCs and OERs adoption and adaptation into mainstream education is to yield desired results. The gaps could also be viewed as opportunities for stakeholders' involvement depending on vantage point that one looks at it. Such gaps include limiting internet infrastructure and related ICT infrastructure like computer or ICT labs, which higher learning institution providers could work on expanding, including coming up with innovate ways that spur uptake and usage of MOOCs. For instance, could make deliberate efforts to support and encourage students' use of OERs and MOOCs using the most suitable and innovative approaches. Moreover, efforts should be made in capacity building learners and/or users of MOOCs ICT skills where and when needed.

On the part of MOOCs developers, deliberate efforts should be cast on guaranteeing that the right curriculum, quality instructional and appropriate pedagogical methods are availed and used in the MOOCs platforms that learners are exposed to.

It is also evident that inequities and inequalities' dynamics in the urban space play an important role in accessing and using MOOCs and related OERs for learning. While it is expected that urban centres, being perceived to have sufficient infrastructural, would have a near universal access to internet and consequently, online learning resources like MOORs and OERs, this is sadly not the case as diverse poverty scenarios and different wealth quintiles determine uptake and usage of online resources. For urban households, only households with internet connections would have consistent access and use of the online learning platforms. Such households are however, the minority with majority of households lacking internet connections, hence making learning in urban areas using MOOCs and OERs to be an imbalanced intervention that further entrench education inequities and inequalities.

Finally, the salient ICT infrastructure challenges notwithstanding, African governments and educational institutions could leverage on the affordability of MOOCs and OERs to mitigate the inherent high cost of learning, particularly in higher learning institutions. This could particularly be effectively and efficiently explored through institution-to-institution collaboration, especially with the institutions in the developed countries, to act as benchmarks and help transform higher education institutions in the SSA region.

7. Recommendation

The following recommendations would thus suffice if efforts to make access to and utilization MOOCs and OERs a universal initiative that addresses aspects of educational inequities and inequalities:

a. Students' uptake of MOOCs and OERs, regardless of context (location – urban or rural, and socio-economic context) is highly dependent on teacher-student support [28, 34]. It is therefore, imperative that instructors, educators or lecturers be at the forefront in supporting learners to use MOOCs or OERs. Such support could relate to students' capacity building on re/use of online enabling resources (ICT) as well as provision of relevant and quality educational contents on the MOOCs' platforms;

b. Enabling resources or environment (e.g. infrastructure related like internet and related technologies' access etc.) is also observed to be a key determinant on uptake of MOOCs [35–39]. It is hence important that education providers, including both basic and higher learning education providers as well as state and non-state education stakeholders to prioritize and re-emphasize the important place of MOOCs in providing quality and affordable learning and teaching. This could be done by through provision of reliable internet access and related e-laboratories for e-learning at institutional level, as well as governmental and non-governmental educational actors support in provisioning household or public internet access primarily for accessing and using MOOCs;

c. Evidence [40], points to a unidirectional relationship between teaching quality and usage of MOOCs. It implies if quality is to be guaranteed in the MOOCs, adoption and enrolments to MOOCs will equally increase. For this reason, MOOCs' developers should endeavor to use and provide educational contents that are guided by an appropriate pedagogy for all learning levels.

For instance, it is observed that MOOCs' providers tend to rely on a pedagogical approach that is cognitive-behaviorist centric [41, 42]. It thus follows that designers of MOOCs' instructional resources ought to take into consideration the need to provide learners with materials for learner(s)'s assessment, giving and obtaining feedback, provide materials that are applicable for remote usage, and materials that highlight the learning outcomes at the onset of the online lessons [43]; and,

d. Ease of utility is another determinant of uptake and use of MOOCs [35, 38, 44]. This shows that the performance of MOOCs in terms of its user-friendliness and ease of accessing the sought educational contents is integral in MOOCs' utility to learners. To address this concern, MOOCs' providers and developers of its contents should ensure existing MOOCs' systems are user-friendly. This can be attained by having place a system that is easy to navigate, accessible even via smartphones (or any other hand-held gadgets), fast-loading site, learning sites that are visually appealing, and easy to utilize.

Author details

Vollan Ochieng'*, Maurice Mutisya and Caroline Thiong'o
African Population and Health Research Center, Nairobi, Kenya

*Address all correspondence to: vochieng@aphrc.org; vollan88ochieng@gmail.com

References

[1] Atiaja, L. M., and Proenza, R. S. (2016). MOOCs: Origin, characterization, principal problems and challenges in higher education. Journal of e-learning and knowledge Society, 12(1), 65-76.

[2] Downes, S. (2008). Places to go: Connectivism & connective knowledge. Innovate: Journal of online Education, 5(1), 1-6. Retrieved from https://nsuworks.nova.edu/innovate/vol5/iss1/6

[3] Lange, C., and Costley, J (2015). Opportunities and Lessons from Informal and Non-formal Learning: Applications to Online Environments. American Journal of Educational Research, 3(10):1330-1336. DOI:10.12691/education-3-10-20.

[4] McAuley, A.; Stewart, B.; Siemens, G.; Cormier, D. (2010). The MOOC model for digital Practice. Retrieved from http://www.elearnspace.org/Articles/MOOC_Final.pdf.

[5] Laurillard, D. (2014). Five Myths about MOOCs. Times Higher Education, 16 January. Retrieved from http://www.timeshighereducation.co.uk/comment/opinion/five-myths-about-moocs/2010480.article

[6] Chai, W. (2021). Definition: massive open online course (MOOC). Retrieved from https://whatis.techtarget.com/definition/massively-open-online-course-MOOC

[7] De-Waard, I. (2015). MOOC factors influencing teachers in formal education. Revista Mexicana de Bachillerato a Distancia, 7(13), 1-8. Retrieved from http://oro.open.ac.uk/44528/3/MOOC%20and%20teacher%20developmen%20final.pdf

[8] Margaryan, A., Bianco, M., and Littlejohn, A. (2015), Instructional quality of massive open online courses (MOOCs). Computers and Education, 80, 77-83.

[9] Ochieng', V., and Gyasi, R. M. (2021). Open educational resources and social justice: Potentials and implications for research productivity in higher educational institutions. E-Learning and Digital Media, 18(2), 1-20. DOI:10.1177/2042753021989467

[10] Oyo, B., and Kalema, B. M. (2014). Massive open online courses for Africa by Africa. International review of research in open and distance Learning, 15(6): 1-13. DOI:10.19173/irrodl.v15i6.1889

[11] Materu, P. (2007). Higher Education Quality Assurance in Sub-Sahara Africa Status, Challenges, Opportunities and Promising Practices. The World Bank.

[12] Osokoya, I. O. (2007). Privatization of university education in Africa: Lessons from the theories and practices of the United States of America and Japan. International journal of African and African American Studies, 6(2), 1-10. Retrieved from https://ojcs.siue.edu/ojs/index.php/ijaaas/article/view/94/154

[13] Emanuel, E. J. (2013). Online education: MOOCs taken by educated few. Nature, 503(342). Retrieved from DOI:1010.1038/503342a

[14] Lewin, K. M. (2004). Mapping the Missing Link: Planning and Financing Secondary Education in Sub Saharan Africa. Lead Keynote, World Bank Africa Regional Conference on Secondary Education in Africa. Dakar, Senegal.

[15] Pityana, N. B. (2009). Open distance learning in the developing world: Trends, progress and challenges. University of South Africa. Retrieved from http://uir.unisa.ac.za/bitstream/handle/10500/411/ICDEMaastricht250609.pdf;sequence=1

[16] Gérard, E., Noukakis, D., and Aebischer, P. (2014). Boosting Higher Education in Africa through Shared Massive Open Online Courses (MOOCs). In Education, Learning, Training: Critical Issues for Development (pp. 195-214), International Development Policy series No.5. Graduate Institute Publications. Retrieved from https://journals.openedition.org/poldev/1790

[17] Ngware, M. N., and Ochieng, V. (2021). Keeping class in session: A case study of EdTech and the COVID-19 response in Kenya. APHRC. Retrieved from https://aphrc.org/publication/keeping-class-in-session-a-case-study-of-edtech-and-the-covid-19-response-in-kenya/

[18] Ngware, M., and Ochieng, V. (2020). Education Technology (EdTech) and the COVID-19 Response in Kenya. Case study. EdTech Hub. Retrieved from https://docs.edtechhub.org/lib/SMLIMS2X/download/UBFPWLAX/Ngware%20and%20Ochieng%20-%20 2020%20-%20EdTech%20and%20 the%20COVID-19%20response%20 A%20case%20study%20of%20.pdf

[19] Lawton, W., and Burrows. A. (2013). Is there a technical fix for sub-Saharan universities? Observatory on Borderless Higher Education. Retrieved from http://www.obhe.ac.uk/newsletters/borderless_report_june_2013/is_there_a_technical_fix_for_subsaharan_universities

[20] Lane, A. (2013). The potential of MOOCs to widen access to, and success in, higher education study. In The Open and Flexible Higher Education Conference 2013 (pp. 189-203). EADTU.

[21] Bervell, B., and Umar, I. N. (2017). A decade of LMS acceptance and adoption research in sub-Sahara African higher education: A systematic review of models, methodologies, milestones and main challenges. Eurasia journal of mathematics, science and technology Education, 13(11), 7269-7286. DOI:10.12973/ejmste/79444

[22] Ng'ambi, D., and Bozalek, V. (2015). Editorial: Massive open online courses (MOOCs): Disrupting teaching and learning practices in higher education. British Journal of Educational Technology, 46(3), 451-454. DOI:10.1111/bjet.12281

[23] World Bank. (2019). Improving Higher Education Performance in Kenya: A Policy Report. World Bank. Retrieved from https://documents1.worldbank.org/curated/ar/831821566966279688/Improving-Higher-Education-Performance-in-Kenya-A-Policy-Report.pdf

[24] Jacobs Foundation (2015). The State of EdTech in Ivory Coast. Jacobs Foundation. Retrieved from https://jacobsfoundation.org/app/uploads/2019/06/The-State-of-EdTech-in-Ivory-Coast_2018.pdf

[25] Sawahel, W. (2015). Cote d'Ivoire: Government Announces Plan for a Virtual University. University World News. Retrieved from https://www.universityworldnews.com/post.php?story=20150108131544806

[26] EdTech Hub (2020). The effect of Covid-19 on education in Africa and its implications for the use of technology: A survey of the experience and opinions of educators and technology specialists. EdTech Hub. DOI:10.5281/zenodo.4018774. Retrieved from https://www.elearning-africa.com/ressources/pdfs/surveys/The_effect_of_Covid-19_on_Education_in_Africa.pdf

[27] World Bank (2015). Côte d'Ivoire Urbanization Review: Diversified Urbanization. World Bank. Retrieved from https://openknowledge.worldbank.org/bitstream/handle/10986/22896/Final0Output.pdf?sequence=1&isAllowed=y

[28] Fianu, E., Blewett, C., and Ofori, K. S (2018). Factors affecting MOOC usage by students in selected Ghanaian universities. University of KwaZulu-Natal. Retrieved from https://www.researchgate.net/publication/324648110_Factors_Affecting_MOOC_Usage_by_Students_in_Selected_Ghanaian_Universities

[29] Porter, S. (2015). To MOOC or Not to MOOC How Can Online Learning Help to Build the Future of Higher Education? Elsevier. ISBN 9780081000489

[30] Awidi, B. I. T. (2008). Developing an E-learning strategy for public universities in Ghana. Educ. Quartelry, 31, 66-69.

[31] Taddese, A. (2020). EdTech in Ghana: A Rapid Scan. (EdTech Hub Country Scan). DOI:10.5281/zenodo.3830951. Retrieved from https://docs.edtechhub.org/lib/4TKSDH2I/download/TUM48CS3/Abeba%20Taddese%20-%202020%20-%20EdTech%20in%20Ghana%20A%20Rapid%20Scan.pdf

[32] Jaiyeoba, A. O., and Ademola, A. I. (2014). Re-engineering tertiary education (university) for sustainable development in Nigeria. Reforming Higher Education in Africa, 46-57. DOI:10.1.1.558.750

[33] Yunusa, A. A., Umar, I. N., and Ussher, J. (2020). Leveraging Massive Open Online Courses (MOOCs) for Increased Access and Quality Education in Nigeria. Universiti Sains Malaysia. Retrieved from https://www.researchgate.net/publication/341192760_Leveraging_Massive_Open_Online_Courses_MOOCs_for_Increased_Access_and_Quality_Education_in_Nigeria

[34] Magsamen-conrad, K., Upadhyaya, S., Youngnyo, C., and Dowd, J. (2015). Computers in human behavior bridging the divide: Using UTAUT to predict multigenerational tablet adoption practices. Comput. Human Behav, 50, 186-196. DOI:10.1016/j.chb.2015.03.032

[35] Decman, M. (2015). Modelling the acceptance of e-learning in mandatory environments of higher education: The influence of previous education and gender. Computers in Human Behavior, 49, 272-281. DOI:10.1016/j.chb.2015.03.022.

[36] Dulle, F. W. (2015). The suitability of the unified theory of acceptance and use of technology (UTAUT) model in open access adoption studies. Information Development, 27, 32-45. DOI:10.1177/0266666910385375.

[37] Juinn, P., and Tan, B. (2013). Applying the UTAUT to understand factors affecting the use of English E-learning websites in Taiwan. Sage Open, 3(4), 1-12. DOI:10.1177/2158244013503837.

[38] Pynoo, B., Devolder, P., Tondeur, J., Van Braak, J., Duyck, W., and Duyck, P. (2011). Predicting secondary school teachers' acceptance and use of a digital learning environment: A cross-sectional study. Comput. Human Behav, 27, 568-575. DOI:10.1016/j.chb.2010.10.005.

[39] Wang, Y. S., Wu, M. C., and Wang, H. Y. (2009). Investigating the determinants and age and gender differences in the acceptance of mobile learning. Br. J. Educ. Technol, 40, 92-118. DOI:10.1111/j.1467-8535.2007.00809.x.

[40] Lee, B. C., Yoon, J. O., and Lee, I. (2009). Learners' acceptance of e-learning in South Korea: Theories and results. Comput. Educ, 53, 1320-1329. DOI:10.1016/j.compedu.2009.06.014.

[41] Bali, M. (2014). MOOC pedagogy: Gleaning good practice from existing

MOOCs. MERLOT J. Online Learn. Teach, 10, 44-56.

[42] Bayne, S., and Ross, J. (2014). The pedagogy of the massive open online course (MOOC): The UK view. Higher Education Academy. Retrieved from http://www.heacademy.ac.uk/resources/detail/elt/the_pedagogy_of_the_MOOC_UK_view

[43] Alzaghoul, A. F. (2012). The implication of the learning theories on implementing e-learning courses. Res. Bull. Jordan ACM, 11, 27-30.

[44] Ramayah, T., Ahmad, N. H., and Lo, M. C. (2010). The role of quality factors in intention to continue using an e-learning system in Malaysia. Procedia – Soc. Behav. Sci, 2, 5422-5426. DOI:10.1016/j.sbspro.2010.03.885

Chapter 12

Metacognitive Assessment Model for Student Project-Based Learning through the Blended Learning Practice MOOCs

Ridwan Daud Mahande, Fitrah Asma Darmawan and Jasruddin Daud Malago

Abstract

Online or blended learning assessments through LMS-MOOCs carried out in the world of education today tend to be multiple-choice assessments that are only based on low-level cognitive. In fact, to measure the metacognitive of students is quite difficult, if only using the form of multiple choice questions. Therefore, it takes the form of questions and assessments that allow students to explore their reflective and metacognitive thinking according to the characteristics of the education they are attending. Vocational education tends to apply a project-based learning (PjBL) model that requires authentic and performance-based learning assessment methods. Therefore, it is necessary to develop an appropriate blended metacognitive skill assessment rubric instrument for vocational education. Metacognitive assessment was developed using research and development procedures, with students as subjects in vocational education in Makassar, Indonesia. The integration between elements of metacognitive skills: planning, monitoring, and evaluation with self-peer-teacher assessment can be an assessment method to measure students' metacognitive thinking skills in PjBL. Especially metacognitive assessment through blended learning practice MOOCs that are in accordance with the characteristics of vocational education and can be adopted by general education.

Keywords: metacognitive skills, blended learning, PjBL, MOOCs, vocational education

1. Introduction

The world of work that is dynamic and develops in accordance with the direction of technological progress, requires workers not only to have hard skills in their respective fields, but also to have soft skills [1]. In the context of a dynamic and complex world of work, intelligence and soft skills are needed that are relevant to the world of work today and the world of work in the future [2]. These soft skills are of course in the form of adaptability, problem solving ability, analytical thinking, creativity, collaboration, and communication. The International Labor Organization (ILO) released several soft skills that are currently needed in the world of work such as analytical skills, creativity, problem solving, communication, collaboration, and entrepreneurship [3]. Some of these soft skills, such as analytical skills, creativity, and problem solving skills, are classified as critical thinking which is regulated by the ability to think reflectively or think metacognitively (metacognitive skills) [4]. Therefore, the ability to think metacognitively is very important for workers because it can help them maintain their work ethic in a very dynamic world of work with change and uncertainty.

Vocational education as an educational institution that aims to prepare a competent workforce is required to have an awareness of the demands of today's world of work. UNESCO-UNEVOC has set one of the main priorities of vocational education in the world, namely to prepare a competent young workforce according to the demands of today's global workforce. Vocational education or globally known as Technical and Vocational Education and Training (TVET) is required not only to equip students with hard skills but also to equip them with creativity skills, analytical thinking, problem solving, and leadership [5]. To support this, higher education should carry out various learning innovations, both in learning planning, learning processes, and learning evaluations. Digitization is one of the best choices because it is the demand of the current digital era that leads to learning 4.0 [1].

Learning 4.0 has now been promoted at various levels of education, not least at the higher education level. The use of online learning is one of the learning media used to assist the digital learning process [1]. The implications of online learning or e-learning in learning present new forms of learning and allow learners to collaborate and interact socially online [6]. In addition, online learning can increase the level of motivation of students [7] as well as helping students to access information and learning resources from anywhere and anytime [8]. The use of e-learning in vocational education has also been widely used and researched. The use of digital-based teaching materials that are integrated in e-learning can improve mathematics learning outcomes in vocational education [9]. From the aspect of users, teachers and students use mobile devices for vocational learning purposes [10]. Learning evaluation is of course also possible to do online with the help of e-learning. The advancement of internet technology and the increasing interest in online learning, issues around e-learning and its assessment methods are also getting more attention among educators [11].

Online learning evaluations carried out in the world of education today tend to measure using multiple choice-based questions [1]. Multiple choice-based questions are often used in summative and formative tests in education (online and offline or blended) [12]. In fact, to measure the higher-level cognitive of students is quite difficult, if only using the form of multiple choice questions. Because in practice, the use of multiple choice-based tests only touches low-level cognitive [13]. Therefore, it takes a form of evaluation and form of questions that allow students to explore their subjective and objective reflective and metacognitive thinking. Through this metacognitive thinking process, it is hoped that students will be able to reflect on their own learning and make adjustments so that students can achieve a deeper understanding [14]. In addition, a form of formative assessment that focuses on teaching students' metacognitive processes is needed to evaluate their own learning and make adjustments to the learning process [15].

Several research results have examined the methods of assessing and measuring students' metacognitive thinking through the online environment [1]. Online metacognitive thinking assessment in certain domain assignments and settings, can measure students' metacognitive thinking abilities [16]. Researchers used measurement tools in the form of otter tasks, multiple choice questions, and open-ended questions. Another researcher conducted an assessment using an online-based group metacognitive scaffolding (GMS) to measure the metacognitive behavior of students in a small group in class [17]. The results show that GMS has a significant impact on changes in the metacognitive behavior of learners in a small group. Furthermore, Altıok et al. [18] measuring metacognitive thinking using an online environment integrated video portfolio and the results show an increase in the level of students' metacognitive thinking in foreign language learning. The results of this study only focus on the measurement and assessment methods of learning in general education, not yet on learning in vocational education which has its own learning characteristics. In vocational education, appropriate learning models are used, namely work-based learning, project-based learning, or contextual teaching and learning so that authentic and performance-based learning assessment methods are needed [19]. The development of rubrics and assessment models uses a student-centered assessment approach where students are the subject and object of the assessment to reflect on their own learning, as well as peer assessment and teacher assessment approaches [20]. The results of the development of rubrics and metacognitive skills assessment models through blended learning MOOCs can be a reference for PjBL assessment methods that are in accordance with the characteristics of vocational education.

2. Technical and vocational education

Technical and Vocational Education and Training includes theoretical and practical learning content developed in schools, training institutions, or companies. Based on this limitation, the knowledge and skills referred to here can be understood not only as technical knowledge and skills, but also knowledge of values and identity in a complex world of work [1]. This vocational education paradigm is also not only a learning process in the school environment, but can be carried out in non-formal training environments such as training institutions and in agencies or companies [21]. The main purpose of vocational education is to prepare graduates directly for work. Vocational education should provide specialized training that is reproductive in nature and based on teacher instruction, with an emphasis on knowledge of certain industrial sectors and includes specific skills or tricks of the trade. Vocational education has played a central role in supporting the transition from school to the world of work for youth. Vocational education for productive work is considered essential for economic and social development [22]. An important emphasis of vocational education is on developing specific work-related skills or skills to prepare students for entering the workforce, while general education emphasizes on equipping students with broad knowledge and basic skills in mathematics and communication [23]. Based on these theories, it can be concluded that in general, vocational education aims to prepare graduates to work in certain sectors. The function of this education is to carry out the process of transforming work competencies, knowledge of the world of work, as well as the ability to collaborate and interact between workers.

3. Metacognitive skill

The study of metacognitive thinking has been widely associated with John Flavell as an expert in the field of cognitive development since the 1970s. The term metacognition as proposed by Flavell et al. [24] used to refer to awareness, monitoring and regulating of one's cognitive processes. In line with this, Yusuf et al. [25] explained that metacognition refers to the principle of organizing thinking through the process of controlling one's cognitive. The metacognitive component consists of self-awareness, as well as monitoring and evaluation. These components can improve students' ability to solve problems.

Furthermore, Jacobs and Paris [26] explained that metacognition refers to thinking about thinking. Metacognition focuses on self-regulated thinking, namely what people know and how they apply that knowledge to certain tasks. Metacognitive theory as a systematic framework used to explain and direct cognitive processes, cognitive knowledge, and cognitive regulatory skills [27]. A fundamental distinction is made between metacognitive knowledge and metacognitive regulation. Knowledge of cognition refers to what individuals know about their own cognition or about cognition in general. It consists of declarative knowledge (knowing about things), procedural knowledge (knowing how to do things), and conditional knowledge (knowing why and when). Cognitive regulation refers to metacognitive activities that help control one's thinking or learning. Three important skills that are widely recognized are planning (strategy selection and resource allocation), monitoring (awareness understanding and task performance), and evaluation (assessing the product and process of one's learning arrangements) [1].

Schraw and Moshman [28] explain the classification of metacognitive knowledge and metacognitive regulation. In metacognitive knowledge, declarative knowledge includes knowledge about oneself as a learner and about what factors affect one's performance. Procedural knowledge refers to knowledge about the implementation of procedural skills. Conditional knowledge refers to knowing when and why to apply various cognitive actions. Meanwhile, the regulation or metacognitive regulation is categorized into three domains, namely planning the cognitive process (planning), monitoring the cognitive process (monitoring), and evaluating the cognitive process (evaluation). Planning involves selecting the right strategy and allocation of resources that affect performance. Examples include making predictions before reading, sequencing strategies, and allocating time or attention selectively before starting a task. Monitoring refers to a person's on-line awareness of task comprehension and performance. The ability to engage in periodic self-evaluations while studying is an example. Evaluation refers to the assessment of the product and process of setting one's learning. Common examples include re-evaluating one's goals and conclusions. In connection with some of the above definitions of metacognitive, [29] explained that metacognition can be divided into two components: metacognitive knowledge and metacognitive regulation. Metacognitive regulation is the monitoring of one's cognition and includes planning activities, awareness of self-understanding and performance, and evaluation of the efficacy aspects of monitoring processes and strategies.

Based on the description of metacognitive above, it can be concluded that metacognitive or metacognitive thinking is an awareness of thinking about how we think, how we organize thinking strategies in order to complete certain tasks well. Metacognitive thinking can be categorized into 2 sub categories, namely metacognitive knowledge and metacognitive regulation. Metacognitive knowledge is further divided into declarative, procedural, and conditional thinking. Meanwhile, metacognitive regulation is divided into planning, monitoring, and evaluation processes.

In the context of learning in vocational education, these two categories allow to be measured and assessed. However, taking into account the performance-based and project- or product-based assessment methods in vocational education, the measurement of metacognitive regulation (planning, monitoring, and evaluation) is more likely to be measured [1]. As explained by Klerk et al. [30] that vocational education emphasizes performance-based assessment where students learn by doing. This is confirmed by Wimmers [19] that at the end of the vocational education program or professional education program, every student must achieve standardized work competence, so that in this educational program, performance-based assessment is a general method for assessing practical competence in an authentic context. Learners can measure their metacognitive thinking skills through the process of planning, monitoring, and evaluating their performance and the projects or products they make.

4. MOOCs

MOOCs cannot be separated from their early history in 2008 when George Siemens and Stephen Downes provided open enrollment for their Connectivism and Connective Knowledge course at the University of Manitoba. This course is designed as a liaison or cMOOC where students are expected to learn more about connecting with each other in online environments such as classroom learning. In 2012, prestigious educational institutions such as MIT, Harvard, and Stanford began experimenting with offering a MOOC model known as xMOOC, taking a more behavioristic approach to teaching [31]. Then in 2011, a professor of Computer Science at Stanford University, and Peter Norvig, Director of Research at Google, announced that they would offer an open online course in Artificial Intelligence. This course does not use a learning credit system, but students who complete this course will be given a certificate of acknowledgment that they have completed learning. As many as 160,000 people registered, so that the world's attention was given to this phenomenal program and was given the term Massive Open Online Course/MOOCs [32].

MOOCs have attracted the attention of researchers, learning experts, and even governments who have raised various opinions and assumptions regarding the features offered and their advantages and disadvantages. Despite this heterogeneity, dozens of MOOC options emerge every day and thousands of people sign up for the courses available. Besides being free, their motivation is because the course content comes from prestigious universities including Harvard, Massachusetts Institute of Technology, Stanford, University of California, and so on. In addition, research teams from various scientific backgrounds from universities around the world focus daily on finding new alternatives in terms of content access and distribution in MOOCs. It is solely aimed at providing a more engaging learning experience for MOOCs users.

MOOCs have great potential in the world of educational technology so that their use becomes a challenge in itself from the massive aspect, open access, and connectivity which of course must be developed through a multidisciplinary approach. Cyber-socialecology MOOCs can provide a collaborative approach not only among students, but also between educational institutions so that students can adapt their learning models, preferences, and learning needs to MOOCs from different institutions. Another important thing in collaboration between educational institutions is the formalization or recognition of learning in MOOCs. In this way, formal MOOCs can become part of an educational institution's curriculum or tailor a course of study to earn an online diploma. An example of this scenario has been done on the "Mobile Cloud Computing with Android" specialization provided by Coursera [31].

MOOCs can support competency-based education [33]. In addition, MOOCs need to improve the quality and personalization of the student learning experience to further increase the effectiveness of education in general. As well as, Rosé et al. [34] emphasized the need to explore the possibilities of new features, such as collaboration features that encourage collaborative online activities such as structured brainstorming, whole group feedback, group reflections, and other collaborative activities. This activity aims to foster and maintain connectivity support, direction, and a more positive experience for students.

One of the advantages of online courses such as MOOCs is that it is easy to be able to engage in classes from any geographic location at any time you want. Having students spread all over the world in different time zones does not pose much of a problem while studying. This is because it facilitates the delivery of learning asynchronously and synchronously. However, the lack of face-to-face engagement can lead to a sense of isolation and result in students feeling separated from their peers in the classroom [35]. As a result, students in online environments tend to feel like they are taking on independent study rather than being active members of a study group [36]. One way to minimize this sense of alienation is through the use of technology and more interactive content that can enhance collaboration and knowledge construction.

In the learning system through MOOCs, students learn content knowledge by utilizing information and multimedia systems based on the development of learning models and methods. In other words, through learning systems and technology MOOCs require students to use metacognitive skills to manage their own learning pace (metacognitive skills). Students must be active learners in encouraging and sustaining their own learning progress. For example, they should assess the extent to which their learning strategies are effective in facilitating their learning progress, and identify which content has been optimal in terms of helping them achieve their desired learning goals [37]. Tsai et al. [38] conducted research with the aim of proposing an integrated model that integrates aspects of metacognition and interest in learning to investigate student learning motivation through MOOCs. The results of this study revealed that the increase in metacognitive skills was also accompanied by an increase in student enjoyment and encouragement regarding learning in the setting and organization of MOOCs. The findings show that metacognitive aspects can explain whether learners are motivated to learn through MOOCs because of the consequences of cognitive aspects mediated by interest in learning. In the use of MOOCs, the term blended is known which combines learning in terms of the implementation of learning (online or face to face), the delivery of learning content (synchronous or asynchronous).

5. Blended learning practice

Blended learning is a combination of various modalities (on-site, self-directed and web-based learning), delivery media (internet, lectures, powerpoint presentations, textbooks); teaching methods (face-to-face or technology-based/online sessions) and web-based technologies (wikis, chat rooms, blogs, textbooks, online courses) [1]. The combination (hybrid) is carried out depending on criteria such as learning objectives, course content, lecturer experience and teaching style, student characteristics, and others [39]. While, Kaur [40] define blended/hybrid learning from multiple perspectives:

1. Holistic perspective: delivery of learning using various media formats, including integration of learning media into traditional classrooms (f2f) or into online learning environments regardless of the combination of synchronous or asynchronous media

2. Educational perspective: a lecture that integrates f2f lecture activities with online pedagogical content. Some f2f lectures are replaced by online activities, especially in terms of synchronous, and online-asynchronous classes.

3. Pragmatic perspective: lectures are taught both in the classroom and remotely using different pedagogic combination strategies.

4. Corporate training perspective: the use of various learning media formats to deliver a curriculum or course.

5. CLO-Chief learning officer perspective: a learning strategy that integrates several communication modalities (both synchronous and asynchronous).

The success of blended learning depends not only on the quality of the courses and the virtual/online environment, but also on the degree to which faculty and students are prepared to work in a virtual learning environment. It also really depends on the preparation of learning materials and activities by the lecturers and the technical abilities of lecturers and students [1]. In particular, to use all the tools/features offered by the Learning Management System (LMS)-MOOCs, such as related to metacognitive assignments and quiz-essays.

6. Project-based learning (PjBL)

Project-based learning (PjBL) is an approach to teaching science and technology that focuses on investigating questions and problems that students find meaningful and interesting, as well as sparking curiosity about something [41]. By investigating these questions and problems, students are involved in understanding phenomena, recurring natural events, or finding solutions to problems using disciplinary core ideas, scientific and engineering practice, and cross-disciplinary concepts. PjBL involves students and lecturers in finding solutions to questions about the environment around them. Investigating real-world questions in which students investigate meaningfulness has long been touted as a viable learning method. Thus, PjBL triggers the curiosity and active involvement of students to find out what is going on in their environment [41]. The George Lucas Educational Foundation [42, 43], recommend 6 steps of PjBL, namely:

a. Essential questions: provide essential questions related to the focus or scope of the project that is related to the real world and is relevant to students.

b. Designing plans for projects: planning the rules of the game, tools, materials, and selection of activities that can support and answer the important questions of the project focus.

c. Create a schedule: create a timeline and determine project completion deadlines.

d. Monitor students and project progress: Monitor student progress and activities during the project completion process. Monitoring uses a rubric that can record all important activities.

e. Assessing the results: evaluating project progress, providing feedback on the level of understanding students have achieved, assisting lecturers in developing further learning strategies.

f. Evaluate the experience: Lecturers and students reflect on activities and results.

Figure 1 presents a procedural map of the use of metacognitive rubrics in PjBL.
PjBL is a model that organizes learning around projects. Projects are complex tasks, based on challenging questions or problems that involve students in design,

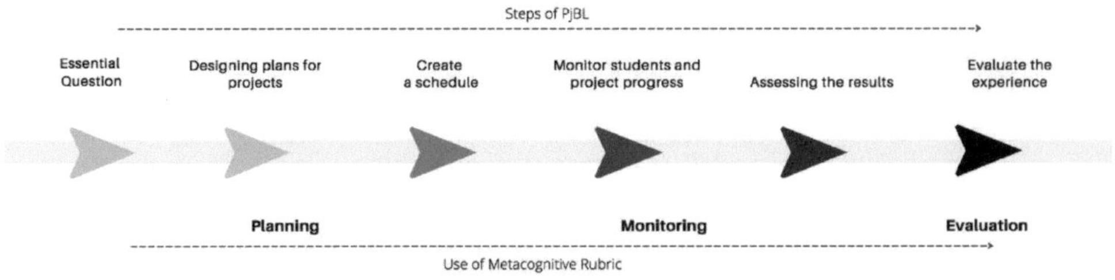

Figure 1.
Procedural map of the use of metacognitive rubrics in PjBL.

problem solving, decision making, or investigative activities, and provide students with the opportunity to work independently guided over a long period of time, culminating in on the final product or presentation. As a learning strategy, PjBL involves students in authentic learning through working on a project. This approach varies greatly from the traditional teacher-centered classroom and provides an interdisciplinary, student-centered activity for students that is integrated with real-world problems and practices, and usually lasts over a long period of time [44].

PjBL, sometimes referred to as project work, can be seen as an extensive problem-based learning activity in which students need to find ways to verify a phenomenon or solve a problem. Thus, aspects of skills are determined to be relevant to aspects of attitudes and abilities needed by students, including abilities such as critical thinking, creative thinking, time management skills and the ability to work cooperatively with others [45]. PjBL is centered on generating questions or inquiries that lead students to see concepts and principles related to their learning. Work on this project requires a long period of time, involving students to generate new knowledge to build on the premise of student inquiry and understanding [46]. Furthermore, Netto-Shek explains that project work, when executed properly, gives students autonomy to make decisions and to work independently and collaboratively in producing solutions for situations that were not previously planned. Netto-Shek argues that in the process of project work by students, monitoring by lecturers provides guidance and advice if needed. As such, project work embeds authentic real-world challenges in student learning experiences.

PjBL allows students to hone and develop skills through knowledge reconstruction when students work together to develop their projects and overcome problems, thereby forcing them to maximize cognitive aspects and overall theoretical understanding and identify theoretical knowledge gaps [47]. This is a more authentic approach to the student learning experience compared to the traditional approach. In keeping with current trends, the Israel Institute of Technology, in 2014 launched an online course on nanotechnology and nanosensors in the MOOCs format, which continues to this day. This course was developed by Prof. Hossam Haick, from the School of Chemical Engineering, is a leading researcher in the field of nanotechnology. The nanotechnology and nanosensors course is the world's first MOOCs in this field, and the first to be presented simultaneously in two languages: English and Arabic. Their purpose is twofold. First, it reaches everyone around the world, even those who live in countries that do not have diplomatic relations with Israel. Second, provide a model for promoting sociocultural learning in the context of technical education, by integrating project-based learning, multicultural teamwork, and peer assessment into a curriculum [48].

Following previous developments on project-based learning in higher education [49], assignments on nanotechnology and nanosensor learning in MOOCs involving features related to the use of authentic questions, inquiry communities, and the use of cognitive aspect support technologies. PjBL involves students in authentic inquiry directly [41, 49]. In order for an activity to be considered as PjBL, it is necessary to involve the construction of knowledge through the development of new ideas, understanding, and/or skills on the part of students. This raises questions about the role of project-based MOOCs in the process of knowledge construction and learning motivation among science and engineering students. More specifically, how to assess the appropriate knowledge construction project for blended MOOCs learning according to the characteristics of vocational education.

7. The development of PjBL metacognitive assessment models

The development of the metacognitive assessment model presented is the result of the author's research, which uses Research and Development steps [1]. Metacognitive instruments and rubrics were developed based on the theory of [28] and Lai [29] previously reviewed, where metacognitive regulation covers 3 aspects, namely: the planning process, the monitoring process, and the evaluation process of the project undertaken.

7.1 Metacognitive scoring rubric for PjBL

Assessment models and rubrics are based on the previously studied metacognitive thinking theory. The results of this study use the theory of metacognitive regulation which is divided into planning, monitoring, and evaluation processes. **Table 1** is a complete rubric that has been compiled based on the theoretical indicators that have been described previously.

The rubrics in **Table 1** are then integrated into the LMS-MOOCs. The following is a metacognitive rubric display on planning aspects that have been integrated into the LMS.

Figure 2 shows a metacognitive rubric consisting of 4 rating scales where each scale contains several assessment criteria from the planning aspect of project work which is one of the metacognitive aspects. Students and teaching staff directly choose one of the points in accordance with the contents of the student project project planning report being assessed.

7.2 Implementation of PjBL metacognitive assessment rubric through blended learning MOOCs

This learning process applies the Blended learning method that combines two learning cycles, namely online-based and face-to-face. The online-based learning cycle is used to strengthen basic materials or theories before students work on projects directly in the laboratory [1]. In addition, online methods are also used to integrate metacognitive assessment instruments and rubrics. The following is a display of the results of Peer, Self, and Teacher Assessment from students (**Figure 3**).

The picture above shows the results of peer assessment (Grades received), self-assessment (Grades given), and teacher assessment (Grade for Submission and Grade for Assessment). Each student gave a score to 3 other students and received a score from 3 students based on the assessment rubric. After that, the teacher also gives a score based on the same assessment rubric. These scores are then downloaded in an excel file format for further processing by assigning a weight to each score. The score from the self-assessment is given a weight of 20, the score from the peer assessment is given a weight of 30, and the score from the teacher assessment is given a weight of 50 so that the maximum score is 100. The following

Metacognitive aspect	Indicator	Score 1	Score 2	Score 3	Score 4
1. Planning (planning their learning activities according to their ability to understand the material)	• The plan contains the ultimate learning objectives they expect in project work. • The plan contains indicators of the achievement of the final objectives of learning that can be measured well. • The plan contains the prerequisites for the initial knowledge needed in the project work. • The plan contains learning activities that will be carried out in completing the project.	The plan contains the ultimate learning goals they expect in project work.	• The plan contains the ultimate learning objectives they expect in project work. • The plan contains indicators of the achievement of the final objectives of learning that can be measured well.	• The plan contains the ultimate learning objectives they expect in project work. • The plan contains indicators of the achievement of the final objectives of learning that can be measured well. • The plan contains the prerequisites for the initial knowledge needed in project work.	• The plan contains the ultimate learning objectives they expect in project work. • The plan contains indicators of the achievement of the final objectives of learning that can be measured well. • The plan contains the prerequisites for the initial knowledge needed in the project work. • The plan contains learning activities that will be carried out in completing the project.
2. Monitoring (self-monitoring of learning activities)	• The learning monitoring report contains the completeness of learning activities in the form of checklist items. • The learning monitoring report contains the obstacles faced in carrying out learning activities during the project work process. • The learning monitoring report contains things that have helped them complete each learning activity that has been carried out. • The learning monitoring report contains strategies that will be carried out in minimizing the constraints that have been written previously.	The learning monitoring report contains the completeness of learning activities in the form of checklist items.	• The learning monitoring report contains the completeness of learning activities in the form of checklist items. • The learning monitoring report contains the obstacles faced in carrying out learning activities during the project work process.	• The learning monitoring report contains the completeness of learning activities in the form of checklist items. • The learning monitoring report contains the obstacles faced in carrying out learning activities during the project work process. • The learning monitoring report contains things that have helped them complete each learning activity that has been carried out.	• The learning monitoring report contains the completeness of learning activities in the form of checklist items. • The learning monitoring report contains the obstacles faced in carrying out learning activities during the project work process. • The learning monitoring report contains things that have helped them complete each learning activity that has been carried out. • The learning monitoring report contains strategies that will be carried out in minimizing the constraints that have been written previously.

Metacognitive aspect	Indicator	Score 1	Score 2	Score 3	Score 4
3. Evaluation (evaluating the results of his work)	• The report contains clear, coherent, and complete information. • Reports are presented by including the appropriate images. • The report states that all project work processes are carried out in accordance with the stages. • The report writes a good conclusion that summarizes the final goal of working on a previously written project.	The report contains clear, coherent, and complete information.	• The report contains clear, coherent, and complete information. • Reports are presented by including the appropriate images.	• The report contains clear, coherent, and complete information. • Reports are presented by including the appropriate images. • The report states that all project work processes are carried out according to the stages.	• The report contains clear, coherent, and complete information. • Reports are presented by including the appropriate images. • The report states that all project work processes are carried out in accordance with the stages. • The report writes a good conclusion that summarizes the final goal of working on a previously written project.

(Source: [1]).

Table 1.
Rubrik metacognitive.

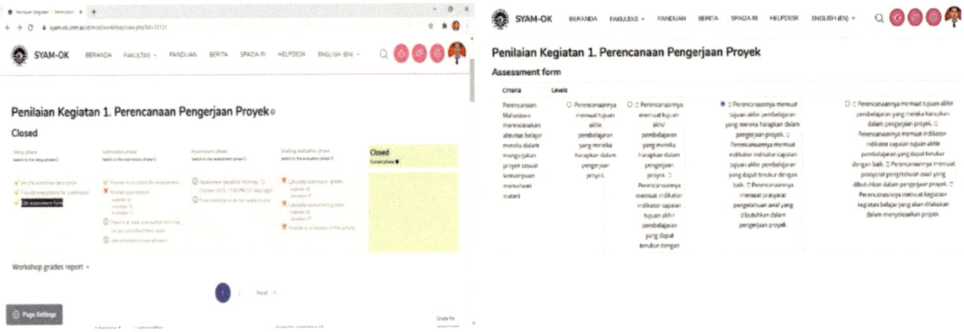

Figure 2.
Metacognitive rubric integrated in LMS. (Source: [1]).

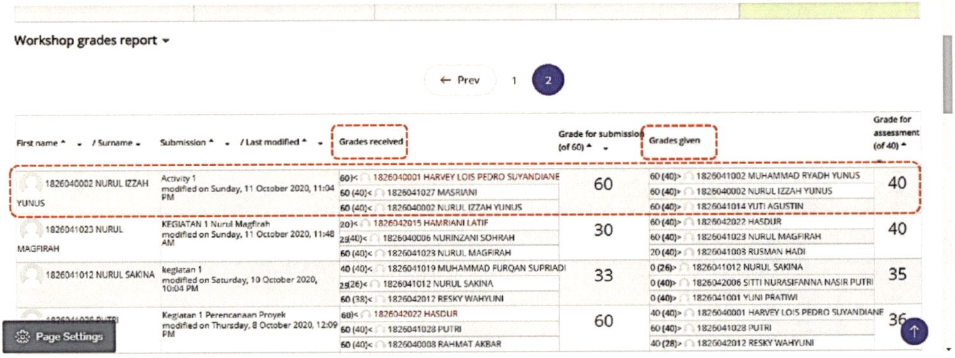

Figure 3.
Peer, self, and teacher assessment.

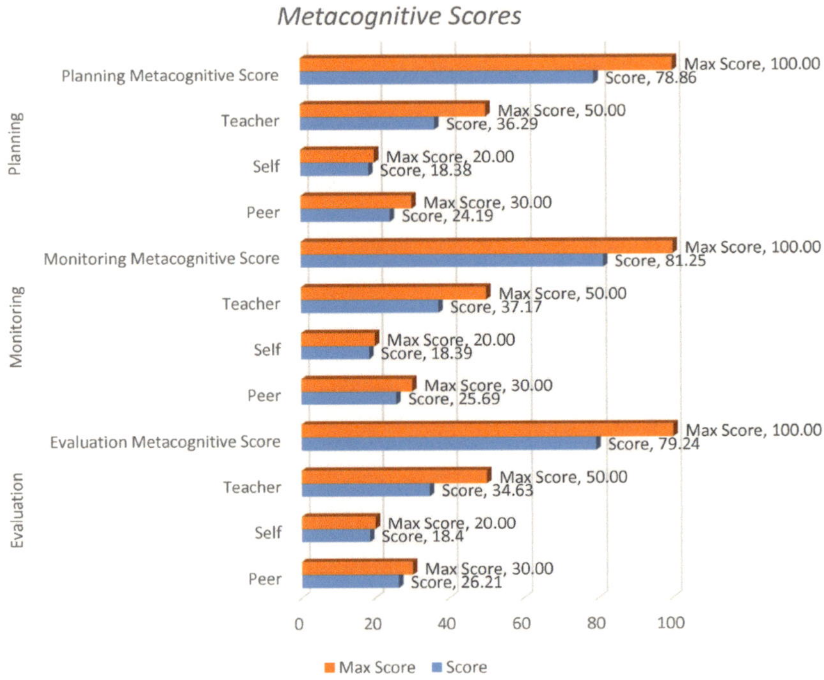

Figure 4.
Results of measuring students' metacognitive thinking. (Source: [1]).

is the final score from the results of measuring students' overall metacognitive thinking in project work (**Figure 4**).

The graph above shows the scores of the three aspects of metacognitive thinking, namely planning, monitoring, and project evaluation. The score comes from three sources, namely peer, self, and teacher assessment. In the planning aspect, the peer assessment score (24.19) is categorized as high because it is close to the maximum score (30). Likewise, the self score (18.38) and teacher assessment (36.29) were also categorized as high because they were close to the maximum scores of 20 and 50. Scores on the metacognitive aspects of monitoring and evaluation also showed high scores from peer, self, and teacher assessment.

The scores in the graph can also be seen that the peer assessment scores from the planning, monitoring, and evaluation aspects are not much different. Likewise, the self and teacher assessment scores do not differ much from the three metacognitive aspects. This means that the metacognitive thinking rubric is effectively used as an assessment guide by students and lecturers in vocational education. These scores have shown the level of students' metacognitive thinking that is in accordance with the characteristics of assessment methods in vocational education based on performance-based assessment and project-based learning models.

8. Metacognitive assessment model for PjBL through blended learning MOOCs

The results of the research on assessment models, instruments, and rubrics that have been integrated with LMS through blended learning practice MOOCs have successfully measured students' metacognitive thinking skills [1]. This is because this assessment model provides opportunities for students to assess their own answers (self-assessment) and provides opportunities for students to assess the answers of their peers (peer-assessment). Students are involved in assessing and evaluating answers based on the assessment rubric given in BLEMS. This encourages students to be more proactive in evaluating their own metacognitive thinking skills so as to support the development of their metacognitive skills. This is in line with the results of Vaughan's research that applies the Triad Approach Assessment (self, peer, teacher assessment) in blended learning where this assessment approach can support the development of students' metacognitive skills [20]. In addition, the results of this study are also in accordance with the theory that has been described previously, namely metacognitive thinking or metacognitive thinking is an awareness of thinking about how we think, how we organize thinking strategies in order to complete certain tasks well. Metacognitive thinking can be categorized into 2 sub categories, namely metacognitive knowledge and metacognitive regulation. Metacognitive knowledge is further divided into declarative, procedural, and conditional thinking. Meanwhile, metacognitive regulation is divided into planning, monitoring, and evaluation processes.

In the context of learning in vocational education, these two categories allow to be measured and assessed. However, considering the performance-based and project- or product-based assessment methods in vocational education, the measurement of metacognitive regulation (planning, monitoring, and evaluation) is more likely to be measured. As explained by Klerk et al. [30] that the vocational education emphasizes performance-based assessment where students learn by doing. This is confirmed by Wimmers [19] that at the end of the vocational education program or professional education program, every student must achieve standardized work competence, so that in this educational program, performance-based assessment is a general method for assessing practical competence in an authentic context.

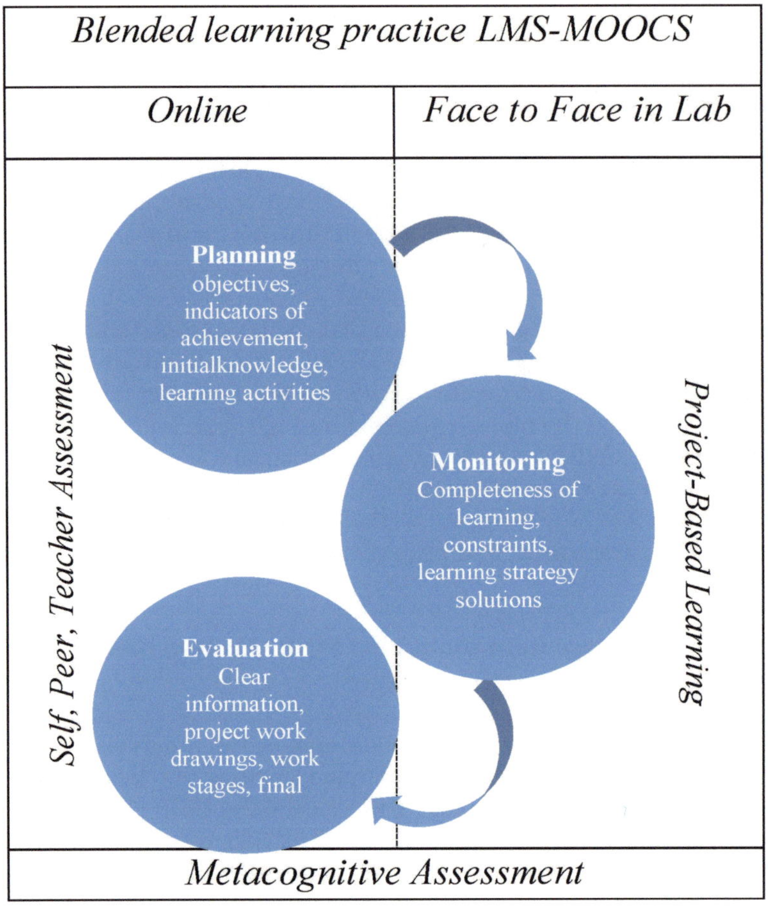

Figure 5.
Metacognitive assessment model. (Adapted from: [1]).

In addition, PjBL is an alternative learning model in vocational education where students can plan, design, and reflect on their learning through projects [50]. PjBL is a student-centered learning model in which students work on a project, make a project report, and communicate the report to their peers and teaching staff [51]. Therefore, students can measure their metacognitive thinking skills through the process of planning, monitoring, and evaluating their performance and the projects or products they make.

In addition, the application of blended learning methods (online and face to face) in project-based learning is able to optimize the learning process carried out. The online method is carried out to strengthen basic theory before students work on projects directly (face to face) in the laboratory so that students are able to optimize the three metacognitive aspects, namely planning, monitoring, and evaluating project work. The following is a metacognitive assessment model that combines self, peer, and teacher assessment in a blended learning environment using a project-based learning model (**Figure 5**).

The picture above shows an assessment model that combines self, peer, and teacher assessment integrated in LMS-MOOCs with a project-based learning model. Blended learning consists of online learning and face to face in the laboratory. The online method is used to assess the three metacognitive aspects, namely planning, monitoring, and evaluation based on metacognitive rubrics that have been integrated in the online environment. While the face to face method is carried out in the laboratory for project work for students. In addition, face to face also allows educators to conduct authentic assessments of the three metacognitive aspects (planning, monitoring, evaluation). The final result of the implementation of this assessment model is the metacognitive thinking score of students in vocational education.

Learning evaluation methods are generally only teacher-centered, not involving students in assessing and reflecting on their own evaluation results. Their answers from carrying out activities at LMS-MOOCs were only judged by one side by the educator. Students only see the score or final score of each test they pass so they cannot see which aspect they lack. However, through this assessment model (self-assessment and peer-assessment), students are actively involved in assessing their higher order thinking skills, namely metacognitive thinking.

9. Conclusions

The assessment rubric aims to determine students' metacognitive thinking skills in project-based learning in vocational education. The assessment rubric was developed for 3 activities, namely planning, monitoring, and evaluation, then integrated into the LMS-MOOCs blended learning practice method. This study also produces a metacognitive assessment model for blended learning models in vocational education. The resulting model is an integration of three activities with self-assessment, peer-assessment, and teacher-assessment assessments for the PjBL learning model [1]. The metacognitive assessment model can be an assessment method to measure students' metacognitive thinking skills, especially in project/work-based learning in vocational education.

Author details

Ridwan Daud Mahande*, Fitrah Asma Darmawan and Jasruddin Daud Malago
Universitas Negeri Makassar, Indonesia

*Address all correspondence to: ridwandm@unm.ac.id

References

[1] Mahande, R. D., Darmawan, F. A., and Malago, J. D. (2021). Metacognitive skill assessment model through the blended learning management system in vocational education. Jurnal Pendidikan Vokasi, 11(1), 1-13. DOI:10.21831/jpv.v11i1.36912

[2] Mane, F., and Corbella, T. (2017). Developing and running an establishment skills survey—Guide to anticipating and matching skills and jobs Vol. 5 Skills for Employment (Vol. 5). Publications Office of the European Union. DOI:10.2816/413514

[3] International Labour Office (2019). A Skilled Workforce for Strong, Sustainable and Balanced Growth (1st ed., Issue November). International Labour Organization.

[4] Gotoh, Y. (2016). Development of Critical Thinking with Metacognitive Regulation. International Conference on Cognition and Exploratory Learning in Digital Age, Celda, 353-356.

[5] Peter Ganter, J. (2019). The Trends Mapping Study on Innovation in Technical and Vocational Education and Training (TVET). the UNESCO-UNEVOC International Centre for Technical and Vocational Education and Training.

[6] Mhouti, A. El, and Nasseh, A. (2017). Enhancing collaborative learning in Web 2.0-based e-learning systems: A design framework for building collaborative e-learning contents. Education and Information Technologies, 22, 2351-2364. DOI:10.1007/s10639-016-9545-2

[7] Kew, S. N., and Petsangsri, S. (2018). Examining the motivation level of students in e-learning in higher education institution in Thailand: A case study. Education and Information Technologies, 23, 2947-2967.

[8] Al-araibi, A. A. M., and Naz, M. (2018). Technological aspect factors of E-learning readiness in higher education institutions: Delphi technique. Education and Information Technologies, 24, 567-590.

[9] Zwart, D. P., Luit, J. E. H. Van, Noroozi, O., Goei, S. L., Zwart, D. P., Luit, J. E. H. Van, Noroozi, O., Goei, S. L., Zwart, D. P., Luit, J. E. H. Van, Noroozi, O., and Goei, S. L. (2017). The effects of digital learning material on students' mathematics learning in vocational education The effects of digital learning material on students' mathematics learning in vocational education. Cogent Education, 29(1). DOI:10.1080/2331186X.2017.1313581

[10] Mahande, R. D., Susanto, A., & Surjono, H. D. (2017). The Dynamics of Mobile Learning Utilization in Vocational Education: Frame Model Perspective Review. *Turkish Online Journal of Educational Technology*, 16(4), 65-76.

[11] Hsu, C. M., Yeh, Y. C., and Yen, J. (2009). Development of design criteria and evaluation scale for web-based learning platforms. International Journal of Industrial Ergonomics, 39(1), 90-95. DOI:10.1016/j.ergon.2008.08.006

[12] Costello, E., Holland, J., and Kirwan, C. (2018). The future of online testing and assessment: Question quality in MOOCs. International Journal of Educational Technology in Higher Education, 15(42), 1-14.

[13] Xiong, Y., and Suen, H. K. (2018). Possibilities, challenges and future directions. International Review of Education, 64, 241-263. DOI:10.1007/s11159-018-9710-5

[14] Earl, L., Katz, S., and WNCP. (2006). Rethinking Classroom

Assessment with Purpose in Mind. In: Learning. DOI:10.4135/9781446214695

[15] Johnson, R. (2004). Peer Assessments in Physical Education. Journal of Physical Education, Recreation and Dance, 75(8), 33-40. DOI:10.1080/07303084.2004.10607287

[16] Veenman, M. V. J., Bavelaar, L., Wolf, L. De, and Haaren, M. G. P. Van. (2014). The on-line assessment of metacognitive skills in a computerized learning environment. Learning and Individual Differences, 29, 123-130. DOI:10.1016/j.lindif.2013.01.003

[17] Zheng, L., Li, X., Zhang, X., and Sun, W. (2019). The e ff ects of group metacognitive sca ff olding on group metacognitive behaviors, group performance, and cognitive load in computer-supported collaborative learning. The Internet and Higher Education, 42(19), 13-24. DOI:10.1016/j.iheduc.2019.03.002

[18] Altıok, S., Başer, Z., and Yükseltürk, E. (2019). Enhancing metacognitive awareness of undergraduates through using an e-educational video environment. Computers and Education, 139(May), 129-145. DOI:10.1016/j.compedu.2019.05.010

[19] Wimmers, P. F. (2016). Innovation and Change in Professional Education 13 Assessing Competence in Professional Performance across Disciplines and Professions (M. Mentkowski, Ed.; 1st ed.). Springer. DOI:10.1007/978-3-319-30064-1

[20] Koc, S., Liu, X., and Wachira, P. (2015). Assessment in Online and Blended Learning Environment. Information Age Publishing.

[21] Sudira, P. (2017). TVET Abad XXI (Hartono, Ed.; 2nd ed.). UNY Press.

[22] Jung, S., Chul, J., and Nam, S. (2019). Impact of vocational education and training on adult skills and employment: An applied multilevel analysis. International Journal of Educational Development, 66(September 2018), 129-138. DOI:10.1016/j.ijedudev.2018.09.007

[23] Hampf, F., and Woessmann, L. (2017). Vocational vs. General Education and Employment over the Life-Cycle: New Evidence from PIAAC. NBER Working Papers Series, 5(10298), 1-17.

[24] Flavell, J. H., Miller, P. H., and Miller, S. A. (1979). Cognitive Development (L. Pearson, Ed.; 4th ed.). Prentice Hall.

[25] Yusuf, Y., Rodding, R., Awang, H., and Mukhtar, I. (2017). Metacognitive Strategies in Promoting the Development of Generic Competences in High TVE in Malaysia. Pertanika Journal of Social Science and Humanities, 25, 247-256.

[26] Jacobs, J. E., and Paris, S. G. (1987). Children's Metacognition About Reading: Issues in Definition, Measurement, and Instruction Children's Metacognition About Reading: Issues in Definition, Measurement, and Instruction. Educational Psychologist, 22(3), 37-41. DOI:10.1080/00461520.1987.9653052

[27] Moshman, D. (2017). Metacognitive Theories Revisited. Educational Psychology Review. DOI:10.1007/s10648-017-9413-7

[28] Schraw, G., and Moshman, D. (1995). Metacognitive Theories. 7(4), 351-371.

[29] Lai, E. R. (2011). Metacognition: A Literature Review Research Report. Pearson's Research Reports, April.

[30] Klerk, S., De Veldkamp, B. P., and Eggen, T. J. H. M. (2018). A framework for designing and developing multimedia-based performance

assessment in vocational education. Educational Technology Research and Development, 66(1), 147-171. DOI:10.1007/s11423-017-9559-5

[31] Mendoza, R., and González. (2016). User-centered Design Strategies for Massive Open Online Courses (MOOCs). In User-Centered Design Strategies for Massive Open Online Courses (MOOCs) (1st ed.). Information Science Reference. DOI:10.4018/978-1-4666-9743-0

[32] Haber, J. (2014). MOOCs. In Angewandte Chemie International Edition, 6(11), 951-952. (1st ed.). MIT Press.

[33] Dasarathy, B., Sullivan, K., Schmidt, D., and Porter, A. (2018). P212-Dasarathy. Future of Software Engineering Proceedings, 212-224. DOI:10.1145/2593882.2593897

[34] Rosé, C. P., Ferschke, O., Tomar, G., Yang, D., Howley, I., Aleven, V., Siemens, G., Crosslin, M., Gasevic, D., and Baker, R. (2015). Challenges and opportunities of dual-layer MOOCs: Reflections from an edX deployment study. Computer-Supported Collaborative Learning Conference, CSCL, 2, 848-851.

[35] Willging, P. A., and Johnson, S. D. (2019). Factors that influence students' decision to dropout of online courses. Journal of Asynchronous Learning Network, 13(3), 115-127. DOI:10.24059/olj.v8i4.1814

[36] Lave, J., and Wenger, E. (1991). Situated Learning: Legitimate Peripheral Participation (E. Wenger, Ed.). Cambridge University Press.

[37] Ackerman, R., Parush, A., Nassar, F., and Shtub, A. (2016). Metacognition and system usability: Incorporating metacognitive research paradigm into usability testing. Computers in Human Behavior, 54, 101-113. DOI:10.1016/j.chb.2015.07.041

[38] Tsai Y., Hsun, Lin, C. Hung, Hong, J. Chao, and Tai K. Hsin. (2018). The Effects of Metacognition on Online Learning Interest and Continuance to Learn with MOOCs. Computers and Education, 121, 18-29. DOI:10.1016/j.compedu.2018.02.011

[39] Kofar, Gülten. 2016. "A Study of EFL Instructors' Perceptions of Blended Learning." Procedia - Social and Behavioral Sciences 232:736-44. DOI: 10.1016/j.sbspro.2016.10.100.

[40] Kaur, Manjot. 2013. "Blended Learning-Its Challenges and Future." Procedia - Social and Behavioral Sciences 93:612-17. DOI: 10.1016/j.sbspro.2013.09.248.

[41] S. Krajcik and M. Czerniak (2014). Teaching Science in Elementary and Middle School: A Project-Based Approach. In Interdisciplinary Journal of Problem-Based Learning (5th ed., Vol. 8, Issue 1). Routledge. DOI:10.7771/1541-5015.1489

[42] Husamah, H., and Pantiwati, Y. (2014). Cooperative learning STAD-PjBL: Motivation, thinking skills, and learning outcomes of biology department students. International Journal of Education Learning and Development, 2(1), 68-85.

[43] Sukamti, E. U., Putra, A. P., and Devi, A. C. (2019). Innovation of Project Base Learning (PjBL) on Outdoor Study for PGSD's Student Activity on Education Diffusion. Int. J. Innov. Creat. Chang, 5(5), 546-561.

[44] Joseph, C. T., and Chapman, A. (2016). Project-Based Learning for Academically-Able Student (1, Ed.). Sense Publisher.

[45] Ngeow, K., and Kong, Y.-S. (2001). Learning To Learn: Preparing Teachers and Students for Learning To Learn: Preparing Teachers and Students for Problem-Based Learning. ERIC. ERIC Digest, 20, 1-6.

[46] Netto-Shek, Ho, T. B., and Chang, A. S. (2014). Making Projects Work: Structuring Learning. Managing Project work in Schools: Issues and Innovative Practices. Singapore (1st ed.). Prentice Hall.

[47] Helle, L., Tynjälä, P., and Olkinuora. (2016). Project-Based Learning in Post-Secondary Education – Theory, Practice and Rubber Sling Shots. Higher Education, 51, 287-314. DOI:10.1007/s10734-004-6386-5

[48] Barak, M., and Watted, A. (2017). Project-based MOOC: Enhancing knowledge construction and motivation to learn. In: B. Berenfeld and J. Ginestie (Eds.), Digital Tools and Solution for Inquiry-Based STEM Learning (p. 26). IGI Global. DOI:10.4018/978-1-5225-2525-7

[49] Barak, M., and Dori, Y. J. (2005). Enhancing undergraduate students' chemistry understanding through project-based learning in an IT environment. Science Education, 89(1), 117-139. DOI:10.1002/sce.20027

[50] Doppelt, Y. (2005). Assessment of Project-Based Learning in a MECHATRONICS Context. 16(2).

[51] Marx, R. W., Blumenfeld, P. C., Krajcik, J. S., and Soloway, E. (1997). Enacting Project-Based Science. The Elementary School Journal, 97(4), 342-358.